NIETZSCHE ON THE STRUGGLE BETWEEN KNOWLEDGE AND WISDOM

Also by Keith M. May

OUT OF THE MAELSTROM:
PSYCHOLOGY AND THE NOVEL IN THE
TWENTIETH CENTURY

CHARACTERS OF WOMEN IN
NARRATIVE LITERATURE

IBSEN AND SHAW

NIETZSCHE AND MODERN LITERATURE

NIETZSCHE AND THE SPIRIT OF TRAGEDY

Nietzsche on the Struggle between Knowledge and Wisdom

Keith M. May

M

St. Martin's Press

© Keith M. May 1993

First published in Great Britain 1993 by
THE MACMILLAN PRESS LTD
Houndmills, Basingstoke, Hampshire RG21 2XS
and London
Companies and representatives
throughout the world

A catalogue record for this book is available
from the British Library.

ISBN 0–333–52390–3

Printed in Great Britain by
Ipswich Book Co Ltd
Ipswich, Suffolk

First published in the United States of America 1993 by
Scholarly and Reference Division,
ST. MARTIN'S PRESS, INC.,
175 Fifth Avenue,
New York, N.Y. 10010

ISBN 0–312–08992–9

Library of Congress Cataloging-in-Publication Data
May, Keith M.
Nietzsche on the struggle between knowledge and wisdom / Keith M.
May.
p. cm.
Includes bibliographical references and index.
ISBN 0–312–08992–9
1. Nietzsche, Friedrich Wilhelm, 1844–1900. 2. Methodology.
I. Title. II. Title: Knowledge and wisdom.
B3318.M54M39 1993
193—dc20 92–28792
CIP

To Thomas

Further, every substance is like an entire world and like a mirror of God, or of the whole universe, which each one expresses in its own way, very much as one and the same town is variously represented in accordance with different positions of the observer.

Leibniz, 'Discourse on Metaphysics'

Contents

Acknowledgements

Appreciation is gratefully expressed for the opportunity to make use of the following editions of Nietzsche's works: *Beyond Good and Evil – Prelude to a Philosophy of the Future*, translated with a commentary by Walter Kaufmann (New York: Vintage Books, A Division of Random House, 1966); *The Birth of Tragedy* and *The Case of Wagner*, translated with commentary by Walter Kaufmann (New York: Vintage Books, A Division of Random House, 1967); *Daybreak – Thoughts on the Prejudices of Morality*, translated by R. J. Hollingdale, introduction by Michael Tanner (Cambridge University Press, 1982); *Dithyrambs of Dionysus*, Bilingual Edition, translated and introduced by R. J. Hollingdale (Anvil Press Poetry, 1984); *The Gay Science*, translated with a commentary by Walter Kaufmann (New York: Vintage Books, A Division of Random House, 1974); *On the Genealogy of Morals*, translated by Walter Kaufmann and R. J. Hollingdale and *Ecce Homo*, translated with a commentary by Walter Kaufmann (New York: Vintage Books, A Division of Random House, 1967); *Human, All Too Human – A Book for Free Spirits*, translated by R. J. Hollingdale, introduction by Erich Heller (Cambridge University Press, 1986); *Philosophy in the Tragic Age of the Greeks*, translated with an introduction by Marianne Cowan (Chicago: A Gateway Edition, Regnery Gateway, 1962); *Thus Spoke Zarathustra – A Book for Everyone and No One*, translated with an introduction by R. J. Hollingdale (Harmondsworth, Penguin Books, 1980); *Twilight of the Idols* and *The Anti-Christ*, translated with an introduction and commentary by R. J. Hollingdale (Harmondsworth, Penguin Books, 1978); *Untimely Meditations*, translated by R. J. Hollingdale, introduction by J. P. Stern (Cambridge University Press, 1983); *The Will to Power*, translated by Walter Kaufmann and R. J. Hollingdale, edited with an introduction by Walter Kaufmann (New York: Vintage Books, A Division of Random House, 1968).

Gratitude is also expressed for the opportunity to use the following works: *The Complete Works of Aristotle*, edited by Jonathan Barnes (Princeton, New Jersey: Princeton University Press, 1984); Heidegger, Martin, *Early Greek Thinking*, translated by David Farrell Krell and Frank A. Capuzzi (San Fransisco: Harper & Row, 1984);

Guthrie, W. K. C., *A History of Greek Philosophy*, Volumes I and II (Cambridge, Cambridge University Press, 1962 and 1965); *The Collected Dialogues of Plato including the Letters*, edited by Edith Hamilton and Huntingdon Cairns, Bollinger Series LXXI (Princeton, New Jersey, Princeton University Press, 1961), and *The Presocratic Philosophers*, a critical history by G. S. Kirk, J. E. Raven and M. Schofield (Cambridge, Cambridge University Press, 1988).

Preface

In a note of 1875 Nietzsche refers to 'The Struggle between Science and Wisdom exhibited in the ancient Greek Philosophers'. By 'science' (*Wissenschaft*) he means every form of systematic learning, while by 'wisdom' (*Weisheit*) he means the activity which the first philosophers distinctively loved. This activity or quality has never been satisfactorily defined. Among the Presocratics it was keenly apprehended but they never thought to delineate it and from about the time of Plato it has scarcely found expression in any cultural form. Whatever this wisdom was, it cannot have been what we think of as sagacity, prudence, reasonableness, or any of the other rough synonyms for wisdom, since it is unthinkable that Heraclitus or Parmenides would have regarded himself in such a way. 'Enlightenment' is the nearest, perhaps, though that is still only a word which does not, moreover, convey anything of the hauteur and sheer audacity of these early thinkers. But Nietzsche, a classical philologist who had given courses on the ancient Greek philosophers, knew what *he* meant by 'wisdom'. He gained his idea from his studies and concluded that wisdom once *essentially* took part in a struggle with knowledge.

Anyone reading Nietzsche's notes cannot at first be clear what he is driving at, and the groundplan, though far from the whole, of the following chapters is an exposition of his meaning. One thing is clear from Nietzsche's published works: in his view wisdom ought once again to challenge knowledge – honourably and with the respect one shows to a worthy opponent.

Long before Nietzsche's assimilation of knowledge to will to power, and no doubt before his youthful reading of Schopenhauer (for otherwise he would not have seized on Schopenhauer so eagerly), he understood knowledge to be other than discovery of the world around us. To that extent he was a Kantian, in effect. But our appreciation of this should not lead us to believe that human beings have always sought or produced knowledge; for knowledge, in Nietzsche's (normal and time-honoured) usage, is not to be identified with learning by imitation. Such learning is utterly natural and biologically necessary, whereas the human race managed perfectly well without knowledge until the sixth century

BC. Thus the naturalness of knowledge is merely the naturalness of whatever historically develops as opposed to that of biological necessity.

True to his genius for psychology, Nietzsche tries to work out what might have suddenly caused the Greeks to cultivate the faculty of knowledge. He is sure this must have been a psychical development, not chiefly the result of material changes. He makes four suggestions as follows: knowledge grows as and when the gods are ceasing to be good; it springs from the egoism of individuals seeking their fortunes (for example, through navigation); it is elaborated as a variety of aristocratic amusement; and finally the urge to know arises in those who, becoming tired of the ebb and flow of popular opinion, want something solid to cling to.

These all seem shrewd suggestions but what matters is Nietzsche's assumption that knowledge-seeking originated in something other than the mere desire to know. It is not pure. Nevertheless, the best kind of knowledge, namely psychological knowledge, should take precedence over every other kind because we cannot get 'further back' than psychology. Today we are encouraged to believe, for instance, that physics lies behind everything, or that biology is the fundamental description of life-processes, but to Nietzsche such sciences are psychological data and thus, in turn, part of the source-material for philosophy.

The reason for something or other, though it can never be satisfactorily and finally found, should always be hunted in what Nietzsche calls 'proper physio-psychology'. This is true of the reasons offered in modern physics. This field of study is of great importance, but not as the means of disclosing the cosmos to us. Rather it is a means of disciplining our observations and of showing us how, in an old, late stage of human development, our species confronts the extra-human world. At the end of his career Nietzsche confidently demands that 'psychology shall be recognised again as the queen of the sciences, for whose service and preparation the other sciences exist'. He continues by saying that 'psychology is now again the path to the fundamental problems' – which are of course the problems proper to philosophy.[1] The word 'again' is picked up by Kaufmann in his translation of the work in which they occur, *Beyond Good and Evil*. He suggests that no one before Nietzsche seems to have regarded psychology as the path to the fundamental problems. But this is to overlook Nietzsche's reading of the Presocratics to the effect that these ancient thinkers referred everything back to the human mind or soul. Having very little notion of 'objectivity', they were already on the right lines.

Despite Nietzsche's respectful subordination of the departments of knowledge (the sciences) to psychology, he rates 'Knowledge', in another sense of the word, exceedingly highly. Such knowledge is no longer compartmentalised, specialised, authoritative, or even, in the usual way, progressive. It is eclectic, and non-professional. Nietzsche regards life itself as the means to such knowledge (see *The Gay Science*, No. 324) but, needless to say, such an attitude requires an experimental response to both knowledge and life. Such superior knowledge is, once again, psychological, and is not the sort that once conflicted with wisdom.

In the way outlined above, Nietzsche turns knowledge against itself, or one kind of knowledge against another. Knowledge as we commonly use the term ceases to be what it has long pretended to be – certainty or, at least, the route towards certainty – and becomes instead a purely adventurous way of life. Familiar problems now crop up. If knowledge is purely an adventure, it will be used crudely by the crude, childishly by the childish, in general according to people's inclinations. Artists, anyway, have always adapted knowledge to suit their own convenience. Notwithstanding his aversion to such antics, Nietzsche appraises the procedures foreshadowed in the sixth and fifth centuries BC as a grand, *creative* expedient for perpetuating the species. Seen in this light, knowledge must lose its authority, in the sense that one does not normally bow before one's own creations. And such created items and fields of knowledge can no longer be guided by virtue or the moral law, since these are themselves merely matter of (psychological) investigation. On the face of it, we have arrived at a strictly anarchic position; there seems to be no controlling principle. But this is not so, since Nietzsche proposes another *arche*, another dominant foundation which was possibly sensed, but not brought to light, before the time of Socrates. This *arche* is Nietzsche's response to the nihilism which he himself has adumbrated.

At present, in the late twentieth century, we are presumably in a phase of transition with reference to this very question of knowledge. Consider the opposed attitudes we adopt according to circumstances. On the one hand, all knowledge is good in being preferable to ignorance and perhaps it is absolutely good in itself. Not to know something one might know can be almost intolerable for one who is not overborne by fear or weariness. On the other hand, some knowledge is bad when it militates against something held to be good (for example, genetic research as against the good of family life). There is, further, the assumption that we already understand what must be good for the human race, specifically cooperation and the elimination of suffering. So whatever we light upon which checks or reverses our advance towards these goods is suspect and conceivably 'diabolical'. Such examples emphasise that we are now midway between grasping knowledge as a product of our will and, contrariwise, apprehending it as sovereign over us. For if it is not sovereign, it no longer seems to be 'knowledge'. The crux is this: when knowledge controls us, the ground shifts beneath our feet, but to the extent that we control knowledge, we begin to lose the sense of our own worth.

Nietzsche saw the beginnings of this modern development among the Greeks from Thales to Anaxagoras – the buddings of that which has since grown to monstrous proportions. Those were the ones who so estimably started to 'think for themselves'. At first they recognised a need to discover (uncover, by conceptual as opposed to empirical means) the origins of the universe which had hitherto been explained by the myths. The gods, powerful and sublime though they were, evidently could not reason these matters out; the gods controlled the world but could not understand it. Thus for the first time Thales explained cosmic origins, or rather, being a Greek and the first philosopher, he *declared* the origins to be such and such. How could they be other than what he conceived them to be?

At this point it may be as well to insert a brief comment upon the distinction between Nietzsche's psychological interpretation of all creative work (science no less than art) and our contemporary activity of deconstruction. If deconstruction is concerned with what is unobtrusively taking place in a text or other medium, Nietzsche sets out to trace back from the available signs in both the work and the life of the creator, for instance Thales, to an irreducible core which is an individual will. So while the one engaged in deconstruction is liable to end up with fragments or at most an unordered picture, Nietzsche always aims to reach a clear image. We tend to distrust such images; the less clarity, the less falsehood: that is the unacknowledged contemporary prejudice. Conversely, Nietzsche assumes that the will of the creative being is both discoverable and coherent.

It is plainly true that whatever will Nietzsche discovers, in

Thales for example, is strictly an invention; there can be no external measure of Nietzsche's discovery. We cannot, anyway, postulate a real will in Thales other than the one we hit upon. In certain situations the temptation, therefore, is to allow such ignorance to lead one to refrain so far as possible from the act of positive interpretation which Nietzsche, following Schopenhauer, held to be the very procedure of nature at every level.

Nietzsche's own post-Kantianism is a decisive step beyond Kant in that Nietzsche was sure not merely of the unknowability of the thing-in-itself but even of its existence. Everything thus becomes a matter of interpretation, not of 'mere' interpretation but of interpretation as a resolute act. Nietzsche's own resolution should cause us, not to stray in the direction of weak nihilism but to find out what his foundation consisted of. On what could such a doubter and psychologist found anything? The aim is to uncover the class of Nietzsche's founding notions and see how this class might hold sway over other people also.

What, then, is the measure or the legislator who, for purposes of creation as well as survival (or rather, for survival *as* creation), provides a base upon which one's creative deeds take place? This legislative force is what it always was, the soul itself, understood, however, in a radically different way from that of Plato. This particular question is considered in Chapter 6, on Ariadne. Nietzsche follows Plato in regarding the soul as immortal, but not in likening its condition to that of the sea god crushed and marred by the waves – not, in other words, as preternaturally pure and unchanging beneath its surface disfigurements. The soul, in Nietzsche, evolves and even (or especially) suffers. As in Plato, the soul still lies above and beyond knowledge. Therefore it cannot be known by the usual procedures of knowledge. Nevertheless it can be intuited and will assume the form of an image.

According to Nietzsche, the Socratics started to take the soul seriously, but this was by no means an unambiguously healthy advance in human responses to the world. At the initial stage, taking the soul seriously involved the decadent distinction between the human capacity for questioning and all natural forces other than this capacity. Prior to such Socratic behaviour our rebellious–innovative genius had found its expression in the figure of Prometheus chained by Zeus. But Prometheus was not yet primarily a questioner and of course this agonised Titan had not the slightest notion of a pain-free life. The dialectic as practised by Socrates was indeed understood to be a natural force, yet somehow it led or pointed to a sphere beyond nature.

It is widely appreciated that Nietzsche's task was to find a way by which human beings might *avowedly* re-affiliate themselves with the natural world to which they are in any case affiliated. This task required a pincer movement, as it were, on the Western tradition, at least back to Socrates. One arm of the pincers must reappraise knowledge, appreciating the creativity of knowledge (as indeed the quantum theorists are now doing in physics), while the other arm attempts what must surely turn out to be harder, that is, to understand and value the soul afresh. The latter movement makes use of wisdom, or *is* wisdom, and as such must be in conflict with knowledge of the systematic progressive sort.

Another point should perhaps be added, as follows. Despite Nietzsche's attacks on what he scornfully calls 'metaphysics', meaning Platonic metaphysics, the standpoint here and, for that matter, the standpoint from which alone Nietzsche can be interpreted, is metaphysical in the Kantian sense. This means simply but decisively that *physis*, or nature, obviously cannot be approached by human beings except through *meta*-physics, or, as Kant puts it, metaphysics is 'a natural disposition of the human mind (*metaphysica naturalis*).[2] Nietzsche retained both a theoretical and a direct, 'unphilosophical' awareness of an infinitely larger, Dionysian reality. It will immediately be seen that to deal philosophically with something held to be unphilosophical (basically unworded) is a major problem, but it need not be a quixotic enterprise. In the argument set out below, and especially in considerations of Heraclitus, we come up against the problem of thought-free understanding (as distinct from mysticism). Will to power is seen as a development from Aristotelian metaphysics, thus itself a metaphysical conception. There is also, incidentally, a tacit belief that the celebrated 'last man' is no more than a grossly inferior metaphysician.

On this same metaphysical basis, Nietzsche himself 'circles back', as it were, to certain predecessors and contemporaries of Socrates, notably Heraclitus, Parmenides, Empedocles and Democritus. It is not that he does much in the way of interpreting these figures but that he unearths their long-forgotten quality of wisdom. Even so, the quality remains more or less buried for us, and the question behind the following chapters is how it can be resurrected and brought back into a combative relation with knowledge.

1
Knowledge and Wisdom in the Tragic Age

In the Later Preface to *Philosophy in the Tragic Age of the Greeks* Nietzsche emphasises that his work differs from other accounts of the Presocratic philosophers by virtue of its selectivity; in other words, by its incompleteness. The book is an almost cavalier simplification, bringing out what Nietzsche sees as the noteworthy quality of each of a number of thinkers before Socrates. This is a more readily justifiable procedure than we are inclined to think, for it is evident from our far more thorough accounts of these thinkers from Thales to Anaxagoras that the salient point is often the one elegantly discussed by Nietzsche. The nineteenth- and twentieth-century tendency towards comprehensiveness reveals nothing so much as the difference between our valuations and those of early Greek philosophers. We try to know by methods which they would have judged to be incomprehensively foolish, unwise, a sacrifice of self, insofar as self is focused through choice and will. Are we then right and they wrong? From our point of view their work is a mish-mash of guesswork, logic, intuition and individualistic preference. Yet such work was the self-fulfilment of each philosopher and his supreme task on earth. In an exceedingly short space of time some pioneers of thought passed from treating (mythical) knowledge as a master to treating it as a servant – as tolerable, serviceable or disposable. They began to enlist knowledge in the service of their own personal wisdom. On the other hand, the only control we try to exercise over knowledge is that of morality, but because we are more sure of learning than we are of virtue, learning runs where it will. One argument of this book is that learning needs to be disciplined again. There was once an extremely subtle art of subordinating knowledge while retaining respect for it, an art which we have lost.

Nietzsche is no exception to the rule stated by Bertrand Russell: 'In every history of philosophy for students the first thing mentioned is that philosophy began with Thales who said that everything is made of water.'[1] Russell himself makes little of Thales and does not try to understand why the Greek should be designated the first philosopher. Modern scholars stick to the reported facts and find it hard to reconcile them with our understanding of philosophy. To Russell, certainly, the reputation of Thales is possibly misleading and, anyway, of little interest.

Conversely, Nietzsche accepts that Thales must indeed have been the first Western philosopher and believes it is up to us to discover why he deserves the title. For the reason, whatever it is, will tell us something of interest about Thales, about how philosophy was born, and about its abiding nature.

When it arrived on earth philosophy was necessarily feeble, and somewhat disguised, though from our perspective we can detect the seeds of its future condition. Therefore, when we have recognised the philosopher in Thales (for there is no doubt that he was other things as well), we shall be able to reject false pretenders to philosophy as ones unlike Thales. Contemplating this obscure man will teach us to define 'love of wisdom', which phrase has been devalued for so long that we hardly know what to make of it, except a joke. When on the other hand we contemplate a great and influential thinker such as Plato or Spinoza, or Kant, we are too easily diverted by technique.

Thales was a statesman, an engineer, an astronomer, a mathematician, a cosmologist and one who believed that even the most seemingly lifeless objects are inhabited by gods. In this list the chief originality of Thales lies concealed, for it comes under the heading of cosmology. Our source for this first step in philosophy is Aristotle. In *De Caelo* Aristotle dismissively remarks that Thales is reputed to have said that the earth floats like wood on water. In the *Metaphysics* Aristotle goes further, claiming that Thales, 'the founder of this school of philosophy', believed water to be the first principle of all existing things: that from which they come and into which they are ultimately resolved.[2] The usual modern procedure is to relate this Greek notion to Babylonian, Egyptian and biblical myths about the creation, since these likewise are concerned with water as the medium upon which the earth rests or from which it originally emerged. Now the problem here for us is to distinguish philosophy from myth, for the philosophers were precisely those who set out to replace myth with a new sort of world-conception. The originality of Thales was apparent to his contemporaries, though they could not have analysed it.

A modern solution to this problem is to regard Thales as one who built a bridge between 'myth-thinking' and reason, thus infiltrating reason into mythicism and beginning the journey towards reason and philosophy proper. From our vantage-point it is easy to see that Thales indeed accomplished something of the sort, but how did he do so? The 'how' is all-important and by no means undiscoverable. It is unlikely that reason was either his means or his goal. To say that it was is to assert that philosophers were, and are, essentially rational beings, persons actually motivated by reason. Nietzsche's belief about philosophers is that they leap ahead to some characteristic conclusion, and only then find a chain of reasoning to lead them there.

Perhaps reason was indeed exploited from the beginning. The preference of Thales for knowledge other than myth was not an elevation of reason over unreason, but rather the enthronement of his own vision. According to Nietzsche, Thales 'had seen the unity of all that is' and, giving priority to his vision, he proceeded to find something which could plausibly unify the universe.[3] That something turned out to be water.

Our first reaction to this (our prejudice) is likely to be that no one should be called a philosopher who so readily confuses his vision with an external quality. It is possible to see unity where none exists. Therefore (so we might conclude), if Thales was a philosopher, he achieved that status in a primitive fashion of negligible interest to us. But this line of thought underestimates Nietzsche's perception. Nietzsche means that it is not possible to separate the world as it is from the world as we see it. Two hundred years after Kant, and despite the ramifications of the quantum theory, we still retain a groundless lack of faith in our concepts and intuitions. But Thales possessed such faith, and for that reason was correct, not simply primitive, to trust his vision of universal unity. In other words, humanity perforce shares this vision. And whatever humanity is permanently obliged to discern about the universe is what, at our most thoughtful, we mean by the 'Truth', since humanity is the visionary agency of the universe.

Even so, it is important to understand Nietzsche's intention in his phrase, 'the unity of all that is'. Elsewhere, in *The Will to Power*, he denies unity. Such an essentially modern recognition that the cosmos lacks unity is a feature of the nihilism now stealing over mankind. However, in *The Will to Power* Nietzsche is referring to a post-Socratic and altogether more grandiose kind of unity; he is specifying (and dismissing) the notion of unified purpose and value. The universe, he thinks, has no purpose, hence no overall value that confers value upon each of us as earthly creatures.

Now this value-conferring unity is not the unity that Thales saw. He detected fundamental *sameness*. Everything is alike in its fundamental composition. We cannot call this a purely physical sameness (or 'unity'), since merely to note it and describe it is a metaphysical act. Here is a vision of physical unity given to a human being, who both partakes of the unity and is able to make it the subject of a metaphysical pronouncement.

Thales trusted his own mind, or to be exact, his *psyche*, regarding his psyche as a 'mirror of the world'.[4] A philosopher is thus distinguished from a mythicist or a religious thinker, not by his use of reason (which is merely argumentative or at best scientific) but by the perceived extent of his need for a metaphysical unity reflected in himself.

Nietzsche's belief about the emergence of philosophy may be summarised as follows: while such men as the Babylonian and Egyptian cosmographers were content with their world-pictures, Thales, a greatly creative individual, sought a formula for the universal unity which he had seen. The legends held together as a narrative or work of art holds together, but they were not sharply enough focused and their spirituality lacked a clear reference back from *physis* (nature) to psyche. To be precise, the emergent philosopher then, as every fully-fledged philosopher since, needed a reference back to his own psyche.

The Greeks, says Nietzsche, 'were the very opposite of realists, in that they believed only in the reality of men and gods, looking upon all of nature as but a disguise, a masquerade, or, a metamorphosis of these god-men'.[5] Therefore they found it excessively hard to grasp concepts as such.

We assume they found concepts to be shadowy and unreal: reality meant mortal beings and gods, the latter sometimes transforming themselves into natural creatures. This is why Thales 'saw' rather than conceptualised unity. To him unity had to take a vaguely pictorial as opposed to an abstract form. But in such a world how could philosophy, that discipline of concepts, develop? Thales teaches us that it did so by justifying a vision of unity through the medium of a substance (water). Thales said water and meant water, but in a way he scarcely understood he also meant something more or other than water. Peering at Thales through the ages of science we are inclined to see him as a proto-scientist (he 'promised' science), but really he was an autocrat who declared, 'I, Thales, tell you *this* is the nature of the universe.'

In his heart, that is, in a 'region' more or less successfully concealed from his verbalising mind, Thales took thought seriously *as thought*. I mean he began to apprehend thought as a commanding rather than a subservient activity. All the Presocratics to a greater or lesser extent appraised thought in this fashion and were thus philosophers in the proper sense of the word. Their constant endeavour was to rise above picture-thinking and deification. They were dissatisfied with the myths, or, to put the matter bluntly, with the gods.

But why did the gods gradually fall into disrepute, since they had been 'disreputable' all along? People grew tired of being at the mercy of imperfect deities; hence the faults of the deities loomed ever larger, no longer as characteristics but specifically as faults. This happened not as the expression of an access of moral insight among the Greeks but because pioneering Greeks began to believe they could think their way to the solution of problems. The gods, superhuman beings, increasingly stood revealed as lacking human power of thought. Certainly no one could come near to saying the gods were 'inferior' to mortals, but not a few might begin to detect a new ambivalence in the relation of people to gods. On the one hand gods possessed insuperable powers, while on the other hand they lacked the human ability to investigate nature and values. About a century before Aeschylus, Thales points the way to that ambivalence in human attitudes towards the Olympians which we find in the tragic dramatists.

Since Thales had no rivals in the new sphere of philosophy, he had almost no need for argumentative proof. He became known as the one who says everything rests upon water: that was his saying, his vision and indeed his essential character. In this way the earliest philosophy was plainly personal; it expressed a person in all his uniqueness.

But philosophy must always do that, no matter what the strength of a school of thought, a methodology, a set of assumptions, or even a system of values. If this can be provisionally accepted, we immediately see why there need be no confusion between the philosopher and the seeker after knowledge (the scholar or scientist) even when we are considering the period of five to six hundred years before Christ, when both philosophy and non-mythic studies of nature began. The philosopher does not prostrate himself before knowledge but neither does he, in his character as philosopher, manipulate knowledge after the manner of a politician or an ordinary egotist. At most (and at best) he respects knowledge as that which may be serviceable to his scheme of things. But this scheme is always an elevation and refinement of himself.

It follows that a philosopher, in common with an artist, cannot be rendered obsolete by subsequent revelations. No amount of geographical or astronomical discovery can quite confine Thales to the history of ideas, though we first encounter him in that history. To the contrary, Thales survives in his own right, not just as a figure preceding a parade. He saw what no one will be able to surpass: that human beings perceive a unity embracing themselves and the cosmos – a mode of unification that manifests itself in the spirit of the observer. To note this is not to acquire specific knowledge but to identify the source of all knowledge.

So Thales is not a crude scientist, except, at most, in a subsidiary way. In *Philosophy and Truth* Nietzsche comments that, 'the philosopher is a self-revelation of nature's workshop; the philosopher and the artist tell the trade secrets of nature'.[6] These trade secrets have little to do with what astrophysicists discover about the cosmos. Nietzsche's idea is that the philosopher finds out about nature's secrets by discerning the natural within himself. He ignores the system, the regulation of learning about nature, and concentrates upon himself-as-nature. For he is a sample of nature's creativeness.

In the ways I have indicated, Nietzsche, uniquely, regards Thales not as a point in the history of philosophy, but rather as 'timeless'; we cannot outgrow Thales and it will always be important for the human race to know that he existed. He serves as an exemplar who once thought about the world in a self-fulfilling manner. For to think about the world, as we say, 'impersonally' is not to gain but to lose wisdom. Thales was wise (one of the Seven Sages) and the *sophia* which he loved comprised both learning and an entirely personal (non-collaborative) domination over learning, which we might call 'insight'.

II

The quality of insight is more marked in Anaximander, for the vision he expresses is yet clearer and bolder than that of Thales. Guthrie speaks of Anaximander as a 'fearless and original thinker'.[7] In an interesting sentence Guthrie also observes that, 'The strength of someone like Anaximander lay in the bold flight of imaginative reason with which he sketched the outlines of a cosmos . . . .'[8] These are valuable words, for they define what was then (in the first half of the sixth century) philosophy at its best.

First, note that Anaximander is said to have sketched the outlines of a cosmos, not *the* cosmos. I doubt if Guthrie intends us to dwell on the fact that Anaximander's cosmos was other than the 'real' cosmos as we know it today. The modern scholar is rightly praising a quality of mind rather than its discoveries. There is a suggestion that such speculations are philosophically creditable, even when they are later refuted by science.

Much more worthy of comment, however, is the phrase, 'bold flight of imaginative reason'. It was Anaximander's *reason* that took flight, not his fancy; nevertheless, his reason was powered by boldness and imagination. It was bold because it flew in the face of others' beliefs, and it was imaginative because Anaximander simply imagined a solution to his problem. This process of imagining was subject to reason, first in that it had a certain logic, and second in that it had nothing to do with what Anaximander wanted to believe: it was not in the ordinary sense emotional or self-gratifying.

Anaximander evidently reasoned as follows: that from which the forms of matter come to be and into which each eventually passes away cannot itself be a form of matter (such as water, the choice of Thales), since it is impossible for a material source to produce 'opposing' materials, for example, both fire and water. Fire and water, he reasoned, cannot live together. In addition, every substance is by definition specific. Whether or not it is thought of as having a spatial boundary, it must have a distinctive quality. Anaximander's term, *apeiron*, means the boundless, but it seems likely that he had in mind qualitative indefiniteness rather than endlessness. The point about the *apeiron* is that it cannot be qualified.

Such thinking is plainly logical so that Anaximander follows his path to a conclusion with little or no dependence upon knowledge. As Guthrie says, Anaximander's idea is 'purely conceptual, and has no meaning in the world of immediate sensible experience'.[9] In this way reason now acquires sovereignty. The human mind, an aspect or organ of nature, discovers within itself the ability to interpret and qualify the whole of nature. The mind, or more accurately what Guthrie defines as 'imaginative reason', will use whatever aids are available – facts and observations – but it has no need of these in the last analysis.

Nietzsche also comments upon what we may as well call the 'ethical content' of Anaximander's reasoning. The latter could not understand why everything must sooner or later die, if it is justified in its existent form. Therefore each existent thing and, it follows, the sum of existent things, is in some sense 'unjustified'. Expounding this idea, Nietzsche writes:

> Whence that restless, ceaseless coming-into-being and giving birth, whence that grimace of painful disfiguration on the countenance of nature, whence the never-ending dirge in all the realms of existence?[10]

Certainly the passage is reminiscent of Schopenhauer, and Nietzsche at the stage of writing *Philosophy in the Tragic Age of the Greeks* had scarcely risen above Schopenhauer's influence, but, despite that, it seems likely that Anaximander thought in some such terms. The Greek speaks of things being destroyed 'according to necessity; for they pay penalty and retribution to each other for their injustice according to the assessment of Time . . . '.[11] Nietzsche's translator, Marianne Cowan, speaks of the 'ordinance of time', [12] but the original might be rendered as either 'assessment' or 'ordinance' and Anaximander indeed seems to be thinking of Time as that which *obliges* us to depart, just as it *obliged* us to enter the scene. Time arranges birth-and-death, coming-to-be and passing-away, each movement (forwards and backwards, so to speak) being both necessary and just. Passing-away is just, because our mere existence is an injustice. Presumably this is an early statement of the understanding which lies behind tragic hubris, namely that one's elementary being-here is an encroachment or assault upon other beings. Thus, whenever one's being-here is pronounced, as it is through undue self-assertion, one potentially angers the Fates.

So far as Nietzsche is concerned in his interpretation of Anaximander, the existence of every being is an affront to other beings; far from 'having a right to life', as we say in modern times, our being here is in some degree criminal and must be expiated by death. However, the same applies to every substance in the universe; hence the universal processes of dissolution – back into the *apeiron*, the indivisible stuff from which all individual things come.

Now here, too, is a sort of reasoning with which we are familiar by means of the nevertheless different conception of death as the wages of sin. In the Christian scheme this is 'our' world in the sense that God has banished us to this place of sin and death. Death happens to us because we are imperfect. In Anaximander's universe death happens also to a mountain, or a star, because they too are 'imperfect'; that is, they impose themselves on other substantial bodies or keep other beings at bay. But this is philosophy, not religion, for Anaximander is describing what eternally happens: there is no Almighty governing the process and redeeming good people for ever. Beyond the cosmos of Anaximander is not a spiritual sphere but a non-existent, quality-less compound of all substances. This 'anterior' world is supposed to be material, not spiritual.

Nietzsche does not discuss Anaximenes, normally regarded by doxographers as the successor to Anaximander, and while Nietzsche makes no apology for this omission, we can possibly guess his reason and make an apology on his behalf. Nietzsche's concealed theme (the theme I am bringing to the surface) is the ascent of creative thought. It is necessary to bear in mind that this thought of the tragic age is overwhelmingly constructive; if it takes its rise in *critique* – in an objection to a traditional idea or a predecessor's idea – it promptly leaps to a new idea. No one is satisfied with pure critique. Thus Anaximenes, a pupil of Anaximander, evidently felt that, as *arche*, the *apeiron* was unsatisfactory in at least one fundamental way. In fact Anaximenes must appear to us as 'more scientific' than Anaximander, because he is more interested in meeting an obvious objection. Why should the originative stuff be indefinite, since we do not know and cannot properly apprehend whatever is said to be without qualities? Following this route, one imagines (and it is hard to imagine any other procedure), Anaximenes returned to the pre-Anaximandrian assumption, the assumption of Thales, that the *arche* could only be an extension of an existent element. Anaximenes selected air, on the grounds that air could be changed into other materials through condensation or refinement, and is constantly moving.

I fancy that Nietzsche omits Anaximenes simply because the latter is limitedly 'scientific', commonsensical, relatively unaware that the great aim of a philosopher must *now* be to vanquish myth. Thus Anaximenes fails to discern the lofty purpose of philosophy and does not realise that the *apeiron* of Anaximander is admirable just because it has a purely conceptual (myth-defeating) justification.

Let us briefly consider this matter in the light of a modern problem. Today most physicists consider that the universe originated in the Big Bang, when an instant's explosion of energy produced the galaxies which have been hurtling away from one another ever since. At the Big Bang, about fifteen billion years ago, space-time, or preferably 'spacetime', began. Now, as we shall see later, this does not necessarily mean that eternity has lost its meaning, for there may still be – or indeed *must* be according to our powers of reasoning – unbounded duration into which spacetime fits. Of course, this is a monumental paradox, yet those who believe that spacetime is the only mode of duration cannot cope with the question, 'But what happened before the Big Bang?' The 'official' answer, reliant upon some sort of proof, is 'nothing', but, philosophically speaking, this is a non-answer; in other words, it is acceptable to the human mind only if one believes in a Creator independent of his creation.

Moreover, we need to note here that since Einstein few have thought of the universe as having an 'outside', unless indeed our universe is but one of many contiguous universes. The belief is that the entire universe is constantly expanding, because as the galaxies travel further apart they take space with them. Matter belongs in space, of course, but, equally, space belongs between clumps of matter. It is not a question of pieces of matter journeying through space, but rather of matter and space journeying together. It follows that space is never quite empty, because even in the most deserted regions lie ghostly particles of light and matter. It is not easy to decide whether such regions are nearer in constitution to the *apeiron* of Anaximander or the more 'commonsensical' air of Anaximenes.

But of course that is a trivial observation and the proper point to be made here is that the philosopher, as opposed to the man of knowledge, must rely on thought alone. From this exalted point of view Anaximenes' air is a step *down* towards science and is insufficiently a product of 'imaginative reason'.

So Nietzsche has no time to spare for Anaximenes. The latter did not realise that the first philosopher, Thales, set out to illuminate an *envisioned* unity and merely used a substance (water) for his purpose. Anaximander had followed a similar philosophical route and found the *arche*, specifically the *apeiron*. It is still necessary to confront an obvious objection to my style of thinking. How in the modern age can one consider a belief preferable when it is nakedly unscientific? However, that is the whole point: these early thinkers were reliant upon concepts in the first instance – *concepts as opposed to observations*. They had almost no notion of empiricism, but this does not mean they were misguided. In fact they naively, or even dumbly, understood what we find hard to understand: our knowledge is but an interpretation of the world and has no higher validity. What finally matters is that knowledge must serve the philosopher. He needs to maintain his legislative function, not indeed by riding roughshod over science but by grasping knowledge as a means at his disposal. He must play the benevolent tyrant. Such tyranny was part of wisdom before wisdom became first confused, then all but destroyed by sovereign and impersonal knowledge.

III

In his book Nietzsche himself goes straight to the more conspicuously wise Heraclitus. I am now using the term 'wise' to mean precisely the celebrated quality of Heraclitus, the quality of relying upon one's own uncorrupted vision. Heraclitus saw what *is*, because he paid no attention to fashion and opinion. More than any other (non-mathematical) thinker and despite his poetic quality, Heraclitus confines language to its elementary role. He is not carried along on a stream of his own words; rather he rejects wordy notions, not to mention attempts at 'proof'. He makes it plain by the style of his assertions as well as the assertions themselves that opinion and proof are, as he believes, contemptible absurdities. It is true that up to this time no one justified his observations, but Heraclitus alone was the 'obscure', the one whose sayings seemed to require some persuasive sort of exposition. We do not know for sure whether Heraclitus wrote a book, but if he did it is likely to have taken the oracular–aphoristic form of his surviving fragments; in other words, it would have manifested a distrust of continuous expository prose. His solution was not ours – the analysis of language – but to indicate as succinctly as possible that the entities we name do not, as entities, exist: there are no things but only interrelated processes, forces, or, as we now say, energies.

To return to Anaximander for a moment, the weakness in his position, as Nietzsche sees it, is this: since everything that comes to be must pass away, in expiation of the self-centredness of its coming-to-be, why has not everything that has come to be already passed away, given that these countless occurrences have occupied – or indeed, composed – an eternity? Note that Nietzsche's 'time' does not have a history, with a beginning, an end and a story that can be told; rather, it runs backwards and forwards to infinity. Such unboundedness is acceptable to those modern physicists who conjecture not only that the universe must eventually collapse back to a small dense mass but that it might start expanding again; that another Big Bang could, conceivably, then start the universal process afresh.

However, an understanding which it is not too fanciful to compare with Nietzsche's assumption was originally expressed by Heraclitus; here are the most pertinent of the Ephesian's words:

> This world, which is the same for all, was made neither by a god nor by a man, but it ever was, and is, and will be, ever-living Fire, in measures being kindled and in measures going out.[13]

The foregoing fragment has been taken to show that, for Heraclitus, fire was not the originative stuff, as water was for Thales or air for Anaximenes, since the words mean that all existent as well as 'pre-existent' things are either fire or transmutations of fire. Indeed there are no pre-existent things; the very phrase is nonsense. All, for all time, is fire.

Fire turns into 'first, sea; of sea half is earth and half fiery storm-cloud',[14] as Heraclitus declares in the next of his fragments (No. 21). Alternatively, some doxographers (Guthrie, for example[15]) maintain that Heraclitus would have shared the world-view of his age to the effect that surrounding the known cosmos is untransmuted *arche*, either finite or infinite in extent.

Looking back at Heraclitus from his own pre-Einsteinian position, Nietzsche sees the ancient philosopher as postulating a universe finite in size but infinite in duration. This is precisely Nietzsche's 'world'; he takes it over from Heraclitus. It is consistent with our expanding universe at least in the sense that, according to the Principle of the Conservation of Energy, while the galaxies grow further apart, the total quantity of energy in the universe remains constant.

The Heraclitean–Nietzschean cosmos is not an organic unity: it is 'not a unity, to be sure, such as Anaximander sought beyond the fluttering veils of the many . . . '.[16] Nevertheless, Heraclitus famously declares that 'All things are one.' [17] How can this be? How is it that the 'one' is not a unity? The solution to this riddle is that the many must be viewed as taking part, willy-nilly, in an inconceivably vast and endless game. One's participation in the game constitutes one's nature – which is not, therefore, distinct and separable from other natures.

In this sense all qualities are finally the same quality (which Heraclitus regarded as 'Fire'). Nietzsche himself did not accept that individuality is the last word about any organism, including the human individual. He never neatly explained his belief, but it probably took the following form. Through laziness people cause themselves to be more alike than they need be. Beneath the social level lies the valuable part of a human being, surrendered by those who indolently join the 'herd'. People who think about the matter often stop at this point, but Nietzsche goes further, believing that below the superficial sameness and the deeper originality lies a further region where all things truly are *one*. This is the original Heraclitean belief developed by Nietzsche. To Heraclitus the world-process is an ever-moving, never-ending pattern of interlinked processes. The *Logos* tells us this, or rather, such a telling is both a corollary of the *Logos* and the wisdom one derives from heeding it. The *Logos* is primarily a grasp of what *is*, of what is present before one at any instant, together with an awareness that this immediate presence of interconnected things is at one with the universal entirety. However, 'men' prove incapable of understanding the *Logos*. They do not 'hear' it. To 'hear' it means to pay attention to it. The pattern to which we should pay attention is any assemblage of processes that we may perceive. In turn, 'paying attention' means discerning the assemblage intimately but artlessly – without preconceptions. When one thus listens to the *Logos*, one neither breaks the pattern down into components nor explains it in accordance with human wishes and styles of explanation. There is nothing cultural in this Way: indeed it is anti-cultural. Plainly the *Logos* requires more consideration than has been given here and in fact the above points are pursued in the final chapter (pp. 167–71).

Thus the 'All' that Heraclitus, as spokesman for the *Logos*, declares to be 'One' refers to any and every 'All' that presents itself to both mind *and* senses. It is not a conceptualised entirety, not (from a modern point of view) the astrophysical cosmos grasped and explained in theoretical terms. When Heraclitus himself refers to the

Kosmos, as he does in Fragment XX ('This world, which is the same for all . . . '), he has in mind the grand total of visible beings exactly as and when they appear before us. The regular human error is either to narrow one's gaze and proceed to make up stories about whatever one then sees, as though it actually enjoyed a separate existence, or else to invent an 'All' which cannot be other than a falsifying simplification. Such stories or such cosmographies comprise every cultural account of beings – poetical, mythical, religious, political, and, in modern times, scholarly or scientific. These expositions, learned or popular, detach the narrowed perceptions from the true 'All', the *Logos*-as-All, to which they essentially belong. On their own, the beings are uprooted, deformed, or perhaps we might say, 'aborted'. Alternatively the *Logos*-as-All is simply concealed by a scientific (or possibly a mystical) All. We human beings are capable of living in accordance with the *Logos*, whereupon we submit ourselves to the universal condition. We and we alone may comprehend that condition. In this way certain fragments of the universe, a race of 'clever animals', have access to the secret of the universe, which is a secret because other beings, who perforce live according to the Word, cannot receive it – and, moreover, among people only the wise can do so.

Nietzsche points out that Heraclitus saw only a world of becoming: everything arrives already growing, then it develops further, and finally it disintegrates in order to make way for new forms of growth. This is not injustice, let alone punishment, but justice itself. Things die, not (as Anaximander thought) because they are wicked, but because the coming-to-be must ever be justified. It is right that things come into the world; therefore it is necessary that the old things depart. The coming-to-be can fulfil itself only insofar as the already-present is 'ingested' (to speak metaphorically, though perhaps not altogether metaphorically). Each measure of energy – to use modern language – proceeds incorporating predecessors, and, likewise, each moment of time swallows up the preceding moment. But from one human point of view – the best available to us whenever we measure and discriminate – every 'unit' of energy and time (time being an attribute of energy) is eternal. Outside our cultivated perceptions and terms of reference there are no 'multiplicities', because the many amounts to the One.

From another point of view, the *Logos* is the Law, superintended by God, meaning Zeus. Zeus himself is best understood as the deification of all existent things, but this world-encompassing God

does not exactly make the Law according to his whim or convenience. Rather the Law is what he administers; he cannot change or
manipulate it, for it is as dominant and durable as he is himself.
Zeus is the totality of all that is, yet even he cannot, for example,
cause a (necessarily) moving or developing phenomenon to stand
still and simply *be*.

Alongside the Law there is another dominant partner, namely
Dike, daughter of Zeus. *Dike* in this grand sense means justice,
though the word most commonly refers to particular rules and legal
decisions. But justice as the daughter of Zeus bears another ancient
meaning which requires a brief discussion here.

We need to clear from our minds all later moral or reformist
notions of justice, even the tragic notion (such as that of Aeschylus
in his *Prometheus Bound*) of a demand made of Zeus on behalf of
humanity. To Nietzsche justice means the rightness of whatever
is pressing to be born. A plant, a creature, a massive eruption of
earth and fire, a microscopic organism: all these in addition to
human beings are justified in entering the world and justifiably
consume some already existing things. Every being feeds on other
beings. Birth and growth are distinguished from destruction and
death by our discriminating minds, but our minds thus falsify an
actual sameness. The manifold workings of creation – or preferably
of creation as inclusive of destruction – comprise *Dike*, daughter
of God. This joint rule of the Law and *Dike* naturally means that
everything is 'up against' other things, for not only must all things
fight their way into the world, but having gained entry, must
incorporate others encountered on their journey. Sooner or later,
they are themselves incorporated. Whatever precisely happens,
every moment of the thing lives on eternally. Thus no moment
is actually lost; it is devoured but not lost to the universal process.

It will be easy to appreciate that my talk of 'things' and 'moments'
is a convenient manner of speaking. Similarly we must bear in mind
that in Nietzsche's reading of Heraclitus the strife I have mentioned
is purely a human view of how the world works. We see what is
as strife, but because there is nothing else, it is not 'strife' in our
derogatory or resentful sense. This is 'how things are' and 'not-strife'
is either a human dream or a sense of comparative rest. In addition
it is possible, if rare, to have an intuition of all these struggling
and contesting qualities as merging: all *is* one. Heraclitus famously
writes as follows:

Couples are wholes and not wholes, what agrees disagrees, the concordant is discordant. From all things one and from one all things.[18]

The paradoxes of Heraclitus are certainly meant to be other than ingenious; they are verbal pointers to material reality. Even spiritual/material is no longer an antithesis viewed Heracliteanly, for the spiritual is the material seen in a different light. The quick and the dead are the same, not just as stages in the transformation of the same body, but in the sense that both are energy or, as Heraclitus would say, 'fire'. Furthermore, the entirety of energy which we conceptualise as the cosmos or the world is of the same nature as any tiny manifestation of energy. When we examine the nature of any one thing, we see the nature of the whole. Conversely, when we conceptualise the whole, our idea should match what we observe of a single thing, for instance the whole must consist of energy. (Here it is worth reminding ourselves that even a stone is today considered to be frozen, or inactive energy.)

At this point it is a good idea to ask how, precisely, Heraclitus thought of the whole. That he was unable to contemplate the stars as we do does not make his idea fundamentally wrong. In modern times our vague picture of the whole is merely an increase of what we can already see – 'more of the same'. We no longer give the universe a distinct quality since it has a camouflaged quality in the largely quantitative form of our charts and spectacular photographs. We are impressed ('awed' is possibly the wrong word) by our sense of enormous size and by unexplained phenomena. To balance this, however, we are fairly sure of much of our information; we believe we know a good deal about how the universe works. But this means that our rather sterile notion of quality consists of enormous quantity. On the other hand, Heraclitus had a clear idea of universal quality, namely that 'Time is a child playing draughts; the kingship is a child's.'[19] Here 'Time' means an age, an aeon.

Nietzsche makes much of this idea, and does so in a noteworthy manner, though without reference to the actual words of Heraclitus. Nietzsche writes as follows:

And as children and artists play, so plays the ever-living fire. It constructs and destroys, all in innocence. Such is the game that the aeon plays with itself. . . . From time to time it starts the game anew. An instant of satiety – and again it is seized by its need, as the artist is seized by his need to create . . . The child throws its toys away from time to time – and starts again, in innocent caprice.[20]

Thus Heraclitus regarded the whole as the sport of an innocent but irresponsible child, or, alternatively, as a creative artist with no moral intent. 'Time is a child playing draughts' implies that the sequence of time as we normally understand it is meaningless. One thing happens after another not in obedience to a scientific law but as one move after another, with meaning only in terms of the game. Someone might remark that the draughts-metaphor suggests a rigid game, yet for certain the game is not rigid but continuously creative. It is a multitude of activities, the moves of which are fashioned by Time as he proceeds. Heraclitus can be taken to mean that while the aeon plays a game with itself, nothing can alter what we may as well call the 'ground rules'. These are to the effect that energies change their forms; that (for human beings) sorrow is of a piece with joy, and that creation and destruction are the same process viewed from different vantage-points.

Then there is the Law which demands becoming and strife. The 'kingship', meaning sovereignty over all occurrences, is most fruitfully to be thought of as the playful zest of a happy child. That is how Heraclitus, the 'weeping philosopher', saw the world as a whole.

Does all this imply fatalism? In one way, yes, in another way, no. Heraclitus means that it is futile to try to change the essential quality of our lives, because that quality is not affected by social arrangements, beliefs, or scientific discoveries. On the other hand, it is our role to play creatively, since that is what the aeon does. We cannot divorce ourselves from the aeon, and in fact even our gloomiest and most arid attitudes are unacknowledged acts of creation. 'Better' attitudes are likewise fabricated. When we distinguish good from bad, we are, to speak in the terms of Heraclitus, ludicrously distinguishing 'parts' of a flame. To be fair, this procedure would not be ludicrous but right and triumphant, if we could somehow grasp its legislative quality even at the moment of making the distinction. The aim is to make such distinctions, knowing them to be inventive. To put this matter yet another way, the aim is to echo Hamlet's 'There is nothing either good or bad, but thinking makes it so', followed by a decision to *think* one's way to ever-fresh valuations.

'Good and bad are the same', says Heraclitus,[21] meaning that these words denote beliefs, attitudes, moods, feelings, 'mere' valuations; but the flame, or energy, is fundamental and always the same. It is true that energy, being creative, avails itself of such beliefs and modes; indeed it manifests itself in the very distinction between good and bad, as it manifests itself in countless other forms, but the *Logos* points beyond ethics, indeed beyond philosophy itself, as practised by others than Heraclitus.

For these others, before Nietzsche, insist upon a distinction between one being and another – not a convenient but, they suppose, a vital distinction. Contrariwise, Heraclitus famously declares that 'You could not step twice into the same rivers; for other waters are ever flowing on to you.'[22] Somehow we have to adjust our minds to the increasingly obvious fact that the things we isolate from the flow do not exist in isolation. Nietzsche takes this recognition a clear step beyond Heraclitus, asserting, in modern terminology: 'To impose upon becoming the character of being – that is the supreme will to power.'[23] This might be said in alternative words as follows: we aspire to the stable and harmonious recognition of reality as process. We, as seeming individuals, have to 'stand still' in order to appreciate reality as movement. Let us say that we float along in the river, or better still, that we *are* the river, yet we cannot evade or dismiss our perspective on 'the rest' of the river at any given moment. The perspective must apparently be formed from a motionless position. 'Motionless' means supposedly motionless; we depend upon the illusion of standing still. This is the human imperative. In modern times, however, we should progressively learn how to live with this illusion, knowing it for what it is.

IV

Parmenides, whom Nietzsche discusses immediately after Heraclitus, rejects the absolute human dependence upon illusion, maintaining that there is an undeluded way, easy enough to comprehend in theory if impossible to pursue in practice. So in Parmenides a gulf opens between the Truth and the muddled route of mortal opinions, which we must follow in order to live. One who has access to the Truth knows he lives in falsehood. For the most part, living *is* falsehood.

As we have just noted, Heraclitus insists on continuous flow, or becoming: that is the Truth of Heraclitus disclosed by the Word. Now in Parmenides' poem the Truth which the philosopher seeks is of necessity distinct from the flow of impressions. That is to say, it is distinct not only from the impressions and opinions but from the *flow*, from the continuity which is provided by our deceiving minds. At this point it is necessary to proceed much more cautiously.

Parmenides' work is divided into a proem and two parts. The proem recounts how Parmenides is taken in a chariot to the goddess who will tell him 'all things'. The first part then reproduces the words of the goddess, revealing, 'the unshaken heart of well-rounded truth'.[24] No other mortal knows this, Parmenides having been singled out to receive the message. The second part expounds some fundamental opinions as if they were valid, though we have been amply assured of their radical untruth. We merely need to remember that *all* human opinions are untrue.

Parmenides' contention in the first part, the account of Truth, is simply that something either is or is not. To my mind the distinction here is not between substantial existents and fictional or imaginary existents, but rather between anything whatever that may be physically *or mentally* encountered and, on the other hand, that which is utterly without being. It is not so absurd as it sounds to look for an example of nonbeing, since we normally think in terms of nonexistence, especially through the processes of history and memory. That, I believe, is Parmenides' point; he wants to distinguish between an image or a perception that is, and an utterly unreal (as he supposes) mental manoeuvre by means of which existents are linked with nonexistents.

I may remember a pen I had in childhood. This pen now appears to me as an image; *thus* it 'is', as we say. But I would be in error to suppose that the image of the pen is *in any sense* the substantial pen. For the latter, as Parmenides says, is not. He specifically argues that a thing can neither come into being nor depart from being. At any moment the things that are are, and the seeming 'things' that are not are not. It is no good remarking that the pen 'I used to have' persists as a memory, because of course it is the memory that persists, not the pen. The latter merely is not. And the words 'used to have' are strictly nonsensical, because they give an exclusively present or existent image a past or nonexistent signification. The physical pen has not 'passed away' in the sense of gone out of existence, for, according to Parmenides, an item cannot pass from existence to nonexistence. Alternatively (and this is the Heraclitean–Nietzschean alternative), the pen is eternal, though we must not think of it as a static object but rather, correctly, as process. It is not *a* process, nor yet part of a process, but simply process: its very character is processive. In this non-Parmenidean, or fluid, way the pen always 'is'. To Parmenides himself there is no transitional stage between 'is' and 'is not', for we must, logically, draw a line after 'is'. Likewise, there is no phase of transition between the so-called pre-existence of some development and its manifest present existence. As we noted earlier, pre-existence is non-existence.

Then, what of history? Let us continue to make concrete references. For example, the Russian Revolution is not, for what we now have, what now is, consists of images and other present-day constructions. A firm disciple of Parmenides would deny the existence of the 'revolution itself', A concept of the revolution is current, but we should divorce this from a presumed series of actions called the 'revolution itself'. Far from being trivial, the kind of aberrant reasoning I here attribute to Parmenides is momentous, since it invalidates all culture. Culture is a composition of representations, analyses, valuations – many of them 'mortal opinions' in Parmenides' denigratory sense. Therefore culture is largely comprised of nonexistents, insofar as the components of culture are taken to be connected with extracultural nonexistents. Of course, a copy of something or other would be a different matter. Thus Caesar *is* either as a statue or as a portrait in a history, but not as an actual Roman. Parmenides denies the past, and likewise, of course, the future.

Nietzsche accepts the main assertion of Parmenides, namely: 'The existent alone has being; the nonexistent does not.'[25] But Nietzsche thinks Parmenides is wrong to distinguish a way of Truth from mortal opinions and impressions. All our perceptions and beliefs are mobile, which is as much as to say Parmenidean 'untruths', sooner or later contradicting one another. We trust them up to a point for everyday purposes, not because they are true but because they are convenient or even necessary – footholds on an icy slope. The question of Truth remains, however, in the sense which Parmenides unyieldingly employs. This means that if one is to do philosophy one must fix what one knows to be unfixed. Like Heraclitus, Parmenides says Truth alone does not become; that is what makes it Truth. After a great gap of time Nietzsche sees it as his task to reconcile Parmenides with Heraclitus. Nietzsche asks the following question: if the senses dissemble, to whom do they dissemble? For there is no subject distinct from the senses who might be deceived. Either the problem of deception does not arise or else 'seeming' – if that is what we mean by deception – is universal, the norm of all life-forms.

Nietzsche treats Parmenides as a stage in a longer and more complex journey, but the rightness of Parmenides, insofar as he is right, continues to be of the first importance. It remains necessary to defeat delusions that truth is the object of culture (for instance, of history), but it is also important to rid ourselves of the idea that there is an extracultural Truth. Throughout his life Nietzsche addresses the problem expressed in Parmenides (though he and we normally encounter it in its elaborate Platonic form). Nietzsche regularly tries to find a satisfactory answer to the following question: how can one think at all validly, which is to say philosophically, about an ever-shifting reality of which one is an ever-shifting 'part'? On the elementary level (though there is a long way to go from here) Nietzsche's answer is that the test of a position is not its irrefutability but its value for the purposes of living – living being considered as organic self-enhancement rather than mere survival. Parmenides is logically correct but fatal. In a very brief time he took ontology as far as it can go as a logical discipline. But this has emphasised our need to live and grow by means of unphilosophic fictions and images of continuity.

V

Thus for our own maintenance (which means the same as growth) we need to find ever-new explanations of the beginning of the world – or of its lack of a beginning. Our explanations will be fictions or metaphors but we cannot proceed without them. So Nietzsche moves straight to Anaxagoras, who deals with the problem of origins by contending that substances as we encounter them have developed from 'seeds', which once undifferentiatedly existed in an all-inclusive whole. 'All things', he writes, 'were together infinite in respect of both number and smallness; for the small too was infinite.[26] Now this (opening) dictum of Anaxagoras, with its evocation of a primordium, has been taken as a specific refutation of Parmenides. Yet, as we have by now amply seen, nothing can refute Parmenides, except a (Nietzschean) belief that Truth is, like everything in creation, a device and exercise of will to power. In brief, to Nietzsche, Parmenides' Truth is not absolutely fundamental.

For his part, Anaxagoras needs to account for the emergence of substances from original seeds. It is important to note that, 'before these things were separated off' (as Anaxagoras puts it)[27] they were not distinguishable, on account of their smallness, for, he supposes, nothing is so small that smaller things may not lie within it. Now these infinitely small seeds were without the usual attributes of substances except perhaps for size, though even that is a moot point. In that primordial age colours were not distinguishable either, and one cannot properly describe such non-colours as 'plain' because plainness requires colourfulness as its antithesis. Similarly one may not confer upon this complete mixture of beings such qualities as moist, dry, hot, cold, bright, dark, or indeed any exclusive qualities at all, apart (once more) from the unmeasurable 'dimensions' of each seed or particle.

But Anaxagoras goes further than this, claiming that everything that has been, or is, or will be in the future, was already present in seed-form in the first indescribable mixture. This is another purely logical point, revealing that Anaxagoras, like others before him, is willing to take logical inference as far as it will go. For he intends us to understand that nothing can emerge from nothing, so that every substance in existence must have proceeded from the mixture of seeds. Where else can it have come from? That is the confident, inexorable argument. If today we suggest that a present substance is a development from prior substances – or 'forces', or 'energies' – stretching back to infinity, then Anaxagoras is not exactly defeated.

This thinker further maintains that 'All other things have a portion of everything, but mind is infinite and self-ruled, and is mixed with nothing, but is all alone by itself.'[28] The first remark appears to us an attempt to realise and specify the sheer compositness of existents. Now that we know the chemical composition of substances, specifically that a compound is made up of certain elements but not others, we are bound to say that Anaxagoras is wrong, but nevertheless he is aware of an important fact: the most complex organism differs from simpler objects, by virtue, not of its elements but of its complexity. Anaxagoras is implicitly speaking of the *naturalness* of human beings, and this is as much a philosophical as a purely chemical or physical idea in its implications.

But Mind is an altogether more interesting concept. Anaxagoras is trying to explain the mysteries of motion, separation, and knowledge. Things are, but by what means do they move? And how did they come to be separated from one another? It seems that the separation must have been accomplished by an external agency, or an agency both extrinsic and intrinsic to the things, for while we may contend that movement is 'mechanical', we still cannot explain how the first impetus occurred. Anaxagoras maintains that Mind, itself substantial in some ultra-fine way, 'controls all things, both the greater and the smaller, that have life'.[29] It is likely that this phrase includes all moving and developing things, not just creatures. By means of a rotatory movement the original seeds were 'winnowed out', becoming distinguishable. Interestingly enough, the process of rotation has continued and will continue into the indefinite future. Since this is so, Mind is omnipresent, for how could distant heavenly bodies move unless they too were urged and animated by Mind? But though Mind is everywhere, it is not in everything. 'In everything there is a portion of everything except Mind; and there are some things in which there is Mind as well.'[30]

Now, what is Mind or, in the original, *nous*? The Greek word always indicates either perception or intention, or both. *Nous* is sense, awareness, and, often enough, purpose. Therefore Anaxagoras wants us to understand that movement is not mechanical but purposive. However, the purpose does not come from quite outside the physical world. Plainly it is *metaphysical*, because it cannot be perceived, measured, or in any way quantified. Nevertheless, it is not spiritual, as we have come to understand spirituality. The difference between Mind and clearly corporeal matter is that the former is made of finer stuff, so fine as to be forever imperceptible. We shall progressively come to see how Nietzsche used Anaxagoras' elementary notion of Mind, and how fruitful a roughly similar idea might still be today.

It is time to comment briefly upon Nietzsche's debt to the Presocratics. The debt has been recognised often enough, but it remains necessary to understand some of Nietzsche's thoughts in the light of his youthful reading of the figures we have been discussing. First, the term 'debt', needs to be understood in regard to Nietzsche. He did not exactly borrow from the Presocratics, even to the limited extent of taking an idea and modifying it in accordance with nineteenth-century philosophical and scientific views. Rather, he knew what he wanted in the first place, probably from childhood, and when he encountered an idea, say in Anaximander, he realised immediately that here was something he could use. One should emphasise the 'he'; this was not a viewpoint that could, in general be used, but an ancient opinion that might now be moulded into a new *Nietzschean* shape. Of course, it can be argued that the idea as developed by Nietzsche is what the original author 'truly' had in mind, though the latter (Anaximander, for example) lacked a suitable cultural environment in which to formulate it. According to this view, Nietzsche completed an ancient thought, and we know that Nietzsche in fact held the later rather than the earlier exponents of a doctrine to be the best, philosophically speaking. For instance, the Jesuits were far better Christian philosophers than the crude and manic early Christians. Nevertheless, Nietzsche never claimed to be improving, adapting or modernising ancient thinkers. Then, what was his procedure? It seems he simply selected from an Anaximander what was creatively useful to him. His genius, like that of each of the Presocratics, lay in uniting philosophical with purely personal development; in resisting the movement of philosophy towards learning. Nietzsche effortlessly discounts just the assumption that has reigned since the Academy, the belief that philosophy too, is a branch of knowledge to which individuals *progressively* contribute. He refashions, when he does not ignore, the very notion of 'progress'.

In relation to Anaximander, Nietzsche first asks *himself* the question: 'Why hasn't all that came-to-be passed away long since, since a whole eternity of time has passed?'[31] The question is fancifully ascribed to Anaximander, though it is Nietzsche, in the 1870s, who still wants to find an answer. As we know, Anaximander held that fresh things forever come to be from the realm of the indefinite, the *apeiron*. But to Nietzsche the *apeiron* cannot be a satisfactory explanation, if it is regarded as a source 'outside' space. We, at any rate, can say to the shade of Anaximander: nothing lies outside space, although indeed this nothing is continually penetrated by the outermost masses of the expanding universe with their circumambient regions of space. Likewise to Nietzsche in his day the world was surrounded, as he said, by 'nothingness'.[32] Nietzsche, having no idea of universal expansion, was strikingly modern just the same, since he regarded the 'world' as finite in terms of total force. He saw its total energy as conserved, in accordance with the Principle of the Conservation of Energy. But being a philosopher, he went further than the scientists in contending that whatever shape materialises in the universe neither endures nor is ever, in the usual sense, 'lost'. The shape inevitably changes; indeed it only exists as process and cannot be fixed. The idea of perdurance and the idea of loss are alike false. One cannot lose what, as an entity, never was. We need to acknowledge what is correct but unimaginable: a universe of uninterrupted alteration – not alteration from one state to the next, since there are no steady states, but merely unchecked flow and metamorphosis. Thus we shall come to recognise our images as necessary fictions.

For instance, I, sitting at this desk (meaning not some such fabrication as my personality or spirit, but just the psychophysiological activity of sitting at the desk), where do 'I' go? In Nietzsche this question receives the answer that 'I' do not go anywhere because 'I', as postulated, have never existed. Certainly it is impossible to apprehend oneself, or, any other object in this 'Dionysian' fashion, but what Nietzsche expects is that a number of 'oligarchs of the spirit' will grow fully aware that their normal 'Apollonian' apprehension is but a way of living, strictly speaking an expedient. Every action, down to the least perceptible, every instant of spacetime, subsists eternally, but subsists as energy. Energy is process, and process flows on, but the shapes which we carve out of the flow and to which we give such labels as I-sitting-at-the-desk, are entirely human devices.

Nietzsche's thoughts about Heraclitus support the same belief. Heraclitus naturally and humanly sees a world of 'eternal substantive multiplicities', but recognises that such is no more than a human vision. In reality, beyond the bounds of discriminatory human perception, the multiplicities are one, namely fire. In this way, and this way alone, I-sitting-at-the-desk may be said to 'persist'. I go forth to infinity – but as Heraclitean fire. I am not even 'part' of the fire, since there are no parts. Nothing perishes, but then, nothing actually is, as a substantive being. There is but fire, playing endlessly, shaping and reshaping itself by means of its games. At the end of the nineteenth century Nietzsche cannot profitably think in terms of fire, but he can and does think of energy: the world is a 'monster of energy'.[33]

From Heraclitus Nietzsche also derives his own version of *Dike*, that is to say, of the justification of all beings in their unamended forms. If one accepts the Heraclitean justification of everything that comes to be (since *Dike* herself smiles upon all arrivals), then one readily accepts, or even welcomes, the underlying and decisive current of events. 'Nihilism stands at the door . . . .'[34]

Fine, if that is so; if nihilism is now, in 1885–6, waiting to enter, then one's philosophy must be fashioned around that disturbing visitor, not dissipated in attempts to substitute another visitor. For nihilism too must be greeted justly, in the spirit required by *Dike*, daughter of god. Here (as always in Nietzsche) justice means not moral justice but, on the contrary, scrupulous allowance for the nature of whatever one is contemplating. For example, we know that Nietzsche had much difficulty in accepting pettiness of mind and spirit, but in *Zarathustra* he concludes that pettiness endures and cannot not be.[35] The perfectly just way proceeds from a firm refusal to see qualities as requiring alteration: thus pettiness can neither be reasoned nor loved out of existence but plays its own essential part.

By the same token Nietzsche recognises, with Heraclitus, that good and bad are the same. This is a far cry from 'philosophical' indifference or reasonableness. Rather it means, for practical purposes, in Nietzsche and presumably in Heraclitus, that one does not resent ill fortune but uses it for self-enhancement. Thus Nietzsche tells us in *Ecce Homo* how he used his own decadence (meaning his physiological morbidity) to gain subtlety of thought and observation. This was not a deliberate procedure and would have been futile if it had been. Instead Nietzsche found his subtlety increasing with his bouts of sickness. In such a way good and bad are the same. Note, there is no hint of moral elevation in this and no inane pretence that the sickness is enjoyed. On the contrary, the procedure is more classical than Christian; it resembles a Caesar becoming more hardy than many of his soldiers *because* of his epilepsy. Here I suppose is the soil in which Nietzsche's doctrine of *amor fati* grew; if it is one's fate to be decadent, then one must love the decadence precisely as it appears in oneself – which means that periods of decadence must alternate with periods of health. It goes without saying that 'love' implies resolute will rather than anything resembling easy affection. The lesson Nietzsche learned is scarcely in Heraclitus, but we can see how such a lesson can be drawn from Heraclitus if one has the practical desire (which in this case is as much as to say, the wisdom) to do so.

Nietzsche is not at all noted for his logic, but this means that he regarded logic as an instrument to be employed now and then, expediently. Therefore we might be tempted to imagine he had little need for Parmenides. And yet I detect in Nietzsche's treatment of Parmenides a general respect for the latter's adamantine quality and a particular approval of the recognition that everything that is is perfect and cannot be deficient in any way. Nietzsche does not mention this Parmenidean doctrine, but quietly moulds it into his own philosophy. Parmenides speaks as follows (in Part One of his poem):

> Therefore it is right that what is should not be imperfect; for it is not deficient – if it were it would be deficient in everything. The same thing is there to be thought and is why there is thought. For you will not be thinking without what is, in all that has been said. For there neither is nor will be anything else besides what is, since Fate fettered it to be whole and changeless.[36]

Such an understanding girds Nietzsche's philosophy. Whatever is cannot be deficient (or guilty, needless to say) and all existents are fettered to the whole. But in Nietzsche this point of view is not taken to be a transcendent truth, as it is in Parmenides. Nietzsche is more subtle and persuasive. We can say, with Parmenides, that all things are perfect, or, alternatively, we can declare many things to be improvable. Here are simply two opposed attitudes. To Nietzsche the question is: do human beings exercise their powers the more by acceptance of what is, or by striving for improvement? This is undoubtedly a psychological question. That Nietzsche comes down on the side of Parmenides is connected with the former's observations of *ressentiment*. This pervasive quality produces, he supposes, an inferior culture. Paradoxically, of course, an inferior culture is one that might, from the non-Parmenidean standpoint, be elevated, though such elevation could only come about by thoroughgoing Parmenidean affirmation. In this way, to aim for improvement in the sense of reform, as the spirit of *ressentiment* always does, means that one cannot match the heights. The spirit of *ressentiment* drags its own inferiority into everything it produces, thus falling short of the very pinnacles to which it pretends to aspire.

Accordingly, Nietzsche's assertion is not that nothing *can* be different (as in Parmenides), but that a great human being 'wants nothing to be different, not forward, not backward, not in all eternity'.[37] It would be ludicrous for us, at this point of all points, to call Nietzsche's statement an 'improvement' on that of Parmenides. What has happened is that Nietzsche has seized on Parmenides in gratitude and declared to himself, 'But that is greatness in a human being!' Thereafter Nietzsche himself dwells on the greatness of such an attitude, not on its 'truth'.

Finally it is from Anaxagoras that Nietzsche derives what may well be the most important lesson of all: the notion of universal purposive action, which in Anaxagoras is called 'Mind' and in Nietzsche 'Will to Power'. Anaxagoras provides the necessary supplement to science, or rather, the vital metaphysical basis upon which *physis*, or nature itself, can be investigated. Science is not enough, not indeed because it needs to be directed by morality, but because it fails to make sense of anything. That is to say, the sense made by science is mechanical; all is mechanism. A contemporary physicist remarks that, 'The fundamental questions we ask in physics – and in other sciences – cannot address *how* something works or *why* something happens.'[38] The fact is, he says, we do not know whether atoms or quarks are real: these, like all scientific entities and laws, are contrivances and nothing more. But then, neither do we know whether Mind as postulated by Anaxagoras is real; in fact we feel fairly sure it is not. The point is that we still need to provide an explanation, just as the Presocratics did: nonempirically and 'wisely'. Such an explanation must now and always be the legislative act of an individual.

Nietzsche's legislative act is to replace the Mind of Anaxagoras, together with the will of Schopenhauer, by 'Will to Power'. This last is universal and purposive, as I have said, and therefore does not require consciousness. Nietzsche understands consciousness to be at most, the entirely superficial and commonly misleading aspect of will to power. There is always a danger of absurdity in explanations of will to power, because explanation is itself nothing more than a mode of will to power. Realising this, Nietzsche simply made observations and suggestions. For all that, we cannot proceed without asserting at this point that that phrase 'will to power' characterises all forms of spiritual and physical development, or alternatively all forms of energy. Will to power is Nietzsche's 'spiritualisation' of process, so that process is given a non-mechanical meaning. Thus will to power is the modern equivalent of 'Mind', the equivalent for an age trying in vain to survive on mechanistic notions alone.

Such is the paramount understanding that Nietzsche derived from the Presocratics. And let us note at this stage that the understanding incorporates the personal wisdom which, starting with Socrates, is increasingly obscured by an allurement of the selfsame will to power, namely the belief that reason equals virtue. The will to power takes unimaginably diverse forms, since it is what Heidegger refers to as 'the Being and the essence of beings'.[39] Our next stage must be to examine the Socratic equation of reason and virtue precisely as an alluring disguise of will to power.

2

Socrates and Dialectic

I

Early in the Seventh Letter Plato discusses the trial of Socrates, saying that it was simply corrupt, since the real reason for arresting the older man was his refusal to ally himself with the Thirty. Socrates was charged with impiety and this was 'sacrilegious', as he was in fact exceedingly pious. Plato seems to lack subtlety here, for we might expect him to see that in the sense used by the accusers Socrates was 'impious' – or something of the sort. The God of Socrates was an entirely new measure of all things, so that Socrates' proper performance of his religious duties – his piety – was nevertheless steadily undermined. The accusers may have dimly recognised that the life of Socrates had brought a new God into the world, and a new doctrine, specifically a virtuous type of individualism. For some reason modern thinkers have not paid much attention to this God, perhaps associating him a little too readily with the God of Christianity.

The awe which Socrates should arouse even today lies not in the mere views he expresses in the *Apology* but in the fact that they are intrinsic to his nature; he could no more cast them off than he could cast his skin. Socrates is therefore extremely hard to understand, except in a theoretical or extrinsic way. Most of those who seem incapable of adapting themselves to their society are either simple or wilful. The latter sort say in effect, 'I am such and such and will do so and so, even if I die for it.' Such resolution may or may not be admirable, but it seldom appears 'Socratic'. Socrates himself remains in command, not remotely nervous, not in fact wilful and not in the usual sense even heroic. He is lordly, as one who has mastered all absurdity. He has done this by placing reasoned thought, a product of human life, above all life. Socrates calmly judges in this way because he listens to the word of God. Now, who is this God? No universal force can be said to be antithetical to the forces we encounter, yet the God of Socrates is apparently the supreme antithesis. Socrates' practice of reasoning and questioning is thus preferred to growth, proliferation, waste and exploitation – the very processes of energy in our experiences. Socrates himself, the only true follower of this God, weighs and measures worldly things as one apart.

His calmness is a portion of his godliness, a faith in a Being who dwells above the summit of his *personal* vision, a vision quite distinct from culture and the social code. It is important to mark this: God cannot be approached in a general or communal way but only by means of one's singular and most noble vision. Wisdom is the preserve of God; that is why Socrates is constantly aware of the unwisdom of mortals, including himself. God comes first, assuredly, though to nearly everyone else God 'comes first' only as and when their fellow-believers sustain them in their belief. But Socrates, standing alone, absolutely *knows* of a God who gives mortal beings their value. Indeed, God is this value and therefore comes to Socrates, as to the few others he visits, in a fashion that never duplicates itself. There is no question of a Lord of Hosts. In obedience to God Socrates is reverential to the gods, therefore pious; on the other hand, God takes precedence over the gods and Socrates must be impious. Socrates' accusers were thus both right and wrong, not merely wrong as Plato claims.

Socrates is what Nietzsche calls him, the 'theoretical man',[1] because such is his entire God-directed nature. He is this unprecedented creature not just in being the first to subject human life to theoretical enquiry but in examining mortal opinions so thoroughly that he seems bent on an extravagant purpose, namely to subordinate life to thought. Whenever Socrates is not physically distracted beyond all possibility of thought he is questioning something or other. His famed vigour does not, of course, make this a paradox but on the contrary helps to explain it. Only exceptional vitality could so clear the undergrowth surrounding every conception. Almost all things present to the senses and the normal understanding – family, friends, Athens, social requirements – fade as presences in the light of his theoretical probings. To Socrates, then, thought is incongruous or unmanageable only in moments of absolute physical distraction, for example at Potidaea, though we are bound to suppose that he went to that battle in his usual theoretical frame of mind. None of his thoughts could have been 'corrupted' by spears, swords and the cries of dying men. By that I mean that while Socrates is constantly thinking about life, naturally including death in battle and other calamities, his considerations are never dictated, or even influenced by practical desires, such as a desire to rid humanity of calamities.

This unparalleled theorising is not precisely a defence against the pains of life, except in the sense that even the fiercest or most despairing human attitude must act as a shield against the glare of naked existence. It is easy to misread Nietzsche himself on this point when he discusses Socrates in Sections 12 to 15 of *The Birth of Tragedy*. Socrates never claimed – and presumably never imagined – that suffering might ultimately be eliminated in some 'theoretical' sort of culture. That is a modern and essentially scientific dream. What the example of Socrates asserts is that a certain kind of suffering is superfluous. This is the kind that often accompanies bewilderment and the sense of helplessness. It is emotional as opposed to physical. In short such suffering is an affect, specifically the affect of *pessimism*. It is *pessimism* that can be cured Socratically.

Socrates was never afraid of the tragic but presumably (if the story is true) watched only the works of Euripides, refusing to attend those of Aeschylus and Sophocles, because the two older dramatists did not make sense to him. He would have been impatient with Aeschylus and Sophocles, since they did not attempt to explain the world. Instead of observing that all is dark and impenetrable, Socrates shines a light so brilliant that the darkness – the 'true', omnipresent darkness – falls away. And yet the light is one of enquiry, not of discovery. Socrates' whole idea is this: if we think hard enough, we live in virtue, and the rest, in respect of both its evil and its impenetrability, is negated. The darkness is negated!

We are only following the example of Socrates if we presume to question the lack of wisdom he detected in himself. Did he really notice a lack, a void, where others ascribe a positive quality to themselves? Socrates pinned all his faith on *search*, and for that reason needed a complete absence of that for which he searched. But, of course, there are other forms or notions of wisdom and Socrates possessed admirable wisdom according to Nietzsche, who writes as follows in *Human, All Too Human*:

> Socrates excels the founder of Christianity in being able to be serious cheerfully and in possessing that *wisdom full of roguishness* that constitutes the finest state of the human soul. And he also possessed the finer intellect.[2]

It seems, further, that Socrates could participate in every temperament, or, in other words, despite the fact that he was signally not a poet, he possessed that 'negative capability' which Keats assigned to the poetical character. We shall see the point of such participation in due course, but for the moment let us just note that (in Nietzsche's comment upon Socrates, as in Keats's comment upon poets) the emphasis concerns *participation*: a person of this kind does not merely observe every temperament – in a judicious or searching way – but shares in the differing temperaments, 'assumes' them, as it were, and just as readily casts them off. At this stage let us also note that Nietzsche, discussing the dying Socrates, remarks: 'I admire the courage and wisdom of Socrates in everything he did, said – and did not say.' He was 'the pied piper of Athens', enticing young people away from the traditions. He did this by being the 'wisest chatterer of all time', who was 'equally great in silence'.[3]

Here we are plainly concerned with two kinds of wisdom: on the one hand the wisdom that Socrates disclaims, and on the other hand the wisdom that Nietzsche discerns. Now, in the *Apology*, Socrates explains to the court that the Delphic Oracle once announced that no one on earth exceeded him in wisdom. Socrates pondered this utterance for a time and eventually concluded that God alone has wisdom, so that all human wisdom is without value. This conclusion of Socrates was itself 'wise' from a Nietzschean point of view, by which I mean that Socrates interpreted the Oracle's words in accordance with his own self-defining beliefs, yet without twisting the words. Thus he preserved and even enhanced himself but did not depart one whit from the perceived facts – the message from Delphi. To Nietzsche wisdom has two strands: self-determination and undeceived perception of the world. More explicitly: wisdom is not at all an absolute but a talented pursuit. The wise individual gets better at determining him or herself and at fending off deception. But the wisdom consists in the *overriding* desire to follow these strands, as Socrates does, to the end.

'Wisdom' sometimes implies a degree or a sort of shrewdness, but not cunning, exactly; it means the capacity to see how to achieve one's ends *and* the skill to follow the path one has seen. Prudence may or may not be involved, though never as an automatic habit. On the other hand, Socrates goes out of his way to be imprudent and this behaviour is carried to the extreme when he more or less invites his own execution.

Socrates always sees what kind of a situation he is in and what sort of character(s) he is talking to. Accordingly he adapts himself to the circumstances and the person(s), not, of course, to make himself pleasing but in order to secure the effect he desires. What he wants is a commanding effect, in the sense that the interlocutor, of whatever character or rank, departs greatly impressed (if sometimes exasperated). Socrates must command the situation and he does this not vacuously by ignoring the other's personality, but by means of empathy, by noticing in a flash what the other desires. To say that he notices what the other wants implies more than powers of observation; it also implies the power of sharing. Socrates swiftly shares the other's need, then adjusts his own conversation accordingly. Certainly he does not give the other what the other superficially requires; nevertheless the thread of his questioning starts from a point properly (or inwardly) grasped by Socrates, not just assessed from the outside. In this way Socrates nearly always ensures that he alone makes the lasting impression. I suggest that such empathy was part of the celebrated charm of Socrates, this Pied Piper's means of bewitchment.

Now it is certain that Socrates did not make an impression purely for the sake of it, like an actor. A stinging fly is fashioned to hurt and Socrates, from childhood onwards, talked in order to disturb. But to disturb people so effectively one needs to be 'wise'. Anyone can make a disturbance or upset others, but Socrates set out to 'shake people to their foundations', as we say; to make them feel the very ground they walked on was unsafe. All his wisdom was devoted to that end.

The scene of the *Apology* is one in which Socrates is entirely at a disadvantage, accused by rich and powerful men of a crime so vague that it would be excessively hard to rebut the charge. 'Wisdom' merely as cunning would be deployed in order to win the case, but wisdom as Socrates manifests it has the purpose of ensuring his permanent influence. As usual he has weighed up the situation (the actors and the audience) and decided what role he must play. Such discernment is an important preliminary part of true wisdom. In order to make his peculiarly Socratic effect he must, of course, do something other than what anyone else would do. Other people would seek, honestly or dishonestly, to walk free or at least get the sentence reduced to exile. Conversely, Socrates, being concerned with the survival of his influence, decides to be candid. Even today we can accept every word he utters not as 'the truth' but as an honourable role played by one who has consciously worked at his role all his life. Socrates had fashioned himself to this end: everything, the story about the Oracle and the disclaimers of wisdom and knowledge; the unqualified faith in God; the injunction to disobey neither superiors nor the laws of the city; the revelation about his *daimon* and his fated role as gadfly; his awareness that the court positively wants to see him weeping and wailing; the contempt shown towards all forms of politics (indeed the implied contempt for majority decisions), even the attack on Miletus: all these sentiments and attitudes delivered in measured tones (no 'oratory') are designed to perpetuate the personality and *therefore* the message of Socrates, namely that human life needs to be questioned. Such questioning *is* virtue, but it also incorporates wisdom as Nietzsche understands the word. Interestingly enough, it exemplifies what Socrates himself regards as lack of wisdom.

Perhaps I am giving the impression that Socrates was but an infinitely superior sort of actor. I mean, however, that he was far too clever not to act (or to be artless), though, for all that, he was devoted to God, his God, meaning precisely the highest and most authoritative judge.

At this point we can begin to distinguish between wisdom in Nietzsche's sense and wisdom as Socrates understood the word. To Nietzsche wisdom is, in part, the penetrating assessment of the world around one with the object of re-creating that world. Possibly 're-creating' sounds over-ambitious, but it is necessary to recall that to Nietzsche creation of some sort is the natural (though generally unacknowledged) mode of being – of all beings. In addition, to create means to re-create, since one must always represent some existing thing (some earlier created thing) in a fresh light. In order to perform such a deed one has to stand back from the existing thing so as to see it afresh. Socrates stands back from Aeschylus and Sophocles, saying in effect that they are too reliant upon instinct. For all her long premeditation, Clytemnestra kills more by instinct than by decision; Oedipus knows instinctually where and when to die. But Socrates, addressing himself to the problem of Athens in the later fifth century, knows that the citizens will be engulfed by their instincts if they do not learn to give life a more theoretical meaning.

It is clear that, to Socrates, making sense did not mean the same as arriving at the truth. 'Truth' is *not* what one arrives at, and Socrates was among the early thinkers who maintained such a position, each in his own way. As we have seen, Heraclitus made a distinction between the Word (*Logos*) which is 'ever true' and the divisions of nature which mankind habitually observes. Each such division is perceived in some perspective or other and, in any event, is perceived separately from other divisions – since such separating constitutes habitual perception. Alternatively, the divisions are understood by means of a man-made conjunction of divisions, for example, the grand conjunction which is the universe of modern physics. By Heraclitean criteria we must judge modern physicists to have invented a universal scheme which more or less matches their theoretical and practical requirements, but inevitably ignores the *Logos*. For the *Logos* when we pay attention to it, is a radiance that casts the discoveries of physics into shadow. It merely *is* and surpasses or 'marginalises' all learning. Similarly, Parmenides pronounces on a way of Truth which is distinct from mortal opinions. To Parmenides all existents *are*, in one continuous whole, and cannot therefore be contemplated according to trivial human preferences and ingenuity (such as the ingenuity of 'it has been' or 'it will be').

So Socrates is the third of three fateful thinkers who declare that truth is, to say the least, difficult of access. To Socrates one's very pursuit of truth sends the quarry further away. Perhaps this is desirable as well as necessary. Thus when Nietzsche in his 'Attempt at a Self-Criticism' appended to *The Birth of Tragedy* wonders whether 'the resolve to be scientific about everything' might not be 'a subtle last resort against – truth',[4] and when he further conjectures that this might have been the final secret of Socrates, he is attributing to Socrates the realisation that truth ('proper truth', so to speak) would be unbearable as well as inaccessible. Is it conceivable that Socrates thought in such an ultra-sophisticated fashion? Could he have known his own questions and arguments to be, as it were, artifices thrown up by nature, as *defences against nature*?

At this stage it will presumably be helpful to enlarge on the above distinction between two sorts of truth. The first sort is strictly speaking the result of a process of reasoning but a process which swiftly leads us into what we apprehend as the depths of unreason. If we reason without interest in the outcome, we are likely to conclude that what we call 'disorder' and 'purposelessness' are the very conditions of the universe. It is clear to our reasoned thoughts that reason is itself 'merely' a mode of thought – or rather, *the* mode of thought. Therefore, if we try to tell ourselves that the universal truth lies outside our ways of thinking (and just happens, quite arbitrarily and pointlessly, to include those ways) then our conception of the universe will be a conception of disorder. But it is paradoxical to have a conception of disorder, since conceiving consists of putting something in order. When we refer to 'disorder' we are speaking of an order apparently at the edge of our conceptual control. For example, a riot is a departure from a peaceful gathering, but it is still another, if disturbing, kind of order, simply because our minds and powers of perception are fashioned to confer order upon events. At best, then, to speak of 'disorder' is to speak comparatively. When we impute meaninglessness to the universe we are likewise conferring meaning of a sort upon the universe. So what I have loosely called the 'proper truth' remains an idea to the effect that fertile disorder controls everything we think or do. If this state of affairs had a purpose (which there is no reason to assert), it would aim to maintain and enhance itself for ever. This is the first kind of truth, which we may as well call the 'tragic'.

The second kind is Socratic or dialectical, defining itself as that towards which we drive by means of an exchange of opinions. Plainly such opinions have nothing to do with the first, or 'proper' truth and the manifest object of a dialectical exchange is persuasion. In this case the truth is a temporary result of a communication between people. In the *Dialogues* it is generally understood that such limited truth is at best a staging-post arrived at by eliminating views which turn out to be 'errors'. Such 'errors' are shown for what they are in the light of reason. That is to say, they are not necessarily mistakes from the biological standpoint. What Nietzsche did, so much later on, was to bring home to people that ordinary thinking derives from being: such thinking cannot 'turn round', as it were, and take command of being. On the other hand, the highest sort of thinking, namely a vision of what *is*, of what lies before one, apparently does take command, for Nietzsche writes in *The Birth of Tragedy* that the Oedipus of Sophocles produces an alteration in nature as a result of his crimes and his final serenity. Oedipus, in his concluding vision at Colonus, elevates all nature.[5]

Both Heraclitus and Parmenides already thought of thinking as derivative and strictly misguided. Heraclitus asserted, for example, that, contrary to our thinking, opposites not only fail to exclude each other but profitably co-exist; 'It is disease that makes health a pleasant thing; evil, good; hunger, surfeit; and toil, rest.'[6] This suggests that if we did not lead ourselves astray by thinking about the matter, we would instinctually recognise evil as the behaviour that makes good behaviour good. So good is neither self-sufficient nor self-justifying; it is no more than what we apprehend as part of a justificatory pattern. Our thinking contrives as opposites what are at most phases of a rhythmic progression. But, of course, Heraclitus is himself doing some sort of thinking in making this observation. He is thinking with the *Logos* at or near the forefront of his mind. Only the *Logos*, not to be discerned by 'thought' in the usual sense (since it is the sheer perception and 'naming' of beings in their relationships), is 'ever-true'.

Parmenides likewise derives thought from being – from 'what is'. In Chapter 1 we noticed an extract from the first part of his poem, including the words, 'The same thing [that which is] is there to be thought and is why there is thought.'[7] Parmenides appears to be saying that 'what is' comes first, for it includes thinking. 'To be' takes precedence over 'to think', because the latter is a mode of the former. But the above remark also maintains that a being of any kind exists so that certain beings, human beings, shall think it. Thus being includes thinking, but nevertheless exists for the sake of thinking. Even if Parmenides is offering no more than an explanation of thought, namely that it is compelled into being by other beings, we still have to recognise thought as that which confers being. Does he not mean that without thought there would be no being? It follows that nothing can be until it can be seen and said to be. So the statement, 'There are more things in heaven and earth, Horatio / Than are dream't of in your philosophy', is meaningful only on the level of drama and characterisation. Hamlet is postulating the existence of non-existent beings; his assertion exists as an idea, having no reference outside the realm of ideas, for, by definition, there is *nothing* (nothing 'dream't of') outside that realm to which it could point. We should remember, too, that thinking, as being, is fettered by *Moira*, and all being comprises one continuous whole. Nevertheless, Parmenides' main point is that there is no thought of a being without the being to which it corresponds, even if the being is legendary or imaginary. This is indeed obvious, but Parmenides intends to close the gap between being-as-thought and other modes of being. He puts all occurrence, substantial occurrence and thought-occurrence, into one continuous entirety.

The question persists: did Socrates, like Heraclitus and Parmenides before him, know human thought for what it is, or did he 'take it seriously'? Certainly the Platonic Socrates of the *Republic* takes dialectical thought seriously, though he understands it to be no more (and no less) than training for philosophers. More to the point, perhaps, Socrates thinks to the end, with Crito in the prison, not in order to mask the quality of his last day on earth, but because he considers it possible that he will thus go on thinking for eternity. Thinking is *the* way for him, but does this mean that he took it seriously?

II

Nietzsche, to whom Socrates remained a question, I believe (for even in *Twilight of the Idols* Nietzsche is unsure whether or not Socrates truly apprehended his own decadence),[8] is clear that the Socratic mode of thought originated and has remained as a method of controlling the instincts. There is indeed something *abnormal* in Socrates' avoidance of tragedy, and possibly we can discern a great abnormality (rather than courage alone) in his conduct and bearing on the last day of his life. At this point let us see if we can discover something reasonably reliable about the attitude of Socrates towards the power of thought. A promising approach will be to consider, not one of the grandest and most transparently Platonic dialogues, such as the *Republic*, the *Phaedrus* or the *Symposium* but the *Theaetetus* which thoughtfully deals with knowledge.

Why should we do this? What has knowledge necessarily to do with thought? The way of thinking that goes back to Aristotle, the 'scientific way' in a broad sense, takes knowledge to be the goal of thought. We think about a matter in order to understand it, which is to say, 'know' it (and, often enough, when the matter discomforts us, to 'solve' it). This procedure is normal; almost all serious thinking is concerned with acquiring knowledge, so the two activities are intimately connected. But it was not so, or not readily seen to be so, before Aristotle. To Socrates himself, knowledge, far from being acquired by thought, was itself a matter for investigation. But Socrates, contrary to appearances, does not truly think about knowledge in order to know it, but for the virtuous delight of thinking. In Socrates thinking is done, so it seems, for its own sake, and, since it is more or less synonymous with virtue, is its own reward. Neither is knowledge of major importance in Socrates' eyes, though when it comes to the useful arts of mankind, the application of knowledge is of course necessary.

Fairly early in the dialogue, Socrates disposes of the notion that knowledge is to be identified with perception. If this were true, then Protagoras would be right and man would indeed be the measure of all things. Why then should Protagoras set himself up as a teacher of wisdom? Have not others wisdom equally, being perceivers? Why should not a baboon, which also perceives, acquire knowledge? For the most part, at this stage of the dialogue Socrates is tilting against what we nowadays call 'perspectivism', or to be more precise, against the beliefs of the 'men of flux', prominently Heraclitus. Socrates proceeds to show that if all things constantly change, then this applies to the senses themselves; hence all our observations are on a par as regards their soundness or absurdity. Language itself becomes nonsense, or else arbitrariness. Today, certainly, we accept the formal nature of language, but we should not forget that some among the Presocratics likewise recognised a gulf between 'mortal opinions' and the Truth. The *Logos* in Heraclitus is what most people never hear. Thus the 'commonsensical' kind of reasoning carried to an extreme by Socrates was denied before the long reign of his – or Plato's – views, and is again denied by us. For the moment, however, we ought not to be detained by such considerations.

Socrates further argues that we perceive not exactly with the senses but by means of the senses as instruments, for whatever it is that enables us to know a perceived thing must be other than the senses themselves. Knowledge resides not in the senses but in one's reflections upon whatever the senses disclose, and is, in short, a mental acquirement.

At this point, it seems as though Socrates could be on the verge of a fateful discovery: he could step forward beyond Parmenides and point in the direction of Kant. He might conceivably say that knowledge as we understand the term is not possible and that what we call knowledge is a technique of categorisation. The mere example of Parmenides implies the theoretical possibility of such an understanding at that time. Yet two-and-a-half thousand years later Nietzsche is still constrained to debunk 'knowledge'. He writes as follows:

The *proton pseudos*: how is the fact of knowledge possible? is knowledge a fact at all? what is knowledge? If we do not know what knowledge is, we cannot possibly answer the question whether there is knowledge, – Very well! But if I do not already 'know' whether there is knowledge, whether there can be knowledge, I cannot reasonably put the question 'what is knowledge?' Kant *believes* in the fact of knowledge: what he wants is a piece of naiveté: knowledge of knowledge![9]

Throughout the *Theaetetus* Socrates seems to be wrestling with this very problem. It is as if he knows, or at least strongly suspects that knowledge must ever remain a question. Kant may be naive about this matter as Nietzsche says, since while he establishes that knowledge is a function of the human constitution, he still insists that our general understanding of a being validates that understanding, rendering it (as he says) 'objective'.[10] In this way, Kant 'naively' alights upon firm ground, but beyond that I am not sure that he wants 'knowledge of knowledge'. Certainly he would like to explain what knowledge does, how it functions, but then, so would Nietzsche. So far as Socrates is concerned, however, there is no excessive or suspect drive towards solving the riddle of knowledge. When he directs his attention positively towards knowledge, he reaches the temporary conclusion that knowledge consists of a 'true' belief (a belief that is valid) with the addition of the *Logos*, meaning, in this context, an account of the matter in question. The Socratic *Logos*, finally, makes all the difference between knowledge and mere recognition (such as animals experience). Socrates argues that the *Logos* must be a descriptive understanding, not of one seemingly isolated being (which can only be named, not known) but of a number of beings combined. Only a combination can be analysed and thus an object of knowledge. The final, though still unsatisfactory definition of knowledge, reached by Socrates in company with Theaetetus and the elderly Theodorus, is that it consists of a valid belief about a being together with an account of the being which explicates its difference from other beings.

The *Theaetetus* illustrates the importance to Socrates, not of knowledge but of thinking for its own sake, or to be precise, of dialectical reasoning. As we appreciate, Socrates is the virtuous man, not on account of what he knows but solely because he is the man of reason. Knowledge itself (including knowledge of the virtues) is no more than the subject of reasoned enquiry – the mirage towards which reason proceeds. It is not at all certain at the end of the *Theaetetus* any more than at the beginning that knowledge is even a good. Today and indeed for almost the whole of Western history we have tended to assume that knowledge is *in principle* better than ignorance. Knowledge is light, where ignorance is darkness. But Socrates makes no such assumption. For him light is cast by dialectical reason alone. It is the dialectical process that brings light (or *is* light) not the conclusions – namely a sort of knowledge – that the process discovers. It seems, then, that Socrates took thinking seriously, not for its objectives but for its own sake.

Dialectical reason (not any thinking and not any sort of reason) does not lead to virtue. I suggest that this Socratic belief is exhibited most clearly when Socrates tries to detach his thought-process from knowledge itself, because here, supremely, Socrates is prepared to think even about that which, from Aristotle onwards, becomes pretty well the object of all serious thought, hence the master of thought. Here Socrates sets himself apart from the incipient movement towards science, and for that matter, 'progress'. It is in this dialogue that Socrates utters the complete anti-progressionist statement: 'Evils, Theodorus, can never be done away with, for the good must always have its contrary . . . .'[11] To make such a remark is to take thinking very seriously indeed, but now comes our reservation: Socrates can have no intention of reasoning towards a position where reasoning itself forms a barrier across the road to virtue. Socrates is determined to proceed in the direction of divinity; he is beckoned on by the divine. This is not a hard calling, for it comes naturally to him. He reasons purely as an exercise in virtue, or, rather, as *the* exercise of virtue, but what if reasoning might ultimately lead one away from virtue and back towards nature – the natural world that Socrates has always done his marvellous best to ignore? Finally, then, Socrates does not take thinking seriously, for 'too much thinking', or thinking of the 'wrong' sort, would indeed lead him back to nature. A striking comment upon this general point is provided for us by *The Bacchae* of Euripides, which is concerned with the enduring power of the god Dionysus, as opposed to the flimsy sway of rational thought. Euripides was supposed by contemporaries to have been influenced by Socrates, and Nietzsche in *The Birth of Tragedy* treats Euripides as a 'mask' for a new demonic power, 'an altogether newborn demon, called Socrates'.[12] But in *The Bacchae* Euripides apparently discards his earlier Socratic assumptions, and illustrates that the god-denying rationality of the hero, Pentheus, rests upon nothing other than the Dionysian processes of life. In other words, reason cannot devour its own stock, cannot act against the nonrational source of its own vitality. Therefore to take dialectical thought 'too seriously' means failing to grasp that such thought is merely a tool to be used judiciously, in appropriate circumstances. It is not supreme but, on the contrary, the sometimes insolent subordinate of a god. However, Socrates made his career out of an unyielding denial of that very possibility.

Indeed we are invited by Nietzsche to see Socrates as a 'newborn demon' who sets himself against Dionysus. What does this mean in more sober, if less attractive, language? First, Socrates, having the power of a demon, *is* a demon, a superhuman being who aims to overthrow the 'good'. The good, when Socrates comes upon the scene, is still the tragical world-picture, the notions of measure and hubris, and the awe-inspiring acts of tragic heroes. Nietzsche is right to see Socrates as a demon whose very being was calculated to destroy tragedy – and, of course, Socrates succeeded. But in what other than a hyperbolic sense is Socrates 'superhuman'? Perhaps it is almost as accurate as it is hyperbolic to call someone 'superhuman' when he destroys one world and ushers in another.

Socrates should be seen as possessing a twofold drive: on the one hand he needed to subdue his own passions, thence to spread abroad the belief that passions *may* be thoroughly subdued; but on the other hand he also needed to restrain the 'knowledge drive', which had been gathering force for some time in the lands of Greece. That the passions desperately required to be conquered is less than obvious to us because ours are thoroughly tamed; we have little notion of the intensity of feeling originally contained by tragic drama. Here it is necessary only to say that the passions of Socrates must have been formidable, if they obliged him to employ reason as an entire way of life. Left to themselves, Socrates' passions would have led him to monstrous and perverted crimes. At any rate, that is Nietzsche's theory, in support of which he recalls the physiognomist (Zopyrus) who is reported to have said that Socrates was 'a cave of every evil lust', to which Socrates is supposed to have replied, 'That is true, but I have become master of them all.'[13] Let us simply note that there would have been some hidden motive for the abnormal employment of reason by Socrates; there is little sense in our simply admiring his rationality.

However, it is much more important to concentrate our attention on Socrates' restraint of the knowledge drive. He is not generally treated from this point of view, yet it is most promising. We have seen how, in the *Theaetetus*, Socrates disposes of knowledge, not in the sense of solving the riddle of knowledge but in the sense of subordinating it as a human activity. He realises (and this is a feature of his wisdom) that we must control our desire for knowledge. Since the rise of science (or more generally of *Wissenschaft*) we modern people have come increasingly to view knowledge as superior to reasoning. One cannot 'reason away' facts, we say. We confer honours upon those who *know*: historians, classicists, scientists of every description, medical specialists, engineers, even biographers, provided they offer monuments of fact rather than interpretation. If such professional people protest that, on the contrary, they are downgraded in a materialistic society, they should reflect that no one but an esteemed colleague may disagree with them and that to be a specialist is a peculiarly modern form of merit. And yet, after all, it is unthinkable that knowledge in the latter-day academic sense is what it pretends to be. For example, it pretends to authority on the grounds that a member of a knowledgeable group has possession of currently accepted facts and presumably does his work in the approved contemporary style. But there are no hard facts; there are only viewpoints, local definitions and criteria which for *philosophically unsatisfactory reasons* we agree to accept. In theory we recognise that knowledge is not absolute even in its own sphere, but merely categorisation of one sort or another; nevertheless, it is usually convenient to join in the deception. Nothing is taking place here, beyond a certain type of social determination; the authority of knowledge is no more than a division of social authority.

III

At present we can say that it was knowledge of this sort that Socrates opposed, not in the sense that he set out to defeat it (for in the fifth century such knowledge was no more than adumbrated) but in the sense that he realised, by some prophetic means, that as people increasingly questioned beings, they would produce cliquish little answers (in modern terms, physicists' answers, historians' answers, and so on), placing precisely these answers as obstacles across the road to virtue. For virtue, as Socrates understands and practises it, questions nothing so much as the answers currently provided – whatever they are and by whomever provided. Socrates is emphatically not a man of knowledge. It looks as though he had the perfect – if inevitably suicidal – answer to social determination; that, in short, he was creative on a vast and world-historical scale.

But what is this professional or socially-determined knowledge against which Socrates provided a prophylactic? It is what
Heraclitus earlier regarded as the range of notions and conditioned
perceptions which fall as a screen between oneself and the Word.
It is also what Parmenides described as 'mortal opinions', namely
untruths. Socrates' personal and creative solution, so different from
that of any predecessor, consisted of taking hold of each notion (each
piece of knowledge) and subjecting it, in conversation, to rational
enquiry. Unlike Heraclitus and Parmenides, he did not hold out the
prospect of clear, present truth – of *aletheia* in the primary sense of
whatever is discovered by, or to, the senses.[14] To the contrary, the
Platonic Socrates of the *Republic* specifies the real and intelligible as
that which can be reached only by dialectical means. It is, of course,
utterly hidden by unclouded, or 'Heraclitean' observation.

So far as Socrates is concerned there is, then, knowledge, which
must itself be questioned, and dialectic which questions knowledge,
as it questions, or seems to question, all behaviour, with the ultimate
goal of living in accordance with reality. Socrates' reality, we must
repeat, has nothing to do with either knowledge or unclouded
perception. Socrates takes no account of the entirely different mode
of knowing which (as we remarked in Chapter 1)[15] was already
practised by the Presocratics and is mentioned, without reference
to the Greeks, in two key passages of Nietzsche. Consider the
following, in the first of which Zarathustra is addressing the people
in the market square, and in the second of which Nietzsche is making
a confession to his readers.

> I love those who do not first seek beyond the stars for reasons to
> go down and to be sacrifices: but who sacrifice themselves to the
> earth, that the earth may one day belong to the Superman.
>
> I love him who lives for knowledge and who wants knowledge
> that one day the Superman may live. And thus he wills his own
> downfall.[16]

> *In media vita* – No, life has not disappointed me. On the contrary,
> I find it truer, more desirable and mysterious every year – ever
> since the day when the great liberator came to me: the idea that
> life could be an experiment of the seeker for knowledge – and not
> a duty, not a calamity, not trickery. – And knowledge itself: let it
> be something else for others; for example, a bed to rest on, or the
> way to such a bed, or a diversion, or a form of leisure – for me it

is a world of dangers and victories in which heroic feelings, too, find places to dance and play. *'Life as a means to knowledge'* – with this principle in one's heart one can live not only boldly but even gaily, and laugh gaily, too. And who knows how to laugh anyway and live well if he does not first know a good deal about war and victory? [17]

The first passage is a declaration by Zarathustra that he loves those who live for knowledge and sacrifice themselves to the earth. It is clear enough what is meant. Those whom Zarathustra loves sacrifice themselves, not to ideals, distant dreams, or 'improvements' of any kind upon the existing earthly condition, but to that condition as it appears to them. Such a self-sacrificer is also one who lives for knowledge, meaning an understanding awareness of whatever the earth discloses at any moment. Such an understanding awareness seems to be much the same as the Heraclitean *Logos*, precisely what one perceives when one perceives without either learning or any other kind of distortion (including, of course, the distortions of preference). However, for the scene to be knowable, it must also be representable, in words or some other medium. Such is the knowledge that Zarathustra wants in order that the Superman shall live. The Superman will be one who spontaneously lives in such knowledge.

Before we go any further let us just lodge a question here, to be pursued later: is it possible that the real Socrates (I mean the Socrates whom Aristotle distinguishes in several works) sensed the proximity of this sort of knowledge and, through dread, desired to fend it off at all costs? Or, alternatively, is it likely that Socrates truly venerated his own dialectical procedures? He certainly gives every sign of doing so.

Now we should proceed to Nietzsche's observations about himself. One day the 'great liberator' came to him in the form of a realisation that 'life could be an experiment of the seeker for knowledge'. Very few people think in these terms and almost no one succeeds in thus living experimentally. Nietzsche, one feels sure, succeeded up to a point (and Socrates *seems* to have succeeded completely, though we must later consider whether he did so by means of controlling his experiments). For many of us life is, in Nietzsche's words, a duty, a calamity or a trickery. Despite that, it is unnerving to seek to make life into an experiment of the seeker for knowledge; one prefers, for instance, that it should be something of a duty and perhaps, in rare moments of escape, an experiment. Leaving that aside, the main point here is Nietzsche's presumption that knowledge is to be sought or, rather, that knowledge alone is what one seeks.

But can we let that statement stand? It is easy enough to say that knowledge must not serve some other purpose, such as happiness. According to an earlier unpublished note of Nietzsche, Socrates and his followers restrained the knowledge-drive 'out of *individual* concern for living happily'.[18] This was the wrong motive, since – so Nietzsche implies – happiness is a terminus and has no creative possibilities. Nietzsche's view seems to have been that, on the one hand, knowledge ought to be restrained, specifically by philosophy, while on the other hand, it ought not to be checked for the sake of happiness. Happiness, is neither here nor there, but, certainly, uncontrolled knowledge is vulgar, demeaning and a biological error.

Nietzsche's own knowledge-seeking was always under his control; he, somewhat like a Presocratic, selected pieces of knowledge and threw the rest away. This, I contend, was wise, especially since he realised from the beginning that knowledge is, anyway, provisional, fashionable and unavoidably subordinate to some other purpose. In that case, why should the other purpose not be happiness? How, then, can it be knowledge that one supremely seeks? And how can the pursuit of knowledge be the great liberator?

What Nietzsche has in mind is clear, though extremely unfashionable today. One's *a priori* understanding is that all healthy life is a drive towards self-elevation: some beings among a species rise above the rest. This is not something Nietzsche ever bothers to 'prove', because he believes we can all *see* it when our vision is not obfuscated. In any event, the very idea of proof is calculated to discourage the raising of an individual above his fellows. The 'true' (meaning the healthy) *biological* purpose is to elevate the species – not each and every member of the species equally but the possibilities of the species as a whole. In *The Will to Power* Nietzsche writes as follows:

> In contrast to the animals, man has cultivated an abundance of *contrary* drives and impulses within himself: thanks to this synthesis, he is master of the earth . . .
> The highest man would have the greatest multiplicity of drives, in the relatively greatest strength that can be endured.

Indeed, where the plant 'man' shows himself strongest one finds instincts that conflict powerfully (e. g. in Shakespeare), but are controlled.[19]

The proposition is twofold: first, we human beings differ from other animals in virtue of the contrariety of impulses we cultivate and control; second, within the human race the strongest specimen is the one who can thus endure powerfully conflicting impulses. The strength of Socrates, for example, consisted not in his use of reason alone, but in this use as the means of mastering certain base and vicious appetites. In Socrates reason was not the opposite of a base appetite, nor even, in the strict sense, its contradiction, but a corollary: Socrates was extensively rational, because (in Nietzsche's view) he was 'but five steps' from anarchy.[20] The argument is that an epochal figure does something like this; he or she extends the possibilities of the race. And such doings actually alter external nature. From now on, nature appears different and therefore is different. An invented personage thus expresses the epochal will of his creator. This is what Nietzsche claims Sophocles did in creating his Oedipus. Sophocles exalted not the human species alone but all nature: 'every law, every natural order, even the moral world' perished and was transformed into a 'higher magical circle of effects . . . '.[21] Sophocles was lofty enough to fashion a hero who could, through his actions and dreadful sufferings, reinterpret nature on a more sublime plane than had been reached earlier. This was accomplished in the Theban plays, especially in *Oedipus at Colonus*. The 'circle' of nature, in which effect endlessly follows effect not upwards but in a ring – was as a whole transported to a higher plane. By 'higher plane' I mean, of course, not morally superior but more subtle, intricate and replete with nuances. After Oedipus, so Nietzsche's implication runs, our interpretations and valuations were able to grow less superficial and more self-conflicting. If anyone asks why conflict within the self is a good, Nietzsche would reply, I imagine, that this is an evident fact: the more complex the organism the more we value it. The attempt to value simpler, less divided creatures and conditions, fails sooner or later.

Since the above is Nietzsche's primary if unproven assumption (the assumption he regards as *prior* to proof) he treats knowledge in accordance with it. Therefore, if one turns to history, for instance, in pursuit of knowledge, one either rejects or subordinates every fact thrown up by the documents that does not encourage human greatness. As a philosopher one has decided in advance that the interminable documentation of social and political facts is, for the most part, backdrop. It is true, of course, that any such facts might serve one's purpose, but will not and are therefore useless. Now, Socrates is 'great'; accordingly we want those facts about the fifth century that illuminate him. Nevertheless, this procedure in history is far from a 'great man' approach because such an approach overlooks precisely the psychological insights that, for Nietzsche, chiefly constitute knowledge. He penetrates the mask of Socrates, not for the purpose of belittling such a world-historical figure but in order to surpass him – to surpass *even* him. The rest (Athenian life in the fifth century) is of only comparative significance. Athena is thus subsumed under a few decisive figures, not the other way round. But Socrates is still used as a contestant against whom Nietzsche measures himself.

Nietzsche regarded his own knowledge as quite distinct from the specialised and theoretical variety. Even his philological expertise was constantly at the service of his philosophy, which was in turn a *Lebensanschauung* or a *Lebensauffassung*, a way of interpreting life. In any case, the liberator revealed to Nietzsche that life *could be* an experiment of the knowledge-seeker, not of course that life necessarily *is* such an experiment. For Nietzsche this was a liberating view. If one sees life as an experiment, one approaches every experience, not without expectations (which is forever impossible) but with expectations that must always be overturned. Every experience in life, as opposed to the controlled circumstances of the laboratory, gives results other than those hypothesized. Knowledge in Nietzsche's eyes is this stream of fresh findings. Each position in which one finds oneself is also, and primarily, another experiment. So knowledge is not progressive discovery but discovery-as-creation.

The trouble with this way is that even the boldest are too timid and lazy for it. It is an ideal in the popular sense, a supremely desirable, if scarcely possible procedure. But it is supremely desirable, though not in a fashion derived from Christianity; to the contrary this desideratum is *earthly*, since it consists in a creative adaptation of the individual perceiver to what he has perceived. Now this superficially sounds like a passive, receptive procedure, but what I have just called a 'creative adaptation' is really a mode of dominance. It is an absolutely unfounded, or groundless mode of dominance; there is nothing behind it apart from one's nature.

It is one's original nature thus to dominate the scene, which means to perceive the scene as one perceives it. This natural procedure is consistent with the Heraclitean hearing of the Word, the *Logos*. For the *Logos*, when one hears it, is distinguished from mortal opinions by its originality, its lack of viewpoint and explanations provided by the culture. Now there is no overriding criterion (for example an ethical criterion) which declares how things should be perceived.

Our question remains: did Socrates already grasp knowledge along these lines, or did he, contrariwise, control his 'experiments' by means of his elenctic procedures? The latter seem to be restrained by nothing other than intellectual integrity, but perhaps they are a wonderfully effective disguise – and another fashion in which wisdom limits knowledge.

Early in his career Nietzsche made a private note about Socrates as follows: 'With Socrates truthfulness gains possession of logic. It notices the infinite difficulty of correct classification.'[22] This remark certainly seems to pinpoint Socrates' habitual procedure; he notices what others fail to notice: the infinite difficulty of correct classification. What Nietzsche means here by 'truthfulness' is contained in the observation. 'Truthfulness', according to this usage, is the allocating of a quality or substance to its proper category, the category which defines it and nothing else. People have talked for long enough about courage, but what is this 'courage'? Socrates probes the question in the *Laches*, finally forcing the soldiers, Laches and Nicias, to concede that he and they, the principal speakers, have managed to reach only a contradictory conclusion, namely that courage is the whole of virtue, while at the same time it is no more than part of virtue. An apparently impressive definition is offered earlier in the dialogue by Laches, who at that stage maintains that courage is a 'sort of endurance of the soul' (192c). Nevertheless, this will not do, for there are both wise and foolish sorts of endurance of the soul; can they both be creditable, as (according to Socrates) courage undoubtedly is? Then, in what sense are we now using the word 'wise'? So the dialogue proceeds with no sign of an honest, as opposed to a socially convenient conclusion. When Socrates thus works towards his aporetic endings, he deprives people of their supports. But this, it seems, urges people ever so slightly in the direction of virtue. The brave Laches no longer knows what his bravery consists of, or how, within his personal make-up, it should be allocated. Thus to his acknowledged virtue of courage is added the possibility (no more) of a further, or larger quality of Virtue, as the condition of his soul. And still the original courage of Laches persists; it is an actual quality which distinguishes him from many others. If we simply assert that courage (along with other virtues) is not by any means hard to recognise but impossible to analyse, we are stumbling a few steps along behind Socrates. But Socrates is a paragon in knowing this to be an infinite process. It may continue after the death of the individual and will certainly continue as long as the human race concerns itself with good and bad.

So far as Socrates is concerned, the way of Virtue is not even especially wise, for it is merely not flagrantly unwise. However, it is directed towards truth. On the other hand, sophists have absolutely no interest in truth. In the *Euthydemus* the distinction between the arguments of the sophists, Euthydemus and Dionysodorus, is clear. But how may we explain this difference? The two sophist brothers argue for the sake of scoring points, but then, Socrates does so as well. In general Socrates is also required by God to push towards a flawless conclusion; he constantly reaches upwards to the divine. Today we cannot see that he had any purpose other than this care for his own soul. Perhaps it is possible to call Socrates (not in the least a 'saintly' man) a 'genius of Virtue'.

As we have seen in the previous chapter, philosophy begins as pure (and admirable) self-assertion: Thales and Anaximander merely declare something or other to be true. Likewise, though in ways that still seem satisfactory, Heraclitus and Parmenides distinguish between the human being as creative voice of the world – the one who sees and declares what *is* – and the human being as mouther of opinions. Next, logic begins as a sport (not a very aristocratic sport), but Socrates enters the world-scene and shows how holiness might shine through logic. All one needs to do, apparently, is *take logic seriously*. It is no longer a sport but a procedure for maintaining one's soul at the highest level above the customs of the multitude. Language is intrinsically deceptive, but one can stand guard against all the deceptions by an especially tough and exacting use of language. If this is rare even in philosophy, at least in philosophy there is nothing else.

Such a use Socrates takes to be dialectic as he practises it. This is care of the soul and it apparently guarantees the greatest degree of happiness. Socrates implies that one cares for the soul in order to be happy. Happiness is certainly subordinate to the good – to knowledge of the good – but the supreme value of the good cannot be divorced from the happiness it requires. Reasoning is the way to happiness, and it goes without saying that if ever the goal tempts one to take a short cut, namely to 'leap over' a piece of reasoning, then one's leap fails. Many people know in theory that there is little chance of happiness along the populous route where happiness is directly sought. But Socrates teaches that the direct search for happiness includes not only the obvious sorts of pleasure but even the ways of self-abnegation. People deny themselves, 'unselfishly', for the sake of ultimate happiness, and this too is an error in Socratic terms, a virtuous miscalculation. Socrates' way aims to be happy *now*, in the present, by reason of its mask- and myth-destroying tendencies, in short its *light*.

In our appreciation of Socrates (who, incidentally, is said by Aristotle to have been a melancholic man)[23] we have not so far specified the normal condition of the soul he so effortlessly avoided. This condition consists of reaching out for *eudaimonia* by means of the imagination and then taking steps to realise one's images. But Socrates reasons *ab initio*; the reasoning has no external impetus or, for that matter, goal. To Socrates all praxis exists for the sake of theory. As we know from Aristotle, and would probably guess anyway, the Forms themselves exist, so far as Socrates is concerned, purely in the course of discussion. The Forms are not *his* desideratum; nothing is his desideratum. Socrates talks rather as an animal frisks in a field: *pointlessly*, in the sense that the talk is self-sufficient.

I have used an animal simile, a natural simile, in order, finally, to bring home the profoundly unnatural manner of Socrates' life. Interestingly enough, it is the sophist despised by Socrates, namely Hippias, who could reasonably be said to put his finger on the weakness of Socrates' dialectic. Naturally this weakness is also a strength – the strength that has immortalised Socrates. Hippias speaks as follows in the *Hippias Major* (301b):

> You see, Socrates, the fact is that you yourself do not consider things as a whole, nor do those with whom you habitually converse; you test beauty and each general concept by taking it separately and mentally dissecting it, with the result that you fail to perceive the magnitude and continuity of the substances of which reality is composed.[24]

Socrates responds to this facetiously, with the result that we cannot tell how well he takes the point. He says in words at once evasive and sincere that we all do what we can, rather than what we wish. Socrates really cannot do what Hippias suggests he should do: consider things 'as a whole'. But Hippias is making the profound general point that things do not exist, and strictly cannot be dissected, in the isolation that Socrates attributes to them. Courage, for example, cannot be separated from someone's entire constitution. And that constitution is in turn continuous with everything it encounters. Hippias grasps that beauty is of a piece with its context, so that to distinguish each beautiful sight or sound is already an artifice. Thence to move towards the Form of beauty is yet more exploitative in relation to the instincts: it is frankly to divorce oneself from the instincts by whose agency the beautiful element first announced itself as beautiful. That is why so many of the dialogues are aporetic; they must be so, because whatever answers the speakers propose cannot meet the impossible demands of the question. And, of course, Socrates, having introduced truthfulness into logic, specialises in showing up the deficiencies of answers. He catches himself as well as others in his trap, and seems perfectly happy to do so.

For all that, if we are to take the supremely favourable view of Socrates that Nietzsche often expresses (expresses far more often than not, according to Kaufmann),[25] we can do so only by believing, in the end, that Socrates was indeed a demon who knew what he was about. Possibly he sensed and feared the superior 'truth' of tragedy, realising, unlike the awed spectators of Aeschylus and Sophocles, that unless the human race spurns this monstrous truth in favour of the truth of reason, the race is doomed. If tragic drama is a making-sense of the intrinsically senseless, then it may be in some fashion 'truthful'. But Socrates regards human beings as elevated above nature precisely in virtue of their capacity to 'make sense'. Our doing this requires the notion of a gulf between people and other beings. Socrates knows exceedingly well that humanity is rooted in nature, as are all other creatures, but he believes that developing, and indeed perfecting the notion of a gulf is virtue. That is what virtue is: not attempting to extricate oneself from nature, but commanding nature by preserving at all costs the sense of a gulf. Note: this is a *sense*, an interpretation, not *otherwise* a reality. As we moderns might (too comfortably) say, the division is not a fundamental biological division, but merely a biologically employed perspective – a perspective developed by a species for its own protection. Thus it is a reality in its capacity as a shield against the larger reality of which human beings, alone of beings, could be fatally, if fitfully, aware.

Nevertheless, the wisdom of an individual consists, so far as Socrates is concerned, in his doing something so unnatural as testing each general concept by taking it separately and mentally dissecting it – to use the words of Hippias. But notice what Hippias adds: this Socratic technique means that one must fail to perceive the magnitude and continuity of the substances of which reality is composed. To Socrates, such a failure actually is wisdom to the limited extent that human beings are capable of wisdom. At least, it is the road towards wisdom. How could one wisely take into account the magnitude and continuity of reality? To admit the continuity is to live in darkness, and no one needs to be so utterly unwise as that. For wisdom is *command* and it is not possible to command the continuous. In this way Socrates makes his wisdom out of a rejection – or perhaps more strictly a perversion – of his natural perceptions. He makes it also out of a dissection and relegation of knowledge. Our insistent question from now on must be: was the way of Socrates enduringly valid? Does it remain the only way for the human race? In other words, are we post-Socratic people obliged *by nature* to break nature into fragments, not instinctively but for the purposes of dissection? Can we not 'know' as a creative exercise, appreciating the blackness from which the brightness of our knowledge emerges? Are we compelled to 'denaturalise' nature, especially by a more or less conscious refusal to acknowledge its continuity?

3

Plato's 'Real World'

When, in *Twilight of the Idols*, Nietzsche sets forth six stages of what he calls the 'History of an Error', he summarises nothing less than the groundwork of Western culture from Plato to modern times. It has merely been a mistake to suppose that another world of truth determines our familiar world. Now, how did this mistake come to be made in the first place? Nietzsche describes the critical stage as follows:

> 1. The real world, attainable to the wise, the pious, the virtuous man – he dwells in it, *he is it*.
>   (Oldest form of the idea, relatively sensible, simple, convincing. Transcription of the proposition 'I Plato, *am* the truth').[1]

In 1888 Nietzsche takes it for granted that most of his readers have no use for another world; reality is manifest, since what else could be 'real'? Thus Plato's fateful error has come to the end of the line, though its implications linger forcefully in the patterns of our speech and thought. Those of us who have put aside the 'real world' are nevertheless lost and bewildered without it.

Plato assumes that reality must be other than what we encounter and is attainable only to wise and virtuous people. Here, undoubtedly, is the oldest form of the idea, because no one before Plato mentioned an immaterial reality beyond both the senses and the imagination. This reality seems to be Plato's personal invention, since, according to Aristotle, Socrates had earlier sought universal definitions purely as the 'starting-point of deductions'.[2] It was Socrates' successors who gave such definitions an independent existence, thus conferring a prior reality upon them.

Socrates wanted to make deductions and for that purpose needed universal definitions. His primary purpose was in fact ethical; it was imperative to look for an all-inclusive definition of courage, for example, not solely so that people might become more courageous, but because the search itself, if honest and relentless, constituted Virtue, the source and substance of all virtues. Therefore, assuming Aristotle to be right, Socrates regarded the Forms, the components of Plato's real world, as means to an end. They were a device of dialectic, hence a sort of stepping-stones through the swamp of vice and ignorance.

But Plato gave universals a separate existence. Plato's reality is stable, lucid and everlasting. These are the attributes of reality, for how should a meaningless leaf that falls from a tree be 'real', either in itself or in its relations? And reality is 'attainable to the wise', only to the wise, because the wise are defined as those who yearn for it. The rest of us are caught up in the passing show, having no desire for permanency and perfection.

At present I am presenting Plato loosely, in keeping with Nietzsche's presentation. Nietzsche cannot here be bothered to do justice to Plato's realisation that if the world is Heraclitean (flowing and self-contradictory), then human beings must postulate an antithetical truth even in order to see the world, correctly, as flowing. The fiery universe of Heraclitus can be seen for what it is only from a standpoint of otherness. Plato's belief is that philosophy *is* in virtue of its standing apart – and that human beings depend for their survival on philosophy. But before we move closer to proper thought about Nietzsche's treatment of Plato, it is important to clarify further what Nietzsche says about the first stage of Western culture.

Nietzsche asserts that Plato (in common with his philosophic predecessors down to Socrates) does not regard himself as distinct from the truth which he announces: he *is* the real world; 'I Plato, *am* the truth.' Contrariwise, a modern philosopher often interests himself in a variety of philosophies, indeed in the 'history' of philosophy, and selects from it what he regards as acceptable arguments. In itself, this eclecticism expresses the philosopher, or 'is' him. But to say that one might be anything whatever that comes along in the guise of reason and decency is paradoxically to limit oneself as a philosopher. No 'great' philosopher ever thought thus. On the other hand, Plato, while searching for irreproachable definitions, has no doubt that the root of his personality (or, more appropriately, his soul) is fully embodied in what he says. To argue that Plato is quite dispersed among the speakers of the dialogues, lurking especially behind the words of the Platonic Socrates, is unsatisfactory, since the dispersal of Plato is possibly less marked than the dispersal of an artist, to whom, nevertheless, we do not hesitate to ascribe a personal vision.

What Nietzsche means is that in Plato there is little sense of a separation of the thinker from his thought. A thought is not so much what a thinker thinks as what a thinker essentially is. And the thinking of Plato, like that of each of his predecessors, is disturbed neither by opinions nor by knowledge. As the founder of the Academy rather than an inheritor of centuries of academies, he is intellectually free and sovereign. If he thinks 'truthfully' (that is, rationally, noncontradictorily and without allegiance to any authority) he may – or indeed, must – readily identify himself with the 'truth'. For what else *could* the truth be?

And yet, despite the above, we might argue that Plato does in fact distinguish himself from his thought, since he sees the latter as attainable – precisely by the pioneer Plato. Plato's 'intelligible realm' (I am thinking of the 'divided line' in Book VI of the *Republic*) is in some degree 'attainable to the wise', to borrow Nietzsche's own phrase. Alternatively, also according to Nietzsche, the pious and virtuous man, as envisaged by Plato, dwells in reality.

Nietzsche has the following awareness at the back of his mind. Plato lives in a society which still lacks 'truth' as a body of implicit belief. Such belief has never yet existed. Up to now there have been the myths which everyone, including Plato, continues to accept. The god of gods is Zeus, and Plato would not dream of questioning that religious datum. But Plato's freedom of thought is not thereby limited. Solely for the purpose of illustration we can note an analogy in our view of history. We do not question history 'as such', even if we dispute about the accuracy of particular items of history. Nevertheless, history lies behind us, as it did not lie behind Plato. In the same way Plato inherits the Olympians and does not find them interfering with his thought any more than our burden of history interferes with our thought. Thus the truth which the philosophers, beginning with Thales, had each discovered within himself was quite other than the mythical data. Plato is here and now, in the fifth and fourth centuries, uttering the truth as that which may endlessly be re-examined but which exists over and above the myths. If we can for a moment see the same idea in a modern light, we will appreciate that philosophic truth subsumes and certainly relegates the entire world of learning and, for that matter, perception; indeed, all that merely exists. Plato, followed by other members of the Academy, partakes of the truth, while the rest babble mortal opinions.

The error starts as a way of achieving two deeply desired things. First, the wise man separates himself from the multitude, not (as will be the case in later centuries) in virtue of his learning and sense of rectitude, nor even through his possession of the truth, but by means of his complete self-identification with the truth. As Nietzsche says, this is 'relatively sensible'; this is a relatively valid self-identification, because at this stage the truth is recognised as that which such a man distantly glimpses. It is stable, above all, and what the wise man faintly discerns is precisely that: utter stability. Secondly (for we may as well distinguish those strictly inseparable factors), the stability itself is achieved – as an idea. The human race conquers the most dreadful fact of existence, namely that everything passes. Now all that passes becomes unclear, despite its frequent brilliance, while reality itself (without which we could not begin to exercise our unique capacity for thought) cannot pass. For if it could, then our human existence would be meaningless and we might as well throw in our lot with the falling leaves and the howling animals.

But, Nietzsche insists, this belief is an error. I suggest that his non-Platonic or anti-Platonic truth begins to form in childhood. He writes: '"God," "immortality of the soul," "redemption," "beyond" – without exception, concepts to which I never devoted any attention, or time; not even as a child.'³ This does not mean that Nietzsche was a crude atheist when very young. It means just that he already rejected the consequences of Platonism, hence Platonism itself. But, like Plato, he realised that something or other had to be immortal. Note: this is a human point of view, for what else might it be? However carefully one thinks, and despite Kant, there is always the danger that one imagines the universe as it 'must be' without the human mind. One still inadvertently thinks of thought as the process that detects rather than dictates the universe surrounding thought, yet of course one's thought can never be confirmed. However, proceeding on the basis that we are able to think only whatever we think, and that we must (as Plato first recognised) think from a firm position, Nietzsche, when still quite young (aged 28) privately notes that, 'in the world of art and philosophy man cultivates an "immortality of the intellect".'⁴ Nietzsche is not writing hastily and does not mean to say that man aspires to create such an immortality or deceives himself into supposing he has done so.

What is implied here is that there is immortality, but, so far as human beings are concerned, it is of the intellect and is cultivated by man. The sole everlasting factor in existence is the will (which in the later Nietzsche becomes the will to power) but *we* perpetuate our will in the world of art and philosophy. Plato was right to say we require that which endures; consequently, according to Nietzsche, we cultivate it. But how can man genuinely cultivate immortality? He can do so, so far as I can see, by ensuring that (in art and philosophy) he creates images that take everything into account. 'Everything' means, of course, not trivial items but what they signify: all the significations need to be taken for what they are, meaning what they appear to be, and may not be altered out of a desire for happiness. But why is such a work 'immortal', seeing that it will sooner or later crumble into dust? The answer presumably is that the crumbling also, and most importantly, has to be taken into account. For then the intellect itself takes possession of the crumbling and immortalises even that. Mutability is exactly what the intellect immortalises by means of art and philosophy.

Now, immortality is the essential quality which, by means of art and philosophy, confines such notions as 'redemption' and 'beyond' to the finite realm where they plainly belong. Even Plato's 'beyond' (ultimate truth, the 'real world', the Good) is now seen for what it is: an *immortal* work of the intellect. But it is immortal, as opposed to 'real'. 'Reality', not immortality, is the dubious proposition.

The error starts out as the will of the genius Plato to complete a Greek impulse, a racial impulse, the impulse towards order and stability. He perceives that the artists and philosophers up to now have not carried their conceptions through. He decides to complete the Greek task and *thus* identifies himself with the 'real world'. His grasp of reality is, in our terms, 'idealional', but because he looks unerringly towards reality, he is to be identified with reality. The contingent factors in Plato fall away. In this manner the stability which the Greeks have sought is at last achieved – as an idea.

At present I am not thinking of the Greek *eidos*, which normally refers to our designation of a thing as it appears before us. Nor am I chiefly thinking of the theory of Forms but am, rather, considering the Greek understanding of stability as a supreme desideratum. The vital difference between our customary mode of thought and Plato's is that we are inclined to say of something that it exists 'only as an idea', thus assuming that ideas belong to a lower order of reality than substances. However grand and noble an idea may be, however 'superior' to materiality, it must be secondary, derivative and quite possibly false. But to Plato an idea *in any sense* takes precedence over material things because it is durable and illuminative.

At the close of Book VI of the *Republic* Socrates expounds the hierarchy of the soul as follows: intellection or reason is the highest activity; understanding comes next; belief is the third, while the fourth and lowest process consists of conjecture or picture-thinking. Plato's words need some explanation. The topmost movement of the soul is that which propels us towards our conclusions by means of pure reason; neither our desires nor the sensible world is supposed to enter the process at any point. Secondly, 'understanding' refers to the comparatively common route by which we reach 'reasonable' conclusions, but fail to question our original assumptions. In politics, for instance, a vast amount of reasoning takes place on the basis of unexamined assumptions, especially assumptions about values. Thirdly, 'belief' indicates widely accepted notions of all kinds which are not reasoned out, or are but crudely supported. Fourthly, conjecture and thinking in pictures are the same as jumping to conclusions without the pretence of reason. This last and commonest process barely masquerades as thinking but remains an activity of the soul. Today we easily recognise these procedures and still put them in a vaguely hierarchical order, but we no longer regard intellection as *absolutely* superior to the rest on Plato's grounds that it alone is untrammelled. To Plato, clarity is all; the shadowless vision is what the wise man seeks.

In modern philosophy Plato is carefully discussed by specialists, but these scrupulous discussions often overlook the groundwork of Plato's thinking. Sometimes, indeed, the supposed ground is openly dismissed (as, for example, in Tejera's *Nietzsche and Greek Thought*, where Plato is seen as an artist who 'suspends' the assertion of each and every argument),[5] but commonly Plato's development as a metaphysician is more or less argumentatively examined without reference to the assumptions upon which his metaphysics is based. In the late twentieth century these assumptions are implicitly either accepted or rejected. On the other hand, I maintain that the Platonic bases are exactly what we should re-examine and redefine, for they are, to the modern mind, at once 'untrue' and, in a certain sense, all but inescapable. At least one can escape from them only by exceedingly hard thought, and that is what Nietzsche achieved.

At the late stage of the *Philebus* Plato contends that human reason and intelligence are appropriate to what he has Socrates call 'true being'. True being has the attributes of perfect clarity, constancy and purity. It purely *is* and can be approached by means of the reasoning intelligence without interference of any kind. It not only is but is eternally, since it has no admixture of other (inevitably perishable) qualities. We note Plato's emphasis: he finds that reason and intelligence are appropriate to true being, not that 'true being' is a vital creation of reason and intelligence. He does not say, as we might say, that our human intelligence requires true being, hence brings about true being. We moderns can come near to echoing Socrates by stating that our intellectual framework is such that we perpetually drive towards clarity, constancy and purity. Any falling away from these conditions is automatically judged inferior – which is roughly, if not precisely, Socrates' point.

Thus we are able to see a psychological justification of true being. It is the unconditioned condition to which people must, by their presumably unalterable nature, always aspire. Suppose someone denies this, saying that, on the contrary, people seek pleasures and local satisfactions, or else, at their most striking and dynamic, strive for justice, meaning either equality or appropriateness of treatment. But Socrates has already demonstrated that pleasure occurs insofar as the soul is nourished; there are no physical pleasures. For instance, the pleasure of a drink when one is thirsty is a product of the contrast between the sensation of thirst and the present sensation as one drinks. Without the contrast (the 'apprehension of replenishment', as Socrates calls it) there would be no pleasure. And the contrast is an activity of the soul, for the body cannot itself be aware of contrasts. This is not a watertight argument, but what we need to bear in mind is that by the soul Plato means what we still mean by the psyche: one's entire capacity for feeling, judging, comparing, desiring, aspiring; indeed every process of the human constitution that is no longer entirely of the body, since it entails either some degree of distanced awareness of the body or, ideally, complete forgetfulness of the body. A contrasting modern view is that part of the body, say the cerebral cortex, is 'aware of' another part, say the digestive tract. But this anatomical assumption cannot satisfy us, for no one is able to regard himself as an aggregation of pieces of matter. The mere process of so regarding oneself is still seen as distinct and apart.

In other dialogues, for instance the *Phaedo*, 'soul' is contemplated more narrowly in that the bulk of our common feelings and desires are disregarded and all but dismissed as impurities. But at such times even the lowest activities of the soul are located above whatever images the soul is conscious of. At its most elevated the soul is not conscious of, or desirous of, a quality – let alone an image – but is composed of that quality.

Here it is not even necessary to contend in the familiar modern fashion that the so-called soul is nothing other than a term for a variety of apprehensions and impulses. The root of this modern contention lies in Nietzsche himself, for he remarks in *The Anti-Christ* that not only the soul but also the ego, the spirit, and the will are spurious causes of numerous spurious effects.[6] Owing to Nietzsche and others, we now understand this problem. Nevertheless, when we read Plato it becomes clear how and why some human need for which there is no word to rival 'soul' seeks 'true being'. Every imperfection jars against the soul. It is the nature of the soul to reach for perfection, meaning of course not moral cleanliness but wholeness. In brief, human beings tidy up, and this tidying-up is the 'soul'.

But does this mean that there is after all, a 'real world' in a sense not radically different from Plato's? If we aspire by nature after true being, must not this endlessly sought-after being be other than a product of the imagination, as the imagination is normally understood? And yet Nietzsche declares that this real world of Plato has at last become a myth. Moreover, in becoming a myth it has robbed the real world of its believability as well. What has happened is that we no longer think in terms of reality versus apparentness. To us everything is indeed apparentness. I say 'to us', yet this remark will be resisted by many. Nevertheless, it will be resisted by fewer than in Nietzsche's day, and he presents the attitude I mention as his own completion of Schopenhauer's discovery – as indeed it was. 'What is "appearance" for me now?' he writes. 'Certainly not the opposite of some essence: what could I say about any essence except to name the attributes of its appearance!'[7]

There now arises the question of how far we can assimilate Plato to our psychological understanding of true being, namely that true being is a modus of the mind by means of which we apparently stabilise moving things and continually reach out for wholeness. To put the question another way: is the core of Plato a tremendous anticipation not only of Christianity, but also of whatever succeeds Christianity, an anticipation that *encloses* Christianity to the effect that human beings by their very nature stabilise a merely existent, Heraclitean universe? Alternatively, is the core a strictly superfluous yearning for peace and absolute beauty, in other words, for the excision from human life of all distress?

The Platonic Socrates quite often employs arguments which at first seem to be resolutely based on workings of the mind, yet rapidly acquire what we necessarily regard as extra-mental dimensions. Plato does not make our distinction between the mental and the universal; that is why the real world is attainable to the wise and virtuous man. Are we right to make this distinction, or is Plato right not to do so? Ultimately he is right in the sense that the extra-mental universe cannot be postulated. We know this perfectly well, and yet we also know that all our knowledge depends upon the reverse assumption: we 'know' the universe insofar as it is presumed to be other than us.

As an example of Plato's technique of allowing an argument based on psychology to flow off into the universal, consider Socrates' remarks in the *Philebus*. Socrates maintains at one point that there are no limits to qualities of which comparative terms such as 'more' or 'less' are used.[8] Thus there is no limit to 'more hot'; one thing can, in theory, be infinitely more hot than another. Conversely, notions of equality, number, measurement and the like (mensurational notions) are, of course, limiting. To recall Orwell's jibe in *Animal Farm*, some people cannot be 'more equal' than others. So far, we have the unlimited and we have limits: these are two kinds, says Socrates. A third kind is what Socrates terms a 'coming-into-being' and it consists of the ubiquitous mixture of kinds one and two. But there is yet a fourth kind, namely the cause of whatever comes into being. Now, throughout this interesting discussion one might expect to find Socrates sooner or later asserting something which can be compared with the modern understanding that energies are limited as and when they collide with other energies. In this sense limits are, of course, just as original as unlimitedness – which Socrates indeed maintains. But Socrates tells Protarchus that since limits are perceived they must be timelessly present. So a human being is a perceiving agent who sees an ordered universe because, 'obviously', that is what the universe is. Similarly, the above-mentioned fourth kind which causes the other three kinds and thus 'furnishes the elements that belong to our bodies with soul', cannot fail in regard to the entire universe.[9] Therefore the universe is possessed of soul.

From a particular point of view what Plato has Socrates say still cannot be gainsaid. If we perceive limits, as we do, then the perception of limits is a natural proceeding, and of course a necessity. The perception of limits is universally ordered, we might say. No doubt it is also universally ordered and necessary that we perceive an ordered universe. Thus order itself is natural; thus order *is*, in some final way. Nevertheless, we, unlike Plato, are able to regard our setting of limits, our use of number and recognition of quality, our vision of universal harmony, as creative activities to be set against a truly omnipresent chaos, by which I mean a welter of colliding, therefore limited and limiting energies. It is not that the universe cannot be chaos because it gives us the power of ordering, but that the universe must be chaos, since otherwise we could do no ordering. There would then be no disorder to bring to order. In addition, if the universe were already a perfect order, awaiting our passive perception, then – as Nietzsche reasons to himself in *The Will to Power* – it would be in a finished state, that is to say, *dead*.[10]

Perhaps we can at this point note something wrong with Socrates' argument in the *Philebus*. He regards the natural state of any being that admits of 'the more' and 'the less' as a combination of the unlimited and the limited. This means that while there is no *logical* limit to that of which we can use the word 'more', once we apply a limit, we produce a unity of the unlimited and the limited which Socrates nominates a 'coming-to-be'. It is necessary to appreciate that we are not here concerned with the modern biological understanding to the effect that an organism is genetically 'pre-limited', as it were. Socrates simply means that if a thing (or a person) is growing, that is, getting progressively more big, there is no logical limit to this 'more'. But once we impose a limit, we apprehend a being.

In fact in the biological realm the growth of an organism is partly shaped and checked by other organisms, whatever we today understand to be its genetic potential, but this in turn means that a drive, which is not limited *as a drive*, enters into limiting relations with other drives. So far Socrates' argument appears to be still valid. Just the same, it seems to us that at every stage in the development of a being it reaches a limit of some sort. However, there are no 'stages', for these are just a sort of limits imposed by us. In discerning a stage, we impose a limit. Everything organic truly grows and decomposes; and, on decomposition, it flows into its environment more obviously than it did when growing. Where is the limit 'as such'? The limit is a line drawn arbitrarily by line-drawing beings. If Socrates had argued that creation itself proceeds by moving from *seemingly* secure positions, then his argument would have been an advance on, rather than rejection of, Heraclitus, and would have held to this day. But 'Socrates' (in this context, Plato himself) believes limitedness to be a property of created beings alongside, though apart from, the creative process. He will not accept what first Heraclitus, then in the course of time Nietzsche, believes: that the creative process, including the fixing of limits, is unceasing and all-pervasive.

Why will he not accept this all-pervasiveness? The motive is fairly clear in many dialogues, including the *Philebus*, though admittedly we need to detect that motive. At *Philebus* 31–2 Plato has Socrates contend that harmony in a living creature leads to pleasure, while discord causes distress. For example, hunger is a form of both disturbance and pain, while eating is the restoration of harmony and a mode of pleasure. This is indeed a seductive idea, for it seems to be so fundamental, so 'biological'. Apparently, then, pain and pleasure are biologically founded, even though the feelings themselves are of the soul. This is just the kind of argument to appeal to us today. And I suppose that one could take hold of any pleasure or pain and reduce it to the same root of harmony on the one hand, discord on the other.

But the idea is not necessarily valid, because there is a yet more fundamental possibility than this supposedly rockbottom condition of organic balance and imbalance. It is this: pleasure is the feeling one experiences when one compels a confusion into an order. For, after all, everything is either disorder or order according to one's degree of sovereignty over it. In other words, it is not order itself that produces pleasure, but one's sovereignty over a perceived condition. For this reason some people in outwardly comfortable circumstances seldom feel pleasure, while others, in superficially similar circumstances, feel it intensely. Thus Plato seems to us to be following his usual exemplary procedure of thinking matters through to the end, but is then blocked by the question of pain versus pleasure, assuming these feelings to be relatively independent of the capacities of the subject.

But, why did he make this particular assumption, for he, of all people, had a strong capacity for promoting order? One certain factor is that Plato had a quite abnormal, or supernormal, variety of perceptions and drives to organise, and those drives would have been extraordinarily urgent. It is the tension between Plato's ranging, subtle and potent awareness on the one hand, and his need to control the awareness on the other, that has led to the lasting influence of the dialogues. The tension is communicated to us still.

So we now have a possible explanation of why Plato, rather than Socrates, wanted the Forms to be other than a dialectical device; why he wanted them to be supremely real and beyond the world of argumentation. Plato believed that if the Forms are confined to the mind, then we sever the mind from whatever it contemplates. The supposed 'contemplation' must always be a matter of reorganisation, of recreation, as a mental, not a universal deed. Consequently in the *Parmenides* Plato has Parmenides in his sixties demonstrate to the young Socrates that the 'one' of which a 'many' is supposed to partake can never itself occupy time, or, in other words 'be'.[11] (Parmenides makes a logical onslaught, of which this is but one example.) Plato could naturally see that a Form either lies outside our mental scope and is therefore utterly unknowable, or else is entirely mental and thus as 'unreal' as the multiplicity of beings it is held to originate. Plato cannot get past his realisation that beingness is somehow wrapped up with time, with the very evanescence he has long hoped to vanquish. One cannot move forward, one is paralysed, unless one 'holds evanescence down'. Thus, as I said earlier, the 'real world' is both a myth and a dominant need. That we dwell on its mythical aspect in modern times is due as much to an intellectual conjuring trick as to the maturity of our insight.

And yet perhaps such a conjuring trick is all that has ever been required. It is plainly impossible for us to come to terms with our experience, that is to say, to *live*, unless we rigidify and, so far as possible, verbalise the features of our experience. We must perform the trick of limiting the unlimited, thus detecting distinct 'features'. It is not that we cannot know an object except in terms of its connections (Kant), but that we exist only through the fiction of thinghood. The Kantian awareness that an object can be known only in conjunction (with other objects) has to be joined to another, Schopenhaurian awareness that the object itself is, anyway, a human creation.

Yet in order to determine the quality of an object, if not the object itself, we look to its Form, according to Plato. So we look to the 'real world'. The older Plato concedes (in *Parmenides*) that this is not invariably the case, since such things as hair, mud and dirt – trivial and undignified things – exist in our world but not in 'reality'.[12] Socrates candidly admits his puzzlement over this discrepancy and we should not be detained by it.

Our emphasis here is not upon the variations and developments in Plato's treatment of the Forms (the usual contemporary emphasis) but upon what is consistent in his treatment. I believe the consistency is more important than the development; that what matters is Plato's 'real world', and this, of course, is the emphasis of Nietzsche and the tradition. If we plunge straight into that dialogue which is concerned with the relation between the soul and the body, namely the *Phaedo*, we can begin to assess the degree of reality of the real world, and why, or if, we are now obliged to regard it as a myth. We shall find the *Phaedo* more directly useful in this respect than other dialogues.

Socrates begins his argument by *assuming* that death, whatever else it may be, is the release of the soul from the body. This is a key assumption, one which superficially seems to us to require support but fails to receive any. What Socrates has in mind is elementary: something gives intelligent life to human beings, and this something that animates a collection of tissues is other than the tissues themselves, and is termed the 'soul'. Thus there incontrovertibly is a soul. However, someone might suggest that Socrates has no similar warrant for assuming that the soul is released at death, for could it not just as well perish? And why are we to think of the soul as being 'released', meaning that it has hitherto been captive? We are utterly familiar with these notions through Christianity, but they originate here, in Plato, who does not have Socrates 'prove' them.

If Plato had offered a proof, it would be too absurdly superfluous. He means that the soul, being immaterial, cannot perish. Therefore it persists eternally. The soul does not exist, it does not belong to the sphere of existence. Nevertheless it 'is' in a unique fashion, for we as individuals perform the psychical acts that we designate soul-deeds. For example, one loves someone; how on earth does one do this? No amount of psychological analysis truly explains loving but merely does what an analysis does: breaks the subject down into its components. In this way one's love could in theory be what the Greeks already said it was: possession by a god. At any rate, we reject this explanation only because we cannot accept it; we have no 'grounds' for accepting it.

The difference between us and Plato, therefore, is not that we deny soul – since we cannot do so – but that we link bodies and souls rather firmly together. We attach soul to body and thus individualise it. But this is what Plato (unlike Aristotle) was at pains to reject. Certainly we deny soul somewhat as Gilbert Ryle denies mind (both are 'Ghosts in the Machine'),[13] but not as the specification of activities which can be defined only by reference to themselves – or, in other words, cannot properly be defined at all. We question the freeing of the soul from the body because we believe there is no soul without body *in some sense*. The sense we prefer, and frankly may not do without, is that the soul originates in the body, in terms both of the evolutionary development of the human race and of the birth of a latter-day soul. But this modern understanding is far from adequate, since, while one's body disintegrates, the soul cannot likewise 'go away'. The soul perdures because, as Socrates says, it is impossible for it to depart. So far Plato is right, or at least he remains unanswered. A thought, for example, which is an impure, if not a pure product of soul, gives way before another thought, or say, before sleep; but the thought, having occurred, stays within its realm. Since it does not materially live, it cannot die. If and when we forget the thought, does our forgetting kill the thought? Plato would insist that the thought cannot be killed; it is indestructible. Even a material force goes forward (through space, through tremendous light-years), but its form continually changes. Conversely, the 'force' of a soul (and doubtless one is right to call it a 'force') simply is. To Plato the superior quality of the soul – even of the impure soul – is that it has nothing to do with life and death.

Plato insists (without proof, as I have said) that the soul is unconnected with space and time. Strictly it does not require the space- and time-bound body, though it gets entangled with such a piece of matter. At this point let us consider Nietzsche's hypothesis, which is entirely evolutionary. At a certain point in the prehistory of humanity, people found themselves enclosed 'within the walls of society and of peace'; that is, they ceased, quite suddenly, to be roaming, soulless semi-animals and could no longer rely on their 'unconscious and infallible drives'.[14] Accordingly these early people were obliged to cultivate their consciousness. Their instincts turned inwards, since these could not now be gratified outwardly in the usual way of animals. Such internalised instincts developed into what the human being came to call his 'soul'. Nietzsche is thus distinguishing the soul from consciousness and of course from the rudimentary intellect. The soul is what we have and lower animals do not have because we cannot discharge all our energies spontaneously. (Something like this idea is familiar to us through Freud who nevertheless denied that he was influenced by Nietzsche.)

Plato, however, is constrained to note a hierarchical progression from the grossest soul to the most pure. The latter is the least subject to interference from the body; it desires uprightness, truthfulness, health and strength, these qualities desiderated as absolutes, there-fore not taking the relative forms which we detect through the senses and the commonplace workings of our minds. Such relative forms of soul are still too much of the body, too distracted from their goals by the body. Similarly, there are different grades of a virtue such as temperance, for example. In order to purify the soul, one must not indulge oneself even in temperance. One gets rid of all *self*-indulgence through wisdom, that is what wisdom is, or at least how it works: not a so-called self-extinction but a degree of self-resistance. To put it bluntly: Socrates' questions always aim to destroy gratifying arguments, and thus to lead progressively to wisdom (which is precisely *not* gratifying).

Socrates is convinced that if a question is put in the right way, it must yield the right answer, which, he maintains, points to prior knowledge. One always – or the soul always – knows the right answer. Thus knowledge is a clearing-away of confusions, and a recollection. The soul itself, to the extent that it is pure, is right, and automatically takes command. For instance, the soul alone conceives equality. Equality is not an existent but a soul-conception. However, this soul-conception takes precedence over, hence commands, the hopelessly unequal or but roughly equal things we encounter in life. But it is an insight of the soul to find things 'potentially equal'.

Absolute equality as a Form or soul-concept cannot vary. This invariability is what matters above all. The perceptible varies constantly; we cannot look at a pebble two days running and see the same pebble. But the soul-concept 'pebble', being above and beyond perception, cannot vary and eternally is.

Socrates extracts from Cebes the admission that while visible things vary, invisible things do not. Beauty, being invisible, is constant, though beautiful existents, such as some people, horses and clothes, are scarcely ever fixed either in relation to their surroundings or within themselves. We might substitute the word 'perceptible' for 'visible', since Socrates is actually thinking of sense-perceptions in general. Further, when Socrates speaks of 'invisible things' he does not mean what we call 'mental images', for these are every bit as variable as the objects they reflect. Indeed Socrates makes plain to Cebes that each of the invisible things to which he is now referring forms precisely a class, a kind, an *eidos* in that particular sense. In this way, the *eidos* 'beauty', gives to a beautiful sight (or sound, etc.) its very nature.

Plato goes directly to the point that the beauty of something or other is a two-way process between its impingement upon one's senses and one's immediate – not subsequent – placing of the sensory impressions in the category 'beauty'. Plato does not maintain that the category of beauty needs to be intellectually known as a category. The word itself might well be unknown. An infant who has not yet heard of beauty already practises this placing procedure in his own pre-linguistic fashion. This original knowledge, or rather this pre-knowledge, is also what Plato means by the soul, and why he believes the soul to be independent.

We find an incidental but appropriate treatment of this very point in the *Critique of Pure Reason*, where Kant concludes that while we are in possession of the pure *a priori* intuitions of space and time, we also pass beyond those intuitions to *a priori* judgements.[15] Such a judgement might well take the verbalised form, 'Here is beauty!' though among infants the judgement may be made but not yet verbalised; it will be, as we say, no more than a feeling – a 'feeling-judgement'. It seems very likely that an infant's pleasure in a sight is sometimes divorced from any desire to manipulate the sight, in other words, the sight is entrancing as it occurs, in the absence of desire to possess or mould it. Presumably this is because the sight is already perfectly expressive of the infant; it is not in the least what he wants, but what he effortlessly *is*.

Plato makes plain in the *Phaedo* that this kind of perception is 'wise', a condition of the soul in which the soul becomes, as Plato puts it, 'most like' that which is divine;[16] a condition, in brief, which has moved decisively towards one's using-up of oneself in contemplation of the divine. It seems that nothing is wanted, nothing is lacking because all the usual bodily pollutants have departed. Now the soul has its own 'beauties', as Plato calls them: self-control, goodness, courage, liberality and truth.

Now, here comes the vital point: when the soul has, or consists of these qualities, it is at least near the threshold of the 'real world'. We next need to face the question: on what grounds do we prefer our mundane reality to this reality of Plato?

We prefer it, plainly, because it is 'more real'. Can we any longer see the charm of Plato's attitude, its powerful bewitchment? If we cannot, is this because we have lost the capacity to see the illusoriness of our own attitude? Are we stronger than Plato, or weaker? We seem to be stronger because we can do without his real world. And yet, apparently, we ascribe a reality to our own perspectives without noticing or caring how shortlived and unreliable they are. To Plato reality is what one grasps, or that by means of which one comes to terms with Protean existence. How can one seize hold of endlessly shifting perspectives except by means of a firm, hence an eternal reality? Our very test of reality is the reverse of his; we say of something that it has died, therefore it must have been real.

This test applies even to an idea; the reality of an idea is that it changes and dies. Thus there was once a way of looking that we summarise as 'feudalism'. Because this feudalism once was and no longer is, it has a certain (historical) reality. The real is simply a term for whatever apparently occurs. But it does not normally enter our heads that all these occurrences are so despiritualised that they are without standard, measurement, value, and above all, sacredness. For such evaluative qualities – so it seems – must originate outside both ourselves and the occurrences.

Consider, by way of contrast, one of Plato's most celebrated and nobly-considered realities, the reality of love. In the *Symposium* Diotima tells Socrates what love is – what it *always* is. First of all, it is a very powerful spirit, half-way between the mortal and the immortal. It is mortal, naturally, because it enters a human being and subsequently leaves him, but it is immortal insofar as it yearns for immortality and is thus in touch with immortality. Love might profitably be pictured as a deprived, ugly and resourceful person who longs for his opposite, the radiant Aphrodite. (There are, admittedly, other versions of the origins of Love which hold him to be the child of Aphrodite, but Plato disregards such versions here.) Love seizes on beauty and 'brings forth' or procreates upon it. In other words, love seeks to eternalise beauty. What this should be taken to mean is that the lover, the one possessed by the dominant spirit, wants to preserve every moment and gesture of his beloved. In this way, he *creates* the beloved so that he or she will survive.

At present we are no doubt thinking of romantic or erotic love, but Plato's reference is much wider than that. Let us say for the sake of illustration that there are two 'lovers': the first, an historian, loves a period of history, the Middle Ages, while the second, an astronomer, loves a vision of the universe. To be precise, the latter is possessed by a visionary conception of the universe, a theoretical understanding that has in part been formed, and is now supported by vivid images.

In these examples the historian incorporates all his knowledge of the good and the bad of the Middle Ages into a beautiful work of history, or at least into the possibility of such a work; while the astronomer desires above all that his picture of the universe – which he knows to be an entrancing picture of hideous forces – shall endure. In each case, since we are speaking of persons who respect knowledge, there is no question of preferring ignorance for the sake of beauty, but nevertheless the 'lover' compels his studies towards the goal of beauty. This is precisely not a dilettante proceeding but something approaching the highest calling of human beings.

In contrast, our age prefers facts, regarding them as the nearest thing to truth. Thus we believe that a densely factual account of the Middle Ages has the best chance of survival, but in any event is to be rated above those older accounts which relied on fewer facts. What we do here is downgrade the personal vision which is the source of wisdom. On the other hand, knowledge itself is no longer questionable, as it was to Plato when he wrote the *Theaetetus*, but has become the arbiter of almost everything – and our constant aim.

The Plato of the *Republic* would argue that all our knowledge must be confined to shadows thrown by the fire on the walls of the cave. It is knowledge of distortions, half-lights and reflections. One finds words to fit the shape of a shadow and therefore fancies one 'knows' the reality so inadequately shadowed forth. Say that such a shadow comprises the carefully-researched details of an eleventh-century method of driving out heresy. Our question must be: on what grounds is this sort of learning preferred to the vaguer learning of the lover of the Middle Ages who includes such cruelties in his vision, but does so for the purpose of transcending them? What Plato unfailingly stresses is the importance of transcending reality-as-perception in the direction of reality-as-ground-of-perception. The latter reality, far from being limited by perceptions, irradiates them.

There is a moment in the *Symposium* when Plato seems about to embrace a modern (by which I mean primarily a Nietzschean) understanding. At 206e he has Diotima tell Socrates that love is not exactly a longing for the beautiful as such but for the conception and procreation that is brought about by the beautiful. Beauty thus seems to be a means of life, not life a means to beauty. And why all this longing for propagation? Because propagation is the one deathless element in our mortality. By this means Plato tells his readers that love causes one to make eternal what one sees by seeing it under the aspect of what is beautiful in it.

But, of course, this is not the end of the *Symposium*. Before long, Diotima is not merely advocating spiritual as opposed to corporeal propagation (on the grounds that the spirit is 'less mortal' than human seed), but is tracing a hierarchy of beauty which begins with one all-too-human body and leads via the sciences to beauty as eternal oneness and finally to the 'very soul of beauty'.

This climax of Socrates' contribution to the dialogue is so engaging that we are liable to forget that earlier moment when beauty – and therefore everything – was subordinated to procreation as the one and only means of surmounting mortality. We can surely tolerate the priority of spiritual over physical procreation, but we cannot tolerate the belief that there is an end to all procreation – an end that lies beyond the physical, of course, but 'beyond' the spiritual also, since it is perfect and unmoving. Plato, for all his zest for exploration, seems tugged towards an *end*, and that end is his 'real world'.

But there remains one argument, namely the argument of the *Phaedrus*, to the effect that immortality is (absolutely *is*, by definition) not stasis but perpetual motion, which motion can be achieved by the soul alone. By 'alone' I mean 'uniquely' and also 'unaccompanied' – the pure, *voyaging* soul.

At *Phaedrus* 245 Socrates begins to define the soul. It is immortal, since it is constantly in motion, and that which does not come to rest cannot die. Death is inertness, and the soul, unlike the body, can never be inert. An unmoving body is still a body, whereas the ideas of 'inertness' and 'soul' can never coincide. Plato believes the soul may not be moved by anything from the sphere of existence; hence its uniqueness and supreme value. Of course, there are countless corrupt souls but it is one thing to be corrupted and quite another to be *moved*. Objects in existence are moved by other objects, but the soul is a self-mover and the *arche* of all motion. It is impossible for soul to be destroyed, since then the very universe would collapse. I do not see how we can contest Plato's assumption that the universe is essentially in motion and is moved by an agency other than its own physical composition. It is impossible to deny Plato's awareness that the universe works by non-mechanical means, because, otherwise, a mechanical means, human thought, judges other means as mechanisms, and such a 'judgement' negates itself as a meaningful procedure.

At this point one more aspect of the soul needs to be mentioned as follows: when it is perfect, it wings its way over the physical world, but commonly it settles on to a body, thus animating the body but also exposing itself to the body's corruption. The resulting compound is said to be 'alive', or at least (as we might put it) 'organic', and such a being is therefore composed of the mortal and the immortal.

What might we make of this Platonic description? I suggest we can best see it as an attempt to explain that which human beings must ever acknowledge but never, in our scientific or quasi-scientific sense, account for. Plato put into words – into metaphors and almost into a fable – the elusive fact of movement. Why (to use our knowledge as well as Plato's) is the universe expanding? Why the force of gravity? Why, or how, are some things 'alive' and others 'dead'? To Plato the first clue is motion. And motion itself demands a mover who cannot be God, because deity is not a *philosophical* answer.

To Plato there is God the ultimate Good, but God is not a philosopher's solution to the riddle of creation. Plato wants an answer that is neither natural nor theological. The former is, anyhow, impossible, and the second is an anti-philosophical way, a way to stop thinking. So Plato expounds the soul itself, noting first, and obviously, that materiality is not enough, and second, that whatever the philosopher hits upon, it must explain why we, as philosophers, reckon thinking to be better than not thinking and some thoughts better (or purer) than others. His answer is that better thoughts are more guided by soul through the thickets and shadows of falsehood. The best thoughts are the clearest and least contradictory.

Now one does not expect to find anything comparable with such ideas in Nietzsche, and indeed the young Nietzsche roundly declares in a private note: 'To consider the "spirit", which is a product of the brain, to be something supernatural! Even to deify it! What madness!'[17] Here Nietzsche is speaking of *Geist*, not soul, but we can assume that he would likewise dismiss the deification of soul. That too would be nonsense – *from one point of view*. And yet the positivistic conviction that the spirit is a product of the brain is also quite unsatisfactory. No doubt it is a product of the brain, but once something is thoroughly grasped in that fashion, it ceases to have any use as a world-explanation.

Plato, however, once explained the world by means of an indiscernible reality which could be approached by means of the strictest reasoning. This true reality lay behind the everyday workings of human minds, though these workings normally obscure and misrepresent it. Nietzsche's (essentially post-Kantian) view is that the so-called misrepresentations by the mind are our only possible discernments. Such a Nietzschean view is now widespread. Since these are the only discernments, we are right to say that there can be no other mode of being. It is merely the lingering shadow of Plato that makes us entertain the possibility of other modes. What other modes are these? What is unimaginable cannot be.

But Nietzsche, despite his 'positivistic phase', is the first and almost the last to appreciate that a world-explanation of some sort is required to replace Plato's 'soul' and his 'real world'. For the alternative is meaningless cosmic mechanism, and the human species is so constituted that it cannot see the cosmos in such a way. Those who imagine they can, soon come up against unanswerable questions and start talking about mysteries to be 'solved' in the future, or even, in some cases, about God. And our ability to think of the cosmos as mechanical is due fundamentally to two-and-a-half millennia of self-assurance founded upon Plato. That is to say, we 'mechanise' the world only because we do not finally believe in mechanism.

Today, if we try to suggest a meaning, we should realise that our suggestion must be at once a mental product and an entirely satisfactory understanding of how the cosmos 'works'. It works, Nietzsche asserts, by means of will to power: *'This world is the will to power – and nothing besides!'*[18] But Nietzsche realises that for something to replace the immortal soul this something must also be immortal. The one constant in existence, he says, is will to power; it animates all the apparent varieties. Now, was not the immortality of the soul, as Plato conceived it, exactly what was wrong with it from our standpoint? We will today accept continuous change, though we need to perform intellectual conjuring tricks in order to do so. What we cannot accept, so it seems, is a being at the back of all things which actually constitutes them. And such a being is will to power; it is a cosmic, even an eternal explanation. In this way, Nietzsche, instead of circumscribing his own thought as 'merely' philosophy, an activity subordinate to science, or at most on a par with science, places science at the service of philosophy. Philosophers propose, scientists dispose.

It remains for us to see how science – still meaning every rigorous and systematic form of knowledge – can be governed by philosophy, once we have 'invented', as it were, a universal agency called 'will to power'. (This primary force will be considered specifically as the principle of all being – in contrast to Aristotle's belief in the primacy of substance – in Chapter 6.)

To begin with, there is, admittedly, a sense in which Nietzsche replaces Plato's 'soul' and 'real world' with another desideratum, a concept as speculative, perhaps, as Plato's. Will to power is an assumption, as soul is an assumption. One cannot know or prove will to power, as one cannot convince a sceptic about the over-arching truth of soul. The difference, however, is immense, for soul is pure, essentially unconnected with corrupt matter, while will to power belongs essentially with matter and energy. Will to power is anything but pure, since it animates all the impure beings in the universe, and, for that matter, inspires the very idea of purity. Purity (along with soul) is now seen as a strategic device of will to power. Our latter-day belief is that we can no longer use assumptions such as God, cosmic mechanism, or will to power. The unproven is held to be the unacceptable, even though 'proof' must itself rest upon some undisclosed foundation. Therefore Nietzsche proposes another foundation beneath which it is impossible to probe.

Nevertheless, will to power is a postulate and a desired mode of being for all those who wish to explore behind the idea of purity, those who think the good invites explanation every bit as much as the bad. Will to Power is still a metaphysics, for plainly, the idea does not belong to *physis*, or nature as Aristotle investigates the 'science of nature' in his *Physics*. I suggest that Nietzsche's answer to those who would object to his having a metaphysical starting-point must necessarily have taken the following form. It is a useless self-deception to imagine that we can proceed by steadily acquiring 'knowledge'. This is the great modern delusion. For instance, at the conclusion of *Language, Truth and Logic* A. J. Ayer speaks of making a 'substantial contribution towards the growth of human knowledge'.[19] Nietzsche would say, echoing Plato in this respect, that if by 'knowledge' we mean what Ayer calls *human* knowledge, meaning the sort we learn at school and college, then such cannot come first, cannot be that towards which the best efforts of the mind make a contribution, and, above all, cannot truly 'grow'. On the contrary, knowledge of this kind is a procedure for gaining footholds and staying erect. It is a means, and as a means does not grow but simply varies from age to age.

In complete contrast to Plato's denigration and distrust of visible life-processes, Nietzsche decides that his own universal principle must reflect and satisfactorily account for those processes. He believes that the manifest characteristic of all existents is that they seek to extend themselves, which process demands the absorption of other existents and the use of these incorporated others in a fresh way. Extending oneself is naturally not confined to physical enhancement, but, at the other end of the scale from rudimentary to sophisticated forms of development, it means that one radically reinterprets the others whom (for whatever reason) one sets out to absorb.

However, the chief point here is that Nietzsche makes his universal principle out of the mere fact of growth, his idea being that every existent seeks to develop in some sense (physical or spiritual) and that this very activity is the entirety of all that is. The development is not towards a final stage but is endlessly purposive movement without a final purpose. In other words, a purpose is always something towards which one proceeds because one's nature is processive. Though a purpose appears to get one going, it is never more than a means of channelling one's energies. A purpose is thus *selected* by people and perhaps by animals generally, while other, non-purposive beings simply and motivelessly proceed.

This is the real world in contrast to Plato's 'real world', which, on the contrary, is static. It must be static in order to be reliable, and it must be reliable in order to be real. Admittedly, the soul in Plato is dynamic; nevertheless, to the extent that the Platonic soul is pure, its activity cannot any longer consist of growth.

Both the soul in Plato and will to power in Nietzsche are, as we have said, metaphysical and immortal. Will to power is metaphysical since it more or less openly advertises itself as a human interpretation of all processes. Just the same, from another point of view it is at least as much a fact as an interpretation. In his second volume on Nietzsche, Heidegger quotes Nietzsche as saying: 'Will to power is the ultimate fact we come down to.'[20] Nietzsche must here be taken to imply that while interpretations are not facts, and indeed there are no 'facts' as we usually understand them, will to power cannot be traced back to anything else and must therefore be regarded as a fact – indeed as the 'ultimate fact'.

Let us see what the fact of will to power, which is at the same time a metaphysical judgement, involves; that is to say, the sort of thing it involves. The universe is expanding; very well, this is *why* it is expanding, for a piece of matter hurtling away with its accompanying area of space is naturally comprised of will to power. Our usual assumption that the matter has simply been propelled by 'energy' needs to be supplemented, according to Nietzsche, by the ascription to the matter of will to power. Otherwise we are left with nothing but energies empty of spiritual content. If we affect to believe that the cosmos is exactly such a play of energies, then our very belief is nothing but an energy. But the belief cannot at the same time be what it defines itself as being: a valid world-interpretation. Human beings themselves cannot be unless they are energies who give a meaning to all energies. This meaning adds something vital; no one can honestly see himself as nothing more than kinetic energy; therefore being consists of more than kinetic energy. At least human being includes this extra and indeed decisive quality. But – so Nietzsche implicitly reasons – if human being involves this extra quality, specifically will to power, how might other beings lack it? Will to power must be as universal as the *apeiron* of Anaximander, the fire of Heraclitus, and the Mind of Anaxagoras, for it seems preposterous that of all cosmic beings, one species, mankind, or at most one class of beings, animals, should possess and be driven by an irreducible quality denied to all the others. Such exclusivity requires a gulf between animals and other beings, and this is an unsatisfactory assumption since the elements of which all being are composed differ from one another merely as elements. It is more credible to universalise will to power than to postulate a gulf between animals and the rest. For if we do the former, we need only rid ourselves of the notion that will to power must be spearheaded by some degree of consciousness, or, broadly, of awareness. The line has to be drawn between the awareness possessed by an insect, say, and the unawareness of a plant. Perhaps we should push the line away until it merely divides one form of vegetable matter from another. It is now easier for us to relegate consciousness, seeing it as quite inessential (and of course deceptive).

From all this it follows that just as, for Plato, knowledge must be subordinate to soul (see especially the remarks about the *Theaetetus* in Chapter 2) [21] so, for Nietzsche, knowledge is *clearly* subordinate to will to power. Indeed, knowledge is shaped by will to power and has the sole purpose of enhancing the knower. But such enhancement of one's being, which comprises will to power, is also what we are here increasingly liable to define as 'wisdom'. Certainly wisdom is the way of selecting and ordering one's knowledge so as to continue to bear fruit. Will to power is not infallible; it might first select then discard some knowledge or other. Alternatively it might get stuck for long enough with barren knowledge. In this way, wisdom is the *effective* guidance of knowledge towards the will to power of the individual.

Therefore, what Plato generally seems to mean by wisdom, namely, as we have seen, care of the soul, is not different (except in nomenclature) from what Nietzsche still means by it: an accurate sense of 'this is good for me' and 'that is bad for me'. Such a distinction applies to knowledge also. Some forms of knowledge are bad for some people, because they do not help the people to grow – to grow, not towards a finished state, as Plato desired, but *essentially*: the business of growth is viewed as the essential business. It is worth adding that such an exercise of knowledge is not a form of prudence; the hemlock was 'good for' Socrates in the sense that drinking it was an act of growth. Socrates made his dying deed into a step forward, a way of gathering up his life and immortalising himself.

4

The Legacy of Euripides

There is widespread agreement about the nature of Euripides' legacy to the West, and, for sure, this nature includes or implies a value, but Nietzsche is almost alone in casting doubt upon the Euripidean enterprise from the standpoint of value. As usual, Nietzsche does this by means not of logic but of psychological insight. Euripides did not understand tragedy, and that was his starting point. What, he wondered, was this ritualistic, obscure, ill-motivated business that so thrilled the other spectators, not one of whom was remotely represented by masked figures called Orestes or Prometheus or Oedipus? From such bemused beginnings, Euripides, according to Nietzsche, developed his own (relatively unpopular) sort of tragedy, by means of which 'the everyday man forced his way from the spectators' seats onto the stage'. Euripides was painfully faithful to the 'botched outlines of nature'.[1]

Now the value in question which Euripides introduced through the medium of his 'realism' has been all-pervasive and quite fundamental in our history. To query it is to see our entire culture specifically as a culture, by which I mean a way of looking and thinking that will come to an end. It is not 'truthful' but has long served a purpose and might, or indeed must be superseded, now that 'nihilism stands at the door'.

In the terms which are being developed in this book Euripides is to be seen as 'knowledgeable' (observant) but not normally wise. More than anyone else except the towering Socrates, Euripides rearranges the world to suit his own requirements. In the course of time this fresh arrangement becomes vital for mankind in general, or so it seems. We could readily show that it is this (central) aspect of Euripides' work that causes Aristotle to call him 'the most tragic certainly of the dramatists'.[2] To Aristotle, Euripides is more tragic than Aeschylus and Sophocles because his heroes are 'intermediate' persons such as ourselves, whose misfortunes are brought about through particular faults or errors rather than thoroughgoing depravity. Thus Aristotle believes that Euripides' contribution to the art of tragedy was a logical requirement, a development already implicit in the works of his predecessors back to the dithyrambic chorus. On the other hand, in Nietzsche's eyes Aristotle merely joins Euripides in foisting upon all later generations the conception of tragic drama as a critical copy of social behaviour. In this way Euripides is more intelligible than his forerunners, but the point about the tragic spirit is that it does not especially aim at intelligibility. Euripides insists upon intelligibility and for that very reason is, to Nietzsche, the least tragic of the dramatists.

What Aristotle does not mention is that the catharsis provided by a tragedy comes about, so far as Euripides is concerned, through an access of knowledge. If one is cleansed of pity and fear as a result of watching the *Hippolytus* or the *Alcestis*, this is achieved, partly at least, by means of enlightenment. Aristotle's reference to catharsis, or cleansing, suggests that pity and fear, normal and regular emotions, are temporarily eliminated by tragedy. They are not glossed over, readily contained or momentarily forgotten (which in *our* experience are the usual ways of art), but actually removed. This is achieved as a result of showing the spectator that his emotions are a product and mark of his self-deluded separation from the world. Now he no longer feels pity and fear. However, from the point of view of Euripides, pity and fear depart when one 'understands'. But to the extent that one can anatomise a tragic development, showing the pathology of the characters and so forth, one wanders from the track of tragedy. Cause and effect are not clear-cut in tragedy proper, though there is little sense of the fortuitous also. On the contrary, everything is a *doom*.

To Nietzsche, when a poet focuses upon individuals, as Euripides does (thus explaining what tragedy by its nature asserts cannot be explained), he produces comic as opposed to tragic features. It is necessary to proceed a little more carefully here, more explicitly than Nietzsche himself. No doubt a sort of analysis can be offered; even Aeschylus is thought to do that, and people duly discuss, say, the motives of Clytemnestra. But tragedy does not imply that because a tale can be extracted from the past lives of Clytemnestra and Agamemnon, or because the masked Clytemnestra herself gives reasons for her actions, these factors correctly summarise the meaning of the *Agamemnon*. Today we are again inclined to see offered meanings as purely perspectival, thus suggesting there can be no such thing as a 'real meaning'. Aeschylus also excludes real meaning (as we might understand such a term), although for him there is Fate or the relentless play of world-forces.

Nietzsche writes as follows:

> Somebody, I do not know who, has claimed that all individuals, taken as individuals, are comic and hence untragic – from which it would follow that the Greeks simply *could* not suffer individuals on the tragic stage.[3]

Whoever this somebody was, Nietzsche presumably agrees with the observation. Thinking chiefly of Plato's dialogues, we can say that there is, on the one hand, the *eidos*, in the sense of the Form, and on the other hand, the *eidolon*, meaning a likeness, image or copy. To Nietzsche, as to his unknown somebody, Aeschylus and Sophocles held so far as they could to the *eidos* of a tragedy, while Euripides gladly 'strayed' as it were, in the direction of the *eidolon*.

Let us confront what is involved in this question of Euripides as either 'the most tragic or' in Nietzsche's eyes, the false tragic. All depends upon whether the world is truly composed of individual beings, or whether, contrariwise, individuation is a trick of the senses. The second alternative means that all seemingly single beings are essentially composed of their connections with other apparent beings, so that in truth there is only the entirety of Being, or what Nietzsche calls 'the total character of life'.[4] It is easy to underestimate this tragical conception. One can simply say, for example, that the universe is an aggregation of forces. But the idea goes further, declaring that there is no aggregation, since we have already divided the indivisible in order to form units which may subsequently be aggregated according to our needs and preferences. Instead the separateness of beings is no more than a seeming. It is true that the non-separation of beings, their ultimate unity, is, oddly enough, a sort of 'ideal' distantly glimpsed by us; however, Aeschylus and Sophocles unfailingly kept this ideal in mind: this was the basis of their tragic apprehension. For all that, it was necessary for them to pull away from the apprehension in order to make tragedies. Aeschylus must give some individuality to Clytemnestra, Sophocles to Oedipus. Nevertheless, each of these dramatists appreciated two factors: first, that the individuality he created in his plays was itself a dramatic illusion (not so much a copy of social reality as a device), and, secondly, that, in any case, the tragic development was the consequence of an attempt at individuation. In brief, the individuality of Aeschylus and Sophocles is a way of pointing towards the non-individuation of the ultimately real beyond society and the commonplace. This amounts to saying that individuation was already seen as an indispensable human illusion, a way of living for human beings which was very liable to be punished by the Fates. So Clytemnestra and Oedipus both try to distinguish themselves too sharply, thus horrendously, not from mere social rules and conditions, but from what we have come to call the 'natural order'. Each hero endeavours to stand aside from the flowing world-current, from which, plainly, nothing can stand aside. Note, however, that even Aeschylus and Sophocles already betrayed the tragic conception and could not have written enduring tragedies had they not done so. Nevertheless, they betrayed it in order to emphasise its power – really its omnipotence – while Euripides did so because he actually derided its power, up to the time of *The Bacchae*. To stay strictly within the tragic bounds would have been to offer nothing but a dithyrambic chorus, to venerate Dionysus alone, and not to present any mortal personage as a human form of the god.

But can this ancient view still make sense to us after two-and-a-half millennia of individualisation – of art, science, politics, indeed of every branch of human endeavour straining more and more successfully, as it seems, towards the production of individuals? The fact is, we are now obliged to apprehend the pre-Euripidean world-picture, the picture of a world from which individual beings are substantially lacking or else are present as monstrous and criminal, as a *theory*. Only in theory can we now conceive of that which is supremely non-theoretical. It seems so strange to us when, for example, Heraclitus talks of the cosmos as 'ever-living Fire', implying (to stress the point not too insistently, I hope) that you and I and every being can no more be distinguished than can parts of a conflagration. As I have said, this must remain for us a theoretical idea; we cannot live by it in everyday life. Is it nevertheless true, the irreducible truth? And is our everyday, practical perception therefore inescapably truthless?

Could we suggest, if not establish in a roughly scientific manner, the non-existence of separable beings upon which, presumably, all science (in the sense of learning) depends? I suppose we could pursue this objective by remarking that all apparent beings are composed of chemical elements and obey the laws of motion. Reduce perceptible beings to their fundamentals and they are all the same – or, as Nietzsche put it in an unpublished essay of his schooldays, 'all-one'.[5] Thus there is physical being or materiality which merely assumes different shapes. But the ranks of beings also include metaphysical processes: human mental activities and will to power, in both human and non-human beings. Do these processes exhibit sameness or individuality? Philosophers and scientists agree that metaphysical individuality is superficial; once again, the deeper one explores, the more one comes upon sameness. By definition, one will to power clashes with, modifies and absorbs another, but the tragic homogeneity obviously never denied this sort of difference, this natural and never-ending conflict. When Nietzsche famously says: 'And you yourselves are also this will to power – and nothing besides!'[6] he is denying individuality as it is commonly understood. The 'point' of will to power, one might contend, is precisely to universalise the quality of beings, to place the human species firmly back in the physical universe.

Then, it is clear in Plato that the nearer any soul comes to purity, the less it retains traces of its individualistic beginnings. So from both the Platonic and the anti-Platonic sides the idea of individuation is downgraded. We are left with mechanisation, with the universe as nothing but mechanism, and this is yet more blatantly a dismissal of the individual.

For all that, the will to power of a person could not be, and so *he* could not be, unless he distinguished each of his perceptions. This must apply *in some sense* to all instances of will to power; by its nature it distinguishes one thing from another. Nietzsche's idea therefore, is that will to power draws distinctions as a matter of necessity (this is how the world works), although in truth there are no actual and final distinctions.

We can attribute to Nietzsche the belief (constantly implied in *The Birth of Tragedy*) that tragedy both as dithyrambic chorus and as drama, in Aeschylus and Sophocles, firmly grasped the *expedient* nature of individuation. Indeed the great tragedies are fashioned out of their heroes' refusal to acknowledge such expediency. For instance, Antigone places her brother Polyneices, and the decent burial of Polyneices, above all other considerations. She will not accept that neither she nor Polyneices actually matters. No one matters; not Creon, the king, any more than a slave. Antigone thus defies not Creon alone, nor even the trumpery ethical–legal sphere in general but the cosmic law itself which decrees that Antigone is no more than a will engaged in setting up a mere moral desideratum against the Fates. Now, we certainly admire Antigone, as did Sophocles himself. But he never expected her way to triumph; to him she is admirable *because* her will and all such individual wills, whether or not they assume an ethical form, must be punished by the Fates. Why is this so? Simply and solely because an individual will may not endure. As Nietzsche puts it in *The Birth of Tragedy*, we are to regard 'the state of individuation as the origin and primal cause of all suffering, as something objectionable in itself'.[7]

In this way, even Antigone is objectionable in herself – not of course objectionable to us but to the *Moirai*. Now this is not in the least a hard idea for us to grasp, or even to agree with, in our modern fashion. For it is clear that no creature can suffer except individualistically. 'Collective suffering', so called, means either that a group of people is suffering each in his or her own way or that some sort of public expression of suffering has been devised to which individuals *voluntarily* contribute. Insofar as I feel pain of any sort, physical or emotional, this happens as and when I am separated from others. But this separation and this pain are alike unavoidable; hence the tragic pathos before Euripides. Prior to Euripides, suffering was scarcely intelligible, though it was associated with disunity, with one's tearing oneself apart, or being torn apart, from others.

Such anguish and apartness is refined, poeticised and rendered sacred in the sufferings of an Aeschylean Prometheus or a Sophoclean Oedipus. It seems to us excessive and unfair not because it *is* so, as a matter of fact, but because the dramatists have not provided (that is to say, created) adequate explanations. Presumably, therefore, the everyday sufferings of the ordinary people of Athens, were likewise mere features of life, not matters which normally had *avoidable* causes and could be cured. Compared with our view of things, the Greeks had a very imperfect notion of cause, and we can readily maintain that Euripides is at the forefront of those whose work has led us to such a marked reliance upon cause. I am not trying to deny cause, for Kant has stated, unarguably, that the proposition, '"Every change has a cause," is a proposition *a priori* . . .'[8] In other words, while we might amuse ourselves with the proposition, 'Causes are human inventions,' our minds cannot contemplate a world of uncaused events. However, our developed, modern idea of causation consists of a positive faith in specific, discoverable causes, and it is this *faith* that Euripides, in reaction against his forebears in tragedy, signally helped to inaugurate.

Everything has a cause; therefore everything can be changed, quite deliberately and beneficially. One roots out the cause – of a disease, of marital discord, of poverty, or war, of unhappiness itself – and the way to improvement becomes clear. We often think that this 'Euripidean' view of life reached its apogee at the end of the nineteenth century, or in 1914, leaving us today with a merely absurd world from which reasonable cause seems to have fled. But this very flight is considered unaccountable and monstrous; no one insists on such a response more than the witty absurdist author. Indeed what we seek is a cause for absurdity itself: there must be hidden causes – as indeed there may be, since our *a priori* contrivance of the notion, 'cause', does not necessarily imply that 'causation' in some sense cannot occur. Nevertheless, when we think of the hidden we still have in mind the theoretically ascertainable. So what we regard as absurd would have appeared quite otherwise to a pre-Euripidean Greek, because his notion of non-absurdity, of what is to be expected from life, had little to do with reasonableness. The legacy of Euripides is the belief in light and knowledge – 'knowledge' construed much more superficially than it is by Plato in the *Theaetetus*.

At this point it is worth remarking that Nietzsche himself unites Euripides too superficially with Socrates in their common fight against the tragic world-picture. In *The Birth of Tragedy* he argues that Euripides wrote not for the crowd but for just two people: himself in his alternative capacity as critical thinker, and Socrates.[9] Most likely that is a penetrating way of looking at the matter; nevertheless, as we have seen in Chapters 2 and 3, neither Socrates nor Plato treated knowledge as light, or specifically, in Euripidean fashion, as an obvious requirement of the human race. To Socrates the *pursuit* of knowledge spreads light and is therefore the path of Virtue. Knowledge is, thus, a goal, or a series of goals, but it has comparatively little other value. For Plato, on the other hand, knowledge remains a question, and what he seeks surpasses knowledge in the ordinary sense, since it consists of a steady, measured awareness of the Good (see especially Part VII of the *Republic* and *Philebus* 65–6). Worldly perceptions and desires have fallen away. Plato sees knowledge as at best a stage on one's ascent, and it might even be an obstacle.

In complete contrast, Euripides wants to know because something is there, before his eyes, to be known. He is anti-tragic, but in a different sense from the anti-tragic postures of Socrates and Plato. However, Euripides' way of knowing is not yet proto-scientific;

he 'knows' simply by virtue of his hitting upon an explanation. Now in our earlier treatment of the Presocratic philosophers we regarded this same procedure as satisfactory, indeed as a merit. Why, therefore, should it be a demerit in Euripides? Firstly, because Euripides is an artist and ostensibly a tragic dramatist whose aim must be to induce excitement and wonder in his audience. Therefore he uses his pieces of knowledge as and when they are convenient. His explanations, however convincing (and they are convincing), are never submitted to a Socratic–Platonic test of wisdom. Secondly, the artistic Euripides (unlike the philosophic Heraclitus, Parmenides or Anaxagoras) is fascinated not by fundamental matters but by individual psychology: what sort of a person might the 'real' Electra be? He is an observant psychologist for whom the religious rapture of a tragedy is forfeited in favour of intelligibility.

Theoretically we all believe that the intelligible is a far cry from the correct or the true, but Euripides narrows the gap between the first conception and the second, as narrative artists have generally done ever since. We are more or less content with Euripides' explanation of Medea's behaviour, for instance, even though we now (after Kant) know this to be merely a given explanation. Not only is the reason for Medea's behaviour undiscoverable (even supposing there to be a reason), but 'she', as the theoretical sum of her responses and actions, is at one with the universe. She is not 'one' but an apparent 'point' in the universe, so to speak, through which the nature of the whole is disclosed to us. This is what Heraclitus means by declaring that 'all things are one',[10] and also the understanding that Aeschylus and Sophocles both manage to suggest.

In this connection it is important not to distinguish between an aesthetic work such as the *Medea* and what we call 'real life'. For the purposes of the present argument there is no distinction, since, just as Euripides has singled out Medea, we single out real individuals and thus apparently come to know them. But this very tendency, this business of individualisation and characterisation, is irreligious by tragic standards, for it flouts the wholeness of the whole. However, to say that some sort of conduct is irreligious is not discreditable in modern terms. Why must we be religious? In fact Nietzsche means much more than this, or he means something that cannot be reduced to such modern vulgarities. His view is that happiness, by which I here mean the absence of suffering, lies precisely in the promise made by the oldest tragedies of the eventual recovery of oneness. Remember in *The Birth of Tragedy*

Nietzsche remarks that we are to see 'the state of individuation as the origin and primal cause of all suffering . . .'.[11] For this reason, tragedy deals with the most profound wretchedness, yet gives us joy. The joy is not a compensation for the misery but a product of it. The hope, or rather the trust of a spectator of tragedy is that the god Dionysus will be reborn. This rebirth is implicit in the tragedy. Such a hope is absolutely not to be compared with a pitiful yearning or a childish wish that something favourable to oneself will happen. On the contrary, the hope is inescapable and valid even for – or especially for – the most mature and realistic persons. Such people, Nietzsche maintains, are 'pessimistic', meaning not sorrowful but relatively resistant to everyday hopes. Naturally they proceed hoping for this and that, as we all do, but their wishes are carried along on a current of anticipation of whatever the Fates decree. What they fundamentally anticipate is the rebirth of Dionysus, and when Dionysus comes again, their individual sorrows will be resolved in the regained awareness of unity. All things will again be seen to be one.

It is not that things will no longer be seen as distinctive for, of course, they must be so seen, but their apparent distinctiveness will be recognised for what it is: an unavoidable product of the mind. And certainly the oneness beyond our mental tricks is quite other than unity in God, for it is a unity of worldliness, from which unworldliness or other-worldliness, especially the unmoving perfection of God, has quite departed. It is a unity of living processes (including death).

This was the vision that Euripides set out to destroy, and indeed destroyed. Nietzsche is surely right to insist that when Euripides came to retract his lifelong vision and composed *The Bacchae*, that singular drama which asserts the invincibility of Dionysus, Western humanity had been fatefully influenced by the earlier, the presumptuous Euripides. From Euripides onwards we shall believe in our power to dissect the world to our own advantage, even if the Greek poet himself recants to the extent of affirming that the human race can do no more than reach an accommodation with the god. This means that while we can and must divide the universe into multitudinous beings, we should also remember that we are the dividers.

Now, certainly, it is all too easy to assert that the earlier Euripides was wrong; he himself declares as much. But his wrongheaded achievement needs to be reassessed, not in detail after the fashion of literary criticism, but briefly and fundamentally from the standpoint of philosophy. Nietzsche calls the typical Euripidean play (and by inference all the more-or-less realistic literature that has flowed from it) the 'dramatized epos'.[12] The phrase is used to indicate not just a series of events, a story represented by the words of actors, but, additionally, that the point of the events, the message of the sequence, is no longer what matters. The emphasis has shifted decisively. In the *Agamemnon* of Aeschylus the tragic current is all-important, so that the spectator goes away thinking not, for example, of Clytemnestra's motives, but of life as tragedy. Clytemnestra has merely exemplified this universal tragic determinacy. But Euripides alters our gaze so that we no longer see the tragic flow but rather each distinctive event as it appears before our eyes, or to be precise, before our mental vision. These events are linked in a story, but their connection with the world-flow is neither established nor even suggested. Our gaze fixes on them and their connections with one another, while the world-flow, which really determines them, remains hidden until, in the end, we deny its very existence. Note: it is not that the phrase 'world-flow' is supposed to denote a prior, causative process; rather the events belong to the flow, and this is the universal meaning that Euripides excludes.

However, this new, Euripidean perspective undoubtedly raises our spirits. From one point of view – the most firmly-founded view – it is a false perspective, and yet, by confining ourselves to such a *superficial* perspective we are able to delight in all things, including as Nietzsche says, 'the most terrible'.[13] In modern terms we can contemplate, for example, the details of a murder, and imagine by doing so that we are 'facing facts'. We are indeed facing the facts of appearances but we are nevertheless convincing ourselves that the facts in question are controllable. We have woven them into a story and so used them – we, the *masters* of fact – while tragedy before Euripides gave us no such mastery. Thus every horrible episode can be rendered pleasurable by means of art and, more importantly, our learning, the most staunch ally of Euripidean art, can teach us how to amend episodes of this ghastly sort, and also leave them behind as mere history. The overwhelming fact we *now* have to face is that Euripides thus aided Socrates in establishing a world that could be dissected, hence endured. Does this suggest what Nietzsche at the early stage of *The Birth of Tragedy* could not bring himself to admit: that Euripides has been supremely life-enhancing? He has enabled people to live ever more hopefully, even though he has done so by means of error.

What Euripides chiefly teaches us is the almost unlimited extent to which appearances can be manipulated. Here is an appearance; say, a murder of the most squalid and nauseous kind. (Euripides already deals with such a topic in the *Electra*.) Now if we retain our control over this appearance we may omit none of its grisliness and yet actually enjoy it. The only eventuality that must rob us of pleasure, substituting fear and revulsion, would be the loss of control. In that case, of course, the murder would not be art and would be real instead of realistic. Our pleasure lasts so long as we are the masters. In modern absurdist art we can even control our grasp of the uncontrollable, a paradoxical but successful enterprise. Is it not, therefore, that Euripides has done humanity a tremendous service? Was he wise, after all, instead of merely knowledgeable?

But Euripides tacitly acknowledges his own unwisdom in *The Bacchae*. In this play he reverses his earlier stance, confessing, in effect, that he has devoted his life to a display of mastery over that which – or the god who – cannot be mastered. If that were untrue; if *The Bacchae* were nothing more than theatre, it could not have such power. For the force of this work cannot be a product of technique alone. As it is, the important point of the play is no mere contention: in the struggle of Pentheus, King of Thebes, against Dionysus, the god's strength and cruelty increase the more he is resisted, and this is not simply a Euripidean argument. Dionysus grows when someone actively opposes him; in other words rationality based on the device of discrimination turns most horribly into its opposite, beyond a certain point. More accurately, the rational, discriminatory human mind is an outgrowth of the irrational (a nameless sea without divisions or horizon) and has no independent power. Euripides here declares: 'The source of *my* genius is non-human, infinitely changeable and, for sure, mightier than my critical gifts.' Dionysus is inescapably the origin, or indeed the divine being of Euripides' genius, yet Euripides has always supposed himself to be the exploiter of religion, the one who merely uses the gods for his own representational, analytical and sensational purposes.

So far we can say that Nietzsche is right: before Euripides went to Macedonia in his closing years his practice was to bring the ordinary man down from the spectators' seats on to the stage; he looked for plausible motivations and fully explicated stories. This is the obvious, though nevertheless important aspect of Euripides' legacy: tragedy, hence all art, begins to lose its religious and worshipful role, becoming mimetic, diagnostic and critical. If we momentarily consider some later art which appears, on the contrary, to be voluptuous, celebratory and affirmative, say for the sake of argument, the work of Raphael, it soon becomes clear that this too is in line of descent from Euripides. Raphael likewise *contemplates*, and is not ecstatically at one with the fleshly (hence doomed) beauty he paints. For Raphael evinces no true sense of doom but is in love with forms of life from which, so it seems, doom has been excluded. Raphael too is anti-tragic, superbly affirmative for sure, but affirmative because he recognises nothing to be negative about; neither injustice, decay and such matters which commonly arouse resentment, nor (and this is the crucial part) the mere fact that what he sees – however richly he sees it – is still an illusion.

Consider, however, the religion that Euripidean art transforms, or, frankly, opposes. This is the reverse of what we have come to understand by religion. Euripides cannot, of course, contravene a divine other world, a sphere of ethics, a mystical revelation or even, in the later sense, a faith. He sets out to subvert the Dionysiac, the supremely non-rational and non-moral. It is specifically the religion of Dionysus that he seeks to overthrow, on the grounds that it does not make sense. But the rituals of this religion, including its art-works, channel *our* understanding of what passes understanding. Euripides, nevertheless, places himself above and beyond the merely sensuous world – as if there were some other sphere one could occupy. Aeschylus and Sophocles did the same, but *knowingly*. As artists they needed to distance themselves even from Zeus, yet they know this process or distancing to be a contrivance, an artifice.

Consequently, when the later Nietzsche declares, in 1888, that art is the 'countermovement' to the 'decadence forms of man', religion, morality and philosophy, he refers to religion as it has developed since the tragic age.[14] Morality and philosophy are here regarded as subordinate to the Christian religion, since, in Nietzsche's eyes, the religious belief in another world, a 'real world', governs all three. That is what makes them decadent, for they constitute attempts to fixate and deaden life-processes. So it comes about that even the anti-tragic Euripides is part of the countermovement against decadence. He assists life by the mere vanity of his attempts to illuminate it. Can Medea or any murderess be truly illuminated? Certainly not, but when one shines a light by means of art (as opposed to theory, social science, the confessional, and indeed all non-aesthetic forms), life-processes are enhanced, the general health promoted. The other ways preserve individuals, certainly, and many of us would perish without them, but they do not enhance; they do not exalt; they do not encourage us to overcome ourselves. The point to have in mind here is made in *Thus Spoke Zarathustra*. Zarathustra declares to his disciples that Life once told him its secret, as follows: '"Behold," it said, "I am that *which must overcome itself again and again*".'[15] These crucial words indicate that the cosmic process would come to an end in barrenness and nullity if it merely sought and achieved its own preservation. What every energetic process seeks is to become greater tomorrow than it has been today. But becoming greater involves overcoming not others but oneself. For whatever 'oneself' is, one's grasp of this complex must be composed of experience of others, and it is such a composition that needs to be controlled. Art, in contrast to alternative means, assists this essential business of life. When Nietzsche speaks of health he has in mind this activity of self-overcoming; when he speaks of decadence he means whatever retards self-overcoming.

Art takes hold of some supposition of religion, morality or philosophy (the 'decadence forms of man') and transfers it to the side of health. The best-known and indeed most perfect illustrations of this abound in Renaissance art where theological suppositions are time and again sensualised and made earthly. The ascetic ideal of 'goodness' is naturally quite defeated by any artistic attempts to realise it, for it must turn out to be either ugly (that is, life-defeating) or else beautified into its opposite.

However, these later, theological considerations have no bearing upon Euripides himself except to the extent that Euripides' art leads eventually to all individualising art. Euripides thinks of himself as removing the singular individual from the pointless entanglement of nature. In this way, Alcestis and Medea have next to no roots. For Euripides the critical, illuminative artist opposes the darkness, and all art is held by him to stand in opposition to nature. Art and nature continue to stand in opposition to each other, so far as we are concerned, but for Nietzsche this idea is false. The world, he maintains, is not that out of which and contrary to which we make art, since the world itself, meaning the cosmos, is 'a work of art that gives birth to itself'.[16] And, of course, it is both absurd and symptomatic to think of the artist as one apart from nature, as one merely contemplating (or ignoring) *physis*.

For all that, in what conceivable sense can the world be a work of art? Is this assertion not simply reckless, a provocation or a challenge; perhaps a 'spur' in Derrida's use of the term, according to which Nietzsche's varying styles are fronted by spurs? Indeed everyone's personal style is so fronted, although Nietzsche appreciates this fact to an exceptional degree. A style, Derrida says, seems to advance against its chosen object, like the prow of a ship against the sea; or else one's style-spur resembles a rocky point on which waves break at the harbour's mouth. Alternatively, a style uses its spur as a protection against the threat of whatever forcefully presents itself, thus rendering meaningful that which comes to presence.[17] According to such an assessment of style Nietzsche's remark quoted above has of course nothing to do with 'truth' in the old-fashioned sense of the word, and is indeed put forward as a counter to truth. No doubt the world is *not* a work of art but – Nietzsche means to say – since we are obliged to define the world for our own purposes, the best or most human way of doing so is as a work of art. Those alternatives which may still seem to be satisfactory have no support. It is not philosophically coherent to see the world as a mechanical order, if anyone still does. Then, even Einstein needed to understand the universe as a harmony composed by God; that is to say, a 'work of art' (metaphorically speaking) produced by a hidden God, not a work that gives birth to itself. Nietzsche's viewpoint is more compatible with the work of physicists after Einstein, the quantum theorists. To appreciate the question in these terms is to accept that uncertainty informs the universe. The whole does apparently behave in a continuously creative manner, having neither design nor purpose, rather as Nietzsche imagined in the 1880s. Human reason, already understood by Nietzsche as a mode of human creation, is now quite commonly understood as one form out of a myriad acts of creation.

In this fashion Nietzsche's notion of the world as a self-begetting work of art is acceptable, and indeed more than acceptable, for it is the most promising signpost for the human race. The 'world as a work of art' is no mere metaphor in Nietzsche, since for it to be such there would have to be a *known* reality against which its metaphorical status could be measured. Nietzsche has in mind that the universe cannot be apprehended as anything whatsoever in itself; he is completely loyal to Kant. It cannot be described, defined, categorised in any fashion apart from the human will; in this regard Nietzsche is also loyal to Schopenhauer. At this point it is advisable to pause for a moment and take an objection into account. It will be argued that when Nietzsche talks, for example, of the world as will to power he regards himself as perceiving the world from a standpoint other than a mere perspective. That is correct, and for a proper argument about the matter a reader should refer to Richard Schacht's essay, 'Nietzsche's *Gay Science*, or How to Naturalize Cheerfully'.[18] On the other hand, what Nietzsche surely maintains (though not in so many words) is that once one has arrived at the widest, therefore least assailable perspective, one has reached what even today we must still regard as the 'truth'. We can neither get beyond this perspective nor significantly qualify it. Nevertheless, whatever the world is, it can be apprehended only in human, perspectival terms; there are no other terms, therefore there is no other world. Now a perspective such as this, namely one of a width to accommodate all other perspectives, should perhaps no longer be limited by the word 'mere'. As Schacht argues, this is a standpoint which 'transcends ordinary human perspectives'.[19] Even so, it is still an extraordinary and unsurpassable perspective, because nothing else is possible: that is Nietzsche's position. What makes my point more than a quibble is that Nietzsche never ceases to insist on the indeterminable nature of all things, and that insistence has much to do with the relation of knowledge to wisdom. Further, to describe the world either as a work of art or as will to power is less to determine it than to leave its determinations open. It now becomes whatever we, or at any rate more daring philosophers of the future, may wish it to be.

If we now (with the above understanding firmly grasped) regard the world as a work of art, and if we further choose to employ our formal divisions of art, viz., music, painting, literature and sculpture, as analogies for the purpose of comprehending the universe, we come nearer to a human grasp of the universe than we could by any other means. We are *humanly* bound to see it more as art than as textbook knowledge. In the end this too is a matter of psychology: because our minds work better through the medium of art, the universe must be a work of art (that gives birth to itself).

The most thorough investigation of this topic – the world as a work of art – is conducted by Heidegger in his *Nietzsche, Volume One: The Will to Power as Art*. Obviously the lengthiest treatment of a more inclusive thesis, the world as *representation*, is Schopenhauer's, but Heidegger approaches the matter investigatively. Almost at the end of his book, Heidegger quotes from Nietzsche's 'Attempt at a Self-Criticism' appended to the 1872 edition of *The Birth of Tragedy*. In certain vital words Nietzsche now tries to summarise what his 'audacious book' originally set out to achieve, namely '*to see science under the optics of the artist, but art under the optics of life*'.[20] Heidegger maintains in the last two pages of his own work that Nietzsche expects us to grasp the following points: first, 'science' should be understood as 'knowing' (all knowledge); second, the references to the optics of the artist and of life imply that everything amounts to a way of looking; third, art, to Nietzsche, means the vision of the artist, not the response of those who appraise him; and, fourth, 'life' indicates more than biological life, since the term encompasses every perceived and conceivable process. Thus, to see science under the optics of the artist (Nietzsche's effort in *The Birth of Tragedy*) does not mean to regard knowledge as 'art' in the accepted sense but to understand that the mere activity of knowing is creative. Plainly, then, knowledge may no longer be regarded as either absolute or progressive, for it now needs to be assessed according to its power to enhance the knower.

Art in the usual sense (literature, for instance) Nietzsche tries to see 'under the optics of life'. This does not imply that Nietzsche wants us to judge a novel, say, in relation to the social particulars with which it deals (what were the customs of actual courtesans at the time of Balzac?) but rather that a novel should be valued according to its creative-affirmative force. Dostoevsky, Nietzsche says, is better than Zola, because the former is liberating.[21] But have not many people felt liberated by Zola? Nietzsche's answer to such a question may be expressed as follows: Zola and doubtless his genuine admirers find pleasure in the ugly, though this ugliness is dressed up as a crusade for social betterment. Really the entranced reader depends upon Nana's disfigurement or the Morgue in *Thérèse Raquin*, and would be dismayed if he were 'liberated' from the need to contemplate them. Alternatively, Dostoevsky's psychological power puts us in tune with the workings of the human spirit – teaches us, for instance, about such matters as perverse pleasure in the ugly. Zola manipulates his own and the reader's responses, because he fears them in their raw state. He shies away from them and tries to make them into something else. He cannot be liberating when he is thus enslaved by his own fears. It is to the point that Dostoevsky's novels, as compared with those of Zola, do not reduce psychology to anything resembling a schema, or any sort of explanation. Characters think and behave in the strangest ways, which is to say, as people do in life. Someone might ask, 'Is this not more Euripidean? Is not Hippolytus, for example, something of an early form of a Dostoevskian character?' The answer is 'No' since, however odd the behaviour of Hippolytus, Euripides and we ourselves can formulate it without much trouble. Alternatively, we can scarcely formulate Dmitri Karamazov. Dostoevsky does not pretend to *diagnose* him.

In Nietzsche's eyes we should thus judge a novel, or any other work or art, in relation to its capacity to encourage *amor fati*. Nietzsche's definition of *amor fati* is that 'one wants nothing to be different, not forward, not backward, not in all eternity'.[22] Dostoevsky (perhaps alone of great novelists) seems not to preach anything and to accept, above all, the workings of minds. We are probably wrong to read a moral lesson into *Crime and Punishment* or even to read a socio-ethical lesson into *The House of the Dead*. In such a way, when a novel or a non-fictional work urges a reader towards the conditions of life, he is the stronger, or more affirmative, for having read it. Dostoevsky continually suggests that the conditions he is describing, though 'historical' (in a broad sense), are not a basis for improvement: this sort of thing – criminal misjudgement (as in the case of Raskolnikov); virtual enslavement (as in *The House of the Dead*) – will always take place, or, when there are changes in human practices, such changes will not amount to a general improvement. In fact, if anything is recommended by the works of Dostoevsky I have mentioned, it is precisely *amor fati*.

However, to be affirmative it is essential that one goes, willingly or even happily, some way towards acknowledging not just the conditions and behaviour described in a novel by Dostoevsky, but also the chaos out of which the novel has been carved. The novel defines and illuminates some set of appearances, but it does this 'tragically', which is to say, as appearances pure and simple, drawn from a hopeless jumble of indiscernible processes.

So there is no valid external criterion for a work of art, or rather, each external criterion exists to be overthrown. Euripides' belief that Sophocles neither explained enough nor sufficiently imitated the social world is just a limited point of view, helpful to Euripides. The social world which Sophocles scarcely copied was itself a pageant and not at all the object of the work. If, as Plato says, the artist makes a copy of a copy, the tragic viewpoint also maintains that phenomena, bright, clear-etched appearances, change, fade and vanish; they are real *because* we focus our attention upon them, name them, briefly distinguish and characterise them. But we cannot ourselves give them vigour (through technique), for this lies in the tangle from which we have extracted them. Their roots go back into the tangle and eventually into darkness. This is true both of people in life and of characters in fiction. It is perhaps also why the most expert of aesthetic psychologists (Homer, Shakespeare, Dostoevsky) do not seriously pretend to explain, but merely delineate.

The present question turns on the means by which one is supposed to know a character, either in fiction or in life. In the end one's knowledge consists of information about the past. Of course one recognises and effortlessly categorises habitual behaviour, but for *explanation* one looks to the life-story (perhaps in its full socio-historical context). However, according to Nietzsche, this procedure is a sort of laziness; indeed all so-called knowledge comes about because one is tired or lazy. '"Knowledge,"' he writes, 'is a referring-back: in its essence a *regressus in infinitum*. That which comes to a standstill (at a supposed *causa prima* at something unconditioned, etc.) is laziness, weariness – .'[23] This short remark raises several important questions. First of all, is knowledge always only a referring-back? If we distinguish knowledge from recognition, I believe it is, in the sense Nietzsche intends. We explain something by reference to something else behind it. The exclusively human faculty of knowledge defines *homo sapiens* himself as the one created by God (in God's own image) or else as the one evolved from other, unknowing creatures. We know the newer by relating it to the older – by a process of referring back. In Euripides we know Electra by knowing what has happened to her earlier, before we now discover her married to her nameless peasant. Euripides' technique consists of saying to himself, 'What will a spectator need to know about this woman?' and then supplying a pseudo-historical answer. Nietzsche does not deny that such is an answer of sorts, but what is lacking is any appreciation of a *regressus in infinitum*: where and why does one stop? In Euripides' play our curiosity in fact stops at the explanation offered, behind which the complete answer stretches away to infinity. Naturally we have to stop somewhere, for we must get on with our lives, but why is it necessary to suppose that we have arrived at the terminus rather than a mere stopping-place? Tragedy proper suggests that there is no terminus, since Electra is just a form adopted by the eternally recurring Dionysus.

Is scientific knowledge of the same (actually quite arbitrary) kind? It does indeed seem to be. In physics we reach back to causes, thence to causes of causes, and if we come to an apparent beginning, the

Big Bang, then that is that. But as the Big Bang itself demonstrates, nothing has been satisfactorily explained.

Secondly, if knowledge is a referring back, wherein lies its value? It could be argued that its value is rather distinctively 'Nietzschean', because Nietzsche gives a value to forces according to their 'genealogy'. To trace the genealogy of morals by discovering their origins in priestly manipulation of resentful feelings is certainly to revalue morality. Here, however, we are dealing not with knowledge but with psychological interpretation. Time and again Nietzsche confronts questions that cannot be answered in terms of knowledge, by which procedure he implicitly reveals the limitations of knowledge. In truth this is his specialised method, as it was already the method of the Presocratics. A leading feature of his technique is to go behind knowledge. For example, he goes behind our knowledge of the writing of the Gospels in order to speculate about Christ's motives. He considers such speculation to be more important than knowledge. Even from a theologian's point of view, and especially from a philosopher's, what matter about the gospels is not how they came to be written but the light their composition throws upon the intentions, hence the essential message of Jesus. Nietzsche goes straight to the intention, as a philosopher should, even if he has to go behind, or beyond knowledge in order to do so.[24] Nietzsche's explanation is undoubtedly tenable, yet anyone can reject it. On the other hand, by sticking to knowledge no one arrives at an explanation of Christ; in other words, philosophy surrenders. Thus Nietzsche's genealogical method is a way of finding a meaning while stressing the limitations of knowledge. It is an *openly* creative venture; contrariwise, knowledge-seeking of the orthodox sort is at first a concealed or furtive form of creation and later a relinquishment of one's task.

Thirdly, the supposition that something is unconditional is obviously a form that relinquishment takes. One reaches an answer which demands further enquiry, but demands it less imperatively than earlier answers have done. In this way one is provided with an excuse for giving up.

Finally, Nietzsche's remark suggests not that knowledge is always absolutely 'wrong' – for, of course, there is nothing outside the sphere of knowledge to invalidate it – but that it is always only a means of living and growing. In the ages of faith, knowledge could readily be invalidated or inhibited, but at that time there was another way of growing. Potential for growth is all that matters.

We should remember, therefore, that knowledge is never what it pretends to be, and is 'wrong' in that specific sense.

As between knowledge and fatedness (the core of tragedy), Euripides underrated the latter, hence overrated the former. Tragedy deals with the unlimitedly fertile field of fatedness, of the *Moirai*, daughters of Zeus, as the ones who punish us for exceeding our measures. From our logical point of view the *Morai* must therefore give us our measures in the first place, appoint each of us to our specific range of possibilities, but this is not explicit in Greek literature. For example, Ajax is appointed to be a formidable warrior, nevertheless not the first Greek warrior, since that status is allotted to Achilles. It is the insanity of Ajax that causes him not merely to compete with Achilles (which would be acceptable and healthy) but to resent Achilles *excessively*. If we look at this matter in a modern way, we cannot argue that Ajax should have sought an objective measure of his prowess (since as a matter of fact, he was more or less on a par with Achilles), but that he was too eager to be accorded honours, in other words too dependent on the opinions of others.

In effect the Fates punish Ajax for his Ajax-nature. But, logically, where did this nature come from? Is Ajax supposed to be a self-creator? We still do not answer this question about character for it is unanswerable, yet we still blame and punish people. Thus our characters, given us either by the Fates or by no one, are measured and possibly punished 'by the Fates'. This does not make logical sense, though it makes perfect tragical sense.

In Aeschylus and Sophocles tragedy refers to phenomena as 'fated'. Phenomena are fated and therefore significant; however, they are not explainable and so they are incorrigible. To say that a flower must grow into a certain size, colour and shape is to acknowledge its own significance: it is exactly what it alone is. It goes without saying that this is a radically different matter from causing a person (who is also a phenomenon) to 'correct' himself, that is, to torment himself into an alien shape amenable to society or to God. We proceed thus on the questionable grounds that the person is at liberty to choose a self. Ours is the complete anti-tragic assumption. The Prometheus of Aeschylus, on the other hand, is hideously punished by Zeus for stealing fire from heaven and giving it to mortals. At the conclusion of the tragedy Prometheus is still defiant; God (Zeus) himself cannot bring Prometheus to recant. This means that Prometheus is doomed to defy Zeus; that is his calling. By what must strike us as a monstrous paradox, the very fatum of this drama is that Prometheus is determined as the one who must defy Zeus; he is not reformable, for if he were, there would be no tragedy. And there must be tragedy, since without it the world reverts to primordial Chaos.

Contrariwise, Euripides proceeds by means of 'knowing', that is, by referring back to earlier parts of the story in question. (And his personages also appear to know, meaning they are able to trace their motives). Now, this Euripidean procedure rests upon a confident, assertive selection from quite unordered surroundings. What Nietzsche – without reference to Euripides – calls the 'formless unformulable world of the chaos of sensations'[25] is what Euripides reduces to pseudo-tragical meanings, but he does so without self-awareness. In other words, he fails to recognise, or he disdains, the chaos of sensations. He does not acknowledge that 'in the beginning', so to speak, there is only fuzziness and blurredness. According to Nietzsche this condition is *'another kind* of phenomenal world, a kind "unknowable" for us'.[26]

On the one hand there is, in the words of the young Nietzsche, the 'unmeasured and indiscriminate knowledge drive',[27] and this will immediately be recognised as a great mischief and possible the bane of the twentieth century. On the other hand, there is the sort of knowledge for which, to the Nietzsche of 1887, life was a means: '"Life as a means to knowledge" – with this principle in one's heart one can live not only boldly but even gaily, and laugh gaily too.'[28]

Nietzsche is talking about two sorts of knowledge, the first as harmful as it is encouraged, the second more private and fruitful. In the first place 'unmeasured and indiscriminate knowledge' piles up without regard to the innermost needs of the knower; indeed his needs – and to this extent his life – are sacrificed to knowledge. One more or less becomes what one has been taught. In the second place, however, the knower regards all experiences as knowledge. This might well produce a ridiculous image of some sufferer trying to convince himself of the value of his suffering, but it should produce a higher (more inclusive) image of one who has swept past the ridiculous stage and recognises that stage itself as an old piece of knowledge.

Further, this second, self-enhancing kind of knowledge includes our vague awareness of another kind of phenomenal world. But how can we be aware of this unknowable sphere? Nietzsche himself puts the word 'unknowable' in inverted commas. And Nietzsche is right, for we certainly do guess at the existence of this other sphere, or rather, we *know* it by means which have nothing to do with knowledge. Even Kant at his most meticulous distinguishes between original intuitions of external objects and, on the other hand, the forms which our minds instantly give to such intuitions. We shape and classify phenomena even as we receive them. Thus Kant asserts without fear of contradiction that our minds confer upon external objects whatever qualities the objects are supposed to possess: space itself is not a conception derived from experience, and neither is time.

There is certainly a complete difference between what Kant understands as our original intuition of external objects and what Nietzsche speaks of as a blurred awareness of sensations, but my point is that both philosophers think in terms of knowing the unknowable, albeit a different unknowable in each case. Nietzsche's unknowable is nearer the province of knowledge than Kant's, since he has in mind the awareness that seldom disappears entirely but serves only as an unordered and unnoticed background to whatever is recognised in the foreground.

I believe that some people are relatively at ease with such an awareness, while others scarcely tolerate it. Therefore, the first class have a greater understanding of the formative nature of minds than the second. Members of the first category are less liable to want or need to control their sense-impressions; hence they are more truly *tragical*. They manage to accommodate in some fashion not only what can be said but also what cannot be either said or, in the usual sense, known. That is why they may be described as 'tragical'. For tragedy has nothing essentially to do with misery; rather it is connected with primitive receptiveness, with possessing a fairly strong grasp of the wider context stretching away and beyond the communicable.

(Perhaps it should be made clear that the last two paragraphs are not remotely concerned with Kant's *noumena*, or the natures of things in themselves, for the intuitions just discussed, like our normal verbalised intuitions, belong to the domain of phenomena. The difference under discussion here is between objects perceived in a blurred, inchoate fashion and objects perceived and labelled with precision.)

Now, it is Nietzsche, as opposed to Kant, who (following Schopenhauer) regards our apprehension of the 'formless, unformulable world' as worthy of further reflection. To Nietzsche this apprehension should stand at the gateway of all serious thought, although it normally does not do so in philosophy.

At this stage we can discern more clearly than before the nature of Euripides' mimetic techniques. These reproduce, as Nietzsche says, the 'botched outlines of nature', rather than the bold and heroic traits formerly displayed by the dramatists. But Euripides' so-called copying is still a mode of creation; further, it is not less creative than the procedures of his predecessors. It is merely creative in a different style, or creative of something essentially different. In brief, Euripides does not copy the true reality of nature any more than its ideality; he reproduces only its botched *outlines*. An outline is scarcely real, or is at best a superficial aspect of the real. The outlines preferred by Euripides are crude and flawed (comparatively speaking) because, instead of sensing what nature is driving at – the production of fated beings – Euripides rests content with a simplification of the antics of such beings. Reality is the fate he evades, not the manners he represents. In any case, by representing manners, he does in fact create an abstract from life, since he denies life's fuzziness, which is exactly what Aeschylus and Sophocles imply. Euripides' world is distinct and meaningful, because he has made it so. It means what he misleadingly says it means. It is true that neither Aeschylus nor Sophocles refers in any way to the 'fuzziness' of the world and each is indeed more formal and restrained than Euripides. For all that, the earlier dramatists are implicitly conscious of the *reductive* quality of their plays. Naturally this essential tragic consciousness is shared by the spectators, while in watching Euripides we today are encouraged to think that people are more or less as they appear to the discerning eye. People are roughly analysable, so it seems. That a person's actions merely manifest and elaborate a certain force (that he needs to be 'deconstructed', as one might say) tends to escape attention. So does the fact that the force embodied in him both arrives from and departs into the universe of forces: he is but a metamorphosis of the force. Finally he cannot be an individual, but this truth is increasingly overlooked as the post-Euripidean centuries go by.

Thus a long phase of human behaviour is initiated (not to mention ethical considerations). We gain the impression that our own lives and therefore a good deal more are fairly controllable. Certainly we can control what we have already laid aside as 'knowledge'. This way of thinking gives us a certain assurance, but it is unwise and eventually runs into the sands. The unwisdom lies first of all in the fact that the person (the spectator of the drama and more generally the perceiver) is ideally excluded. His own vision, which ranges from the precise to the nebulous, from the brightest light to the deepest shadow, is kept apart, yet of course this vision *is* him for all important purposes. I am certainly treating the word 'knowledge' as though it embraced only public knowledge, but this procedure is correct, since strictly private understanding, understanding garnered into a private vision, is not directly communicable and as a rule does not count as knowledge. The personal vision, described by Nietzsche as 'a strange penumbra which is the mark of one's singularity',[29] must always assume mastery and treat knowledge as a servant. No doubt this attitude amounts to 'egoism' in the philosophic sense and may therefore be thought to be self-indulgent as well as morally unsound. However, Nietzsche's doctrine (which in any case is not preached and is possibly not even a 'doctrine') entails harder and more fearful activity than the usual procedures of social beings, procedures which, in the opening pages of 'Schopenhauer as Educator', he subsumes under 'laziness'. So every piece of knowledge is laziness, unless it is regarded as a starting-point for a new venture. It is an imaginary point, rather as we might imagine a precise position in the current of a river.

Here is a fitting simile with which to conclude our consideration of Euripides' legacy. This brilliant dramatist undoubtedly treated public knowledge as an instrument, insofar as he viewed the myths themselves *purely* as material for his quasi-historical plays. Nevertheless, he failed to realise that the myths at their most noble (Prometheus, Oedipus) were designed to indicate the uncertainty, indeed the positive blackness surrounding every illuminated thing. Euripides did not attend to the implications of his idea of 'explanation'. Unlike Sophocles especially (I am thinking of Oedipus and Antigone), he did not appreciate that the most certain grasp of all, one's 'strange penumbra' as Nietzsche calls it, is and must remain the least known, least analysable form of awareness. In addition it must also be comprehended as a force within the universe of forces; that is to say, somewhat like a point in a flowing river, itself tragic, fated, and imaginary.

5

Aristotle's 'Being' and Nietzsche's 'Will to Power'

When Aristotle speaks of 'wisdom' he has in mind a searching quality which today we scarcely even recognise, let alone desire. He is the first and possibly the last to offer a distinct and satisfactory definition. This is his superior definition and he would not have offered it if it had been commonplace. 'Wisdom', he says in the *Metaphysics*, is a 'science of first principles.'[1] Metaphysics is precisely the study of first principles, but, even so, this study obviously does not amount to wisdom. Aristotle means that while one can think about first principles well or badly, one cannot be wise without a primary yearning to uncover such principles.

In Aristotle wisdom is an activity to which some people are drawn and others are not. The first sort never rest content with customs, beliefs, solutions, ethics, culture or knowledge, for all these are fields to be traversed by the wise. Ethics, for instance, is not at all what wisdom already knows, for wisdom is that which continually refashions ethics. One arrives at ethics by *questioning*, but there is no end to this process. At present, however, we need to hold on to the fact that knowledge in all its forms is supposed by Aristotle to follow rather than precede wisdom – or even, at best, to be questioningly created by wisdom.

Knowledge is distinguished from metaphysics in being concerned with definite beings, though it seeks or posits the universal of each such being. For example, knowledge of buildings and architecture must embrace the fundamental principles of this science, since merely to recognise buildings is not in itself to *know* them. Just the same, architectural knowledge, although it is higher and more theoretical than simple recognition (of which lower animals are capable), is not remotely wise. Wisdom consists of – or consists *in* – access to the first principles of all existent things. So wisdom is certainly not knowledge (which must be specific), because it makes its way towards the first principles of each and every being, or of 'Being' itself.

Aristotle declares that 'the science of the philosopher treats of being *qua* being universally and not of some part of it . . .'[2] What the philosopher wants or seeks, then, is not science, for it is more like the 'science of sciences'. He treats of being, not as this or that (not, for instance, as the specialist field, 'philosophy') but as what it essentially and universally is. 'Being' is not *this* tree, or house or person (these are substances) and not even everything assembled and unified as the All, but purely and simply 'Being'. It is present, naturally, in negative as well as positive concepts, in the concept of absence as well as in presence, in imaginings as well as in plain sight. A void or a vacuum has being. Chaos itself has being in the form of a notion or some sort of confused image. In other words, Being organises and orders chaos, so that 'true chaos', so to speak, is inconceivable, though the Greeks briefly approached it through representations of Dionysus.

Alternatively, what we, to a vastly greater extent than Aristotle's contemporaries, take to be valuable sciences (that is, systems of knowledge within *designated* departments of Being) 'omit the question whether the genus with which they deal exists or does not exist . . .'[3] In these words Aristotle all but takes it for granted that knowledge is only arrangement and to that extent a sort of invention. He himself, for instance, seeks knowledge of poetry in the *Poetics* but does not ask whether there truly is such a kind as poetry. There are certain structures of words we class as 'poetry', but what is this poetry in its essence, apart from a convenient classification? Nevertheless, Aristotle, unlike other literary critics and thinkers, is obviously concerned with poetry *qua* poetry; he tries to get behind it by saying what it apparently is: an art which imitates human actions by words alone. Whether or not we are satisfied with this definition, we recognise that Aristotle makes an initial attempt to get behind poetry, and of course this is his regular procedure in regard to all the sciences he examines.

But how can we get behind metaphysics? If we cannot, is metaphysics a science? If it is not a science, what can we know about it? In any case, how can we know that which must be the ground of knowledge? In the *Metaphysics* Aristotle tries to go to the root of all things, although in doing so he is merely continuing the practice begun two to three hundred years earlier by Thales and his successors. From Thales to Democritus this was the practice, so that Aristotle treats Socrates and Plato as no more than members of a line. He critically considers the doctrine of the Forms (*meta*-physics in that sense) but he wishes to put philosophy back on the road of fundamental enquiry, which should not stop at the level of any doctrine or any science. Philosophy may not beg the question about any genus but must consider Being as and for itself. Perhaps, then, metaphysics is not a science, since while it is easy to say what investigations are not metaphysical, metaphysics underpins everything else. It cannot be a science because we cannot go behind it.

All of us, in common with some animals, know individuals, but only the wise know universals: that is Aristotle's position at the beginning of the *Metaphysics*. Wisdom, he says, deals with 'the first causes and the principles of things'.[4] There are for sure basic principles at the beginning of every science, to seek which is a part of wisdom, but the highest wisdom, which the philosopher alone exercises, is that concerned with the first causes and principles of all things. Aristotle sometimes speaks of God, yet since he is the investigator par excellence and (despite the *Nicomachean Ethics*) not fundamentally a moralist, he regards God as the first cause and principle whose goodness should never be thought of as opposed to a quality called 'badness'. As we shall see later, Aristotle does not think of god as having a character, which is a limiting factor, but rather of God as Being. God, or Being, is without magnitude and is indivisible. He is neither immanent nor transcendent; all such notions should be put aside for he simply and immovably *is*.

In the first three books of the *Metaphysics* Aristotle considers principles as causes. At this stage, his guiding thread is the question: what is cause? Causes are spoken of in four ways. First of all, a cause is a substance or an essence, that which answers the question 'why' of a particular being. If we can say why something or other has come into being, why it is as a being, then we have arrived at its cause. Secondly, the cause of a being is its matter or substratum; it is the 'what?' of that being. In this case, if one explains precisely and exhaustively what a being is, one has brought to light its cause. Thirdly, the cause of a being is the source of change in that being. An example is in order here, since it seems likely that Nietzsche regularly thought of 'cause' in this sense. If, say, we want to know what morals are, we should look to that which accounts for changes and developments in moral attitudes. When we find this, we shall have found the ultimate cause of morals: the 'genealogy' of morals is at least the nearest we can get to their cause. Fourthly, the cause of a being is its purpose, that which answers the question, what is it finally *for*? Once again we can bring in Nietzsche. What is the cause, in the sense of final purpose, of the human race? Thus to Zarathustra the cause of the human race is the *Übermensch*.

Aristotle seems willing, or, preferably he seems *impelled* to ask a question whenever there is a sensible question to be asked. On the other hand, Plato halts at God who produces the Forms, and 'God' has been the name for our stopping-place ever since. Just now, we are concerned with causes, and while God is the First and Ultimate Cause, Plato regards the Forms generally as causes. The cause of a natural being is its Form, and yet, Aristotle remarks, the Form of wood does not make a piece of wood change. Indeed, the Forms cause neither movement nor change; therefore, what use are they? This is the crucial point, as the Presocratics (who never conceived of the Forms) already recognised: what makes something move? In the case of animate beings (not creatures alone), what brings about their internal and external movements? Whence animation or, more bluntly, whence life or, to be as comprehensive as possible (and to the extent that this distinction is still permitted in chemistry), whence the organic? For, says Aristotle in a nicely-worded assertion which should stand at the portals of thought, 'as the eyes of bats are to the blaze of day, so is the reason in our soul to the things which are by nature most evident of all'.[5] To descend to a clumsy paraphrase, Aristotle means that those things naturally most evident – the sun, the grass, bounding or crawling animals, people moving about and chattering – are opaque to our reason. In the terms of astrophysics we know the sun, but our reason does not know *what* it is. We know evident beings (and not so evident ones) by means of specialist sciences, and they still do not 'make sense'. What sense does the sun make? In sum, that things merely *are* is opaque to reason.

Aristotle declares in Book II of the *Metaphysics*: 'Evidently there is a first principle and the causes of things are neither an infinite series nor infinitely various in kind.'[6] On the face of it the logic of this statement is sound. There must be a first principle, we say, because otherwise we are confronted by the unthinkable: an endless causal sequence. That there should be infinitely various causes is likewise unthinkable, for then there would be one or more causes for every event, so that each cause would be no more than a precedent. A series of precedents running off into eternity defeats the (humanly necessary) notion of cause.

Aristotle cannot conceive of an endless world-process, in the sense of a process running off in a line and never coming to a halt. There must be a first principle or cause, he insists. He means what is undeniable: we apprehend, we perform the act of apprehension, by imagining limits. Therefore, *apparently*, there was a beginning and there will be an end. In this way, the 'ever-living Fire' of Heraclitus amounts to a trick of the mind. We form a notion of ever-living Fire precisely by encircling the flames, thus drawing a boundary line around that which is not supposed to have a boundary. Aristotle is the only thinker before Nietzsche who faces up to this question. Aristotle faces up to the supreme question not (in the ways of Heraclitus and Parmenides) by giving a good but still unsatisfactory answer, and not of course by falling back on some sort of Platonic answer – which is a matter of belief – but by taking his strict interrogation as far as it will go. Thus he is honourable and will not provide even a brilliant non-solution. In the end Aristotle can think of nothing short of God, although, as we shall see, this is God-as-solution rather than God in any other capacity or guise. Above all, God is not the consequence of yearning, as he probably is in Plato, but the result of resolute thought.

Nietzsche alone has hit upon the one *logical* answer which, nevertheless, *at first* seems fantastic, and which in any case one is disinclined to recognise as logic, since Nietzsche characteristically does not present it in a formal manner. Which do we honestly prefer: illogical and evasive 'common sense' (the time-honoured response), or watertight, nonempiric logic – that supremacy of the creative mind already demonstrated by the Presocratics? Nietzsche's solution is that the cosmic play of energies can have neither beginning nor end.[7] Since we, like Aristotle, can think of a beginning outside the energies themselves only by uttering the word 'God', we cannot truly think of a beginning as such. A beginning within the energies is nonsense, and, as Aristotle clearly implies, an end in chaos or darkness is as inconceivable as a chaotic or a black beginning. It follows that what we now perceive has always existed in quantum terms. Energies are eternal, although they expand to scarcely imaginable distances and contract to an equally unimaginable, microscopic 'point'. This means that eternity cannot be understood as a straight line, a linear succession of events and forces, but might be contemplated as a sphere growing larger or smaller – a sphere with all space and matter inside it.

Aristotle is right: a line of succession may not go on for ever; therefore a first cause would seem to be required. On the other hand, a first cause is inconceivable, however often we follow Aristotle in fancying that we have conceived such a being. To this enigma the only answer is curvature, which Nietzsche usually refers to as a ring or circle. The ring must not be imagined as a simple ring, for it would be better for us today to picture curved space. Thus Nietzsche's logical idea is not so much 'true' as the intellectual boundary. But what is 'truth' if not the intellectual boundary?

By the close of Book III Aristotle has implicitly decided to postpone looking for a first principle. A possibly profitable way forward is to search for Being, which is to say, not for the being of each individual (say Socrates, or a marketplace, or a battle) but for the universal(s) prior to these beings. At the opening of Book IV, therefore, Aristotle is ready to contemplate the 'science which investigates being as being and the attributes which belong to this in virtue of its own nature'.[8] He proceeds to ask what it means to 'be' – not (for the moment) what a being is, or what Being is, but what it means when we say of something merely that it 'is'. However, the answer must not be individual but universal in scope. This is certainly the most fundamental of all questions and the one which, between Aristotle and Heidegger, no philosopher has tackled as a question. I say 'as a question' because while Nietzsche provides an answer, he never treats the matter as strictly questionable. We are, of course, proceeding towards Nietzsche's answer, but in order to appreciate that answer, it is necessary first to appreciate the range and depth of the question. This is best done by noting some of the points that Aristotle makes – for not all the points are of equal importance, at any rate for us.

Aristotle tackles the matter as follows: being something or other must always be taken as a revelation of its substance or essence, not of any of its accidental qualities. If a man is white, 'man' is substance or essence, and 'white' is accidental. You cannot get further back than 'man', since larger categories such as 'animal' or 'creature' are merely less precise. The gap which we aim sooner or later to bridge is between 'man' and 'Being'; meanwhile, the whiteness of the man is accidental. So far, then, to be whatever something is, is the same as to constitute a certain substance or essence. It is certainly true that the word 'white' by no means always refers to an accidental quality, since white may itself be the substance: everything depends on the context and the usage. What Aristotle is doing here is distinguishing essentiality from contingency, in order to identify being with the former. But this will be only a preliminary identification, and of course the being 'man' is only used here as a way to Being.

So far Aristotle may be said to be clearing the ground. Indeed all twelve books of the *Metaphysics* are a clearing of the ground, though some parts now seem to us more fruitful than others. It is especially promising when Aristotle (in Book IV) attacks the Heracliteans for maintaining that, since everything is constantly changing, nothing can be reliably affirmed. This is promising, not because we anticipate Aristotle's victory over Heraclitus – and in any case we do not yet know which of them is 'right' – but because here is the nub. Cratylus, for example, a 'professed' Heraclitean, has argued that you cannot truly step into a river once, let alone twice. Aristotle breaks the matter down in the following fashion: that which in the process of change is losing a quality retains some of the quality in question, and whatever new quality it will come to have it already possesses in some degree. Now this is more or less what the Heracliteans have always argued. However, Aristotle's solution to the problem is to maintain that it is not the quantity of a being whose truth we affirm, but rather its quality, namely that it is whatever it is. Thus while the 'quantity' of a river (length, volume, etc.) never stops changing, its quality as *a river* – and for that matter, as a specific, named river – remains the same. In this way we have no need to think of 'truth' as a mere consensus of essentially falsified references but rather as qualitative summary: the 'river', or the 'River Danube', is an agreed term which is not false as a reference and need not mislead one.

Nevertheless, Heraclitus and his followers have disclosed a chasm between truth and being, and at present Aristotle is in pursuit of the truth *of* being. He feels it necessary to face the fact that even the entirety of the sensible world, if the entirety suddenly became perceptible, would still be other than the truth. For the truth, whatever it is, must include more than the sensible world. 'And, in general,' he writes, 'if only the sensible exists, there would be nothing if animate things were not; for there would be no faculty of sense.'[9] Animate things are absolutely required for the purposes of sensing the sensible world. If that world were not available to sense, it would not be.

For all its familiarity, we are still not at home with this contention, just because we find it hard to accept even an impeccable argument when it runs counter to the normal understanding. As usual, Aristotle goes to the root of the matter. A sensation, he says, cannot detect or respond to itself. How may a sensation of heat or of greenness detect itself, as distinct from the temperature or the colour of which it appears to be entirely composed? The heat is a sensation-being which is detected by some other being. This other being is what we are looking for, and we need to persist in looking for what is prior until we reach the utmost accessible priority.

Aristotle writes:

'For sensation is surely not the sensation of itself, but there is something beyond the sensation, which must be prior to the sensation; for that which moves is prior in nature to that which is moved, and if they are correlative terms, this is no less the case.'[10]

These words expound but do not solve the problem. 'That which moves' means that which brings about something or other, and it is invariably true that such a something is 'prior in nature' to whatever is brought about. Clearly this is so. It follows that a sensation of heat or greenness (a 'movement') is brought about by something prior to it, meaning not the hot or green object but an unidentifiable being which either immediately precedes the sensation or may be correlative with it. The sensation is thus caused not by that of which it is the sensation but by this other nameless being.

Here we come to what one might readily see as the key point in Aristotle's metaphysics. This nameless being, he supposes, has to be thought of as unmovable, for otherwise it cannot be contemplated at all. Aristotle has long before (in Book I, 7) disposed of the device of calling such a being a Form, on the grounds that while the being, by definition, necessarily causes movement (indeed that is *all* it does), a Form causes movement only incidentally. That is, a Form is held to exist anyway, and now and then, for some reason, it produces a movement. We cannot resolve a being into a Form, or Being as a whole into the Forms.

It is not until Book XII that Aristotle devotes his attention to Being as such. His argument proceeds along roughly the following lines: if substances, which are the first essentials of existing things, 'are all destructible, all things are destructible'.[11] This being so, we must so far presume (since Aristotle does not articulate the point) not merely the possibility but the certainty of universal destruction. But cosmic annihilation has not occurred and, Aristotle believes, cannot occur. What unquestionably has happened is the completion of cycles of events. Indeed cycles constantly commence while other cycles constantly cease. An event, great or small, comes to be and ceases to be. But no matter how many cycles are thus completed, two things, movement and time, cannot have started and cannot cease. Aristotle therefore takes movement and time to be eternal, since a being anterior to movement and time is inconceivable.

We cannot today apprehend an absolute beginning, so that our vague and botched attempts to do so are a compound of fidelity to the observations of physics (the Big Bang) and utter infidelity to ourselves. In this way – by leaving ourselves out of the picture – we so 'unwisely' pretend to conceptualise what lies beyond conceptualisation and so cannot be. What I am saying here is no doubt only a crude offshoot of Kant's awareness that space and time are *a priori* intuitions – the very conditions of our thinking.[12]

Aristotle roundly states: 'Therefore chaos or night did not exist for any infinite time, but the same things have always existed . . .'.[13] By the 'same things' Aristotle probably means the same basic substances – the same physical and chemical elements. The phraseology of the above translation may not be immediately clear: Aristotle wants to convey that nothing whatsoever has existed for eternity except the things that now exist. There was no prior period of chaos or night.

It follows that 'there is a constant cycle [so that] something must always remain, acting in the same way'.[14] On the other hand, generation and destruction manifestly take place; therefore these processes occur *inside* the constant cycle. For all that, and although 'these difficulties may be taken as solved',[15] Aristotle cannot, as we earlier noted, contemplate movement without a mover: 'And since that which is moved and moves is intermediate, there is a mover which moves without being moved, being eternal, substance and actuality.'[16] 'Intermediate' means occupying a position between the 'first heavens' and 'that which is moved' – the existent universe. The last point is of no interest to us, but we are left with a mover which moves without being moved.

The mover is a 'living being, eternal, most good, so that life and duration continuous and eternal belong to God; for this *is* God'.[17] Thus God, who is most good, is the Being of beings; he is life and duration continuous and eternal. Aristotle has logically proceeded to an affirmation of God who, of course, has no character and no morality but is that which animates the entirety of cosmic substance. God is neither external to substance nor immanent but the Being without which substance would not move and therefore (along with time) would not be.

In respect of this thought-sequence Aristotle is finally concerned to discover what God could possibly think about. This procedure is a move towards a characterisation of God, although the divine Being must still be shown to have nothing resembling a character in the accepted sense. What, however, does divine thought think? It cannot 'think objects', as we consider knowledge, perceptions and opinions, for these areas of human thought are merely features of God's world. Divine thought, therefore, thinks nothing but itself. In this way, what becomes the goal in Hegel, Absolute Knowing or Spirit, is omnipresent and eternal in Aristotle – not a goal to be achieved but an eternal *fact*. This fact itself is Being.

II

What now has to be confronted, by way of a transition from Aristotle to Nietzsche, is that Aristotle's 'Being', or God, or eternal fact, is merely what it is and, as we have amply remarked, has no nature. For this reason it forms only part of the solution. If it were possible to ascribe a character to Being (a character protean enough to accommodate all beings) we would establish the foundation of a human ontology and thence an ethics. People would have the chance to *be* in accordance with universal Being and on this basis of whatever people essentially are, we could reach conclusions as to how they ought preferably to behave. This is what Nietzsche attempted when he, in effect, replaced Aristotle's 'Being' with his own 'will to power'.

To be exact, the phrase 'will to power' is put forward as a perspicuous way of saying what Being is. The term is not chiefly meant to be startling but merely observant. Nietzsche believes he has seen better into the heart of things than Aristotle managed in his day. In Aristotelian terms, Being is the mover of substances, but the mover of substances can be yet more accurately called 'will to power'. Thus Being is will to power, and, if we had the confidence to do so, we could now discard the empty word 'Being'.

But Aristotle's Being is also God, so that we might now characterise God himself as will to power. It is plain that I am comprehending
God as Aristotle does, putting aside the narrow and arbitrary
associations of a distinct way of life, the Way of Jesus, which God
has acquired since the Greeks. But all theological interpretations are
narrowings of God-as-will to power just as Being was originally and
remains to this day a superfluous and vacuous widening of will to
power. As Being has too little character, or rather, next to none at all,
theological apprehensions of Being-as-God have 'too much'; that is
to say, the theological and post-theological characterisation of what
animates all beings is far too specific and demands a too-specific
sort of human being.

The vital first point about will to power is that it stands midway
between the excessive vagueness of Being and the excessive particu-
larity of the Lord God who wants all people to follow his Law and
worship him. Will to power animates every being in the universe,
not just the human species who for some three thousand years
have located themselves exclusively on scales of values linked to
the one God.

On the other hand, if anyone today tried to think of God as Being
he would have before him the additional example of Spinoza. Certain propositions in Spinoza's *Ethics* state that God is the indivisible
entirety, and this understanding might well be used as a preliminary
to a consideration of will to power.[18] In this way a thread runs from
Aristotle to Spinoza, and afterwards to Schopenhauer and Nietzsche,
but clearly this thread reduces the moral God of Christianity – and,
incidentally, the humanistic values of the twentieth century. To
Spinoza nothing is 'outside' God or hostile to God, just as to
Nietzsche nothing lacks will to power as its essence. however,
while Aristotle can, as we have seen, include all beings in one
Being, and Spinoza can likewise embrace all substances in the
one substance which is God, it remains remarkably difficult for
modern people to attribute 'will' (in any sense) *equally* to inanimate
matter and to a highly developed human being – a saint, an artist
or a philosopher. I do not, of course, imply that in Nietzsche's
scheme of things one is supposed to think of such varying beings
as having equal wills to power, but rather that each is equally
possessed of will to power, as the quality that makes it what it
is – a pebble on the shore, for example, or a 'great' thinker. My
examples, and indeed any examples one cares to give, make the
proposition seem ridiculous, yet, as I have just mentioned, that is

how Aristotle thought of Being and, in the seventeenth century, how Spinoza thought of God.

Let us see how Nietzsche approaches his notion of will to power. In the *Nachlass* he takes issue with the concept 'force', which was normally used in his day by physicists or natural scientists. According to the *Oxford English Dictionary*, force has been held to be 'the cause of motion, heat, electricity etc., conceived as consisting in principle or power inherent in, or coexisting with matter'. Force was the nineteenth-century forerunner to our term 'energy', although it is true that we use both expressions, energy (since Einstein) being equal to mass, and force being now regarded as a 'field' to which mass-energy belongs. Today we can readily appreciate what Nietzsche maintains in his notes, namely that force, lacking imaginative content, is an empty word. He writes, 'A force we cannot imagine is an empty word and should be allowed no rights of citizenship in science . . .'.[19] Nietzsche is certainly right; when one has said that a force moves something or other, one has only said that the thing moves. The word 'force' adds nothing to our understanding and is completely unscientific.

But might not the same be remarked concerning 'energy'? We speak of the energy radiated by the sun, and while we can define radiation we are able to say of energy only that it is the equivalent of mass. Energy is not exactly an empty word since we equate it with mass, but we still understand it in terms of its effects; for all practical purposes energy is the mere effect of mass-energy. So, for energy, as for force, the referent has not been imagined, and this is presumably because it is unimaginable.

Let us for the moment consider a possibility that Nietzsche does not explicitly consider, namely that force or energy *is* empty, as a matter of fact. That is to say, energy as such has no content and no characteristic other than its power of producing certain observable effects. This perfectly plausible thought takes us straight back to Aristotle's Being: 'energy' then becomes a modern, scientific term for Being. Now this thought might well be the most correct of all thoughts; it could be that energy = Being, each term lacking synthetic or self-contained predicates. In other words, all one can truly say of Being is that 'it' is. Nevertheless, to consider energy as Being – as that without content which moves substances, or better, as the moving quality of substances – is still to try to cut ourselves off from the rest of the universe. This means that we can no longer carry out our function of interpreting the universe, or rather, that we can only do so badly. We, who are ourselves naturally energised, cannot form an analytical definition of energy. Here at least is the point in our reasoning where we have to face a stark requirement: energy cannot have a content unless we ourselves create it. We now begin to realise the extent (and possibly the terror) of our own *natural* capacity, not as riddlers of the universe but as creators.

The alternative is to remain content with the all-too-human mini-misation and travesty of our human function. I feel sure that many philosophers and scientists would say that this is the only available course. It is not only logical positivists who think of philosophy as the logical framework of science, and it is not only scientists who require proofs of their propositions. In this way, Aristotle's notion of 'wisdom' - that it is a 'science of first principles' – is actually held to be redundant, for (so it seems) there are no first principles. To put the matter another way, we are so taken up with our science (our compartments of knowledge) that we block the route towards first principles. It is abundantly clear that first principles need to be *imagined*, even though in a scientific age they must be imagined in accordance with reason and should be supported by intellec-tual convictions that are independent of wishes and may not be overthrown. Such convictions need not amount to proof, and indeed, since one is concerned with *first* principles (which must be prior to proof) they could not do so. Just the same, they should withstand every rational objection. In fact they must already have withstood rational objections before they became convictions. But still they are not proved – or provable. This is the case with Nietzsche's will to power.

Nietzsche is not remotely content with empty understanding, with 'force', since the concept is nothing more than a confidence trick. It is roughly comparable with selling people shares in a nonexistent gold mine, because 'force' has no more content than the shares have value. To talk of either 'force' or 'energy' is to fall short of a satisfactory interpretation, because we cannot reduce ourselves to energy. Nevertheless such talk is an interpretation of sorts. When we call an imperceptible power 'energy', we are following our human destiny, but why not, therefore, go one *decisive* step further and call the same being 'will to power'? By this means we no longer attempt to distinguish ourselves, or sever ourselves, from our universal roots, but humanise the universe instead. Is it somehow worse to humanise the universe than to 'dehumanise' the human race? It will be objected that the universe, whatever else it is, is not 'human', so what can be the value of this flight of anthropomorphism? Is it not merely atavistic, or a least old-fashioned? Nietzsche's argument would be that whatever we are, the universe is also. If we exhibit, or possess, or are composed of will to power, then so is the most rudimentary thing – to recall Aristotle's example, a piece of wood. If we are animated by will, all things are so animated, though we are the only beings to form a concept and a word for this ubiquitous process. But the concept and word are superficial; what alone matters is the will (to power). Of all cosmic beings we peculiarly entertain a concept of what animates us, though all other beings are animated in exactly the same way: the way, clearly, that animates.

Is Nietzsche therefore saying that even inanimate beings are some-how 'animated'? These beings have no power of self-movement, so surely they can have no will to power. Nietzsche's obviously rather tentative explanation is expressed as follows:

> The connection between the inorganic and the organic must lie in the repelling force exercised by every atom of force. 'Life' would be defined as an enduring form of processes of the establishment of force, in which the different contenders grow unequally.[20]

These remarks are a private deduction, a layman's imaginative stab at atomic theory. Nietzsche is following our requirement stated above, that we should use our imaginations in accordance with reason and current knowledge. No wish-fulfilment is involved, beyond the 'sagacious' (by which I mean the first-cause seeking) desire to reintegrate human beings into the natural order. Nietzsche understandably supposes that an atom repels other atoms, since whatever the smallest unit of substance is, that unit must repel others of its kind in order to remain itself. But, Nietzsche conjectures, when this activity of repulsion is unequal, so that some atoms repel others on an enduring basis (a basis that subsists for a distinct period of time), then what ensues is what we call 'life'. This term means simply that the being so constituted is self-moving. It has this quality because the imbalance of its atomic structure makes it restless.

In view of the explosion of knowledge about the atom in the past hundred years, Nietzsche's idea seems quite inadequate, and yet he clearly appreciates that the structure of matter *now* has to be interpreted so that the organic is utterly continuous with the inorganic; the distinction between the two has ceased to be valuable,

or even tolerable. Physicists no longer make this distinction, seeing
inert matter as latent energy, and chemists, as we have earlier said,
scarcely divide their field into organic and inorganic departments.
However, scientists are not the people to draw philosophical, or
more accurately, metaphysical conclusions. Nietzsche's own metaphysical conclusion is summed up in the phrase 'will to power'.
Every moving or living body moves as a result of its internal
composition and not primarily because it is impelled by other
bodies. This self-movement is precisely its will to power. It goes
without saying that each body is *also* impelled by other bodies, but
even in the act of giving way a body moves according to its own
essential constitution. One is even blown, or swept, or crushed in
one's singular way – which way may be called one's essence, or
being, or – best of all – will to power.

'Will to power' is the best term because it is the most explanatory.
By implication it is intended to replace Aristotle's word 'Being',
and it gives 'Being' universal content. Being is redefined as will
to power. For long enough we have imagined that 'will' (*Wille*) and
'power' (*Macht*) are, from one seemingly decisive point of view, the
wrong words for Nietzsche to have used, since (etymologically as
well as currently) the first has to do with intention and the second
with control or authority. On the other hand, 'intention', if not
'control or authority', give absolutely the wrong impression of
Nietzsche's meaning. But he regularly chose his words with great
care, so it is odd to suppose that here, of all places, he was careless.
We should assume, not that he made a bad choice but rather that he
intended to effect a change in our way of understanding the nature of
the will and of power, hence, eventually, of the structure of thought
itself. 'Will to power' has been deliberately and challengingly chosen, so that later thinkers would be forced to work out what 'will'
and 'power' are. Joined in a phrase, they reconstitute Being.

First of all, we have to grasp that in Nietzsche's view each object
is no longer to be divided, Kantianly, into its use as a *phenomenon* (an
object of possible experience) and, on the other hand, a thing in itself,
or *noumenon*. Nietzsche accepts Kant's fundamental argument to the
effect that our minds confer form and meaning upon the objects
of our experience, but Nietzsche goes further in contending that
noumena exist only in the form of rival wills – wills distinct from
other wills, including our own. There are no *noumena* in Kant's sense,
although there certainly are these competing self-wills. However, all
wills finally constitute a shapeless, meaningless flowing-together,

which Nietzsche, following the Greeks, named the 'Dionysian'. To be more accurate, while the Greeks understood Dionysus in a certain way, it was left to Nietzsche, in the modern age, to clarify and specify that way. Nietzsche's definition brings to fruition and clarity what the Greeks themselves, who lived in a 'Dionysian world', barely comprehended. Nietzsche *completes* and in that sense (though possibly in no other) alters the meaning of Dionysus.

Leaving this matter aside, we are in the midst of a problem which we approached in the last chapter and now needs to be pursued further. Kant points the way by regarding consciousness as a manifold, within which representations of objects appear by means of a synthesis. In other words, consciousness synthesises the objects we perceive; they are not 'themselves synthesised', so to speak. If I select an object for individual consideration, then both the original synthesising and the subsequent selection of an object are mental acts. Neither the individual object nor the synthesis from which it has been plucked exists in and for itself. Plainly Nietzsche would agree with all this (though he would also regard it as laborious and unnecessary), but he further maintains that prior to one's observing a scene (a synthesis) there exists a 'fuzziness and chaos of sense-impressions'.[21] Nietzsche does not ponder how one becomes aware of the existence of this condition, and indeed in order to know it one must paradoxically bring it to order. In other words, one must transform it into its orderly antithesis. 'Fuzziness and chaos' cannot be 'known' in the ordinary way of knowledge. How, then, is this condition apprehended (for Kant, likewise, does not deny the connection but instead relegates it as having no consequence)? I suppose it must chiefly be a deduction; one deduces that, since syntheses are constantly produced, they must be fashioned out of chaos. Moreover, one is aware from such states as dreaming, awakening from sleep, illness, exhaustion, terror (in a word, *primitive* states) that the fuzziness and chaos of sense-impressions is the prior reality.

Now this reality is not a synthesis in Kant's sense of the word. Nevertheless, in order to follow Nietzsche it is necessary to believe that *complete* 'synthesis' in quite another sense is the irreducible condition of nature. This indeed is the Heraclitean 'One' which is all things. There can be nothing other than a world, a whole, of undifferentiated activity.

Why is this Heraclitean 'One' other than a Kantian synthesis? For the reasons that Kant himself gives in the section of the *Critique of Pure Reason* entitled 'Solution of the Cosmological Idea of the Totality of the Composition of Phenomena in the Universe'. To simplify greatly: our understanding of the whole is an intellectual conception, not an intuition; that is to say, we think it but cannot, properly speaking, envision it. The 'Totality' in Kant is an idea, nothing more. Most certainly there is a vital difference between Kant's Cosmological Idea and the 'One' or 'all things' of Heraclitus, a difference with which Kant never concerned himself. It is this: the 'One' of Heraclitus is what the Word or Logos discloses and cannot be regarded as an idea, since one encounters it not by way of thought, 'cerebrally', but merely by laying oneself open to the 'togetherness' of everything one perceives. On the other hand, even Kant's 'Cosmological Idea', despite its status as an idea, a mental product, has to be balanced *against* the understanding we arrive at by logic to the effect that, 'The world has no beginning in time and no absolute limit in space.'[22] Thus by logic, we perform the feat of limiting the unlimited, because, of course, our thoughts and our very lives proceed by setting limits. It will be remarked that modern physics asserts a beginning in time and a boundary in space, which nevertheless is not absolute but is constantly widening and may sooner or later contract. But the time of physics is measurable, while Kant has in mind endless 'time' or eternity (into which the physicists' universe fits). However, to speak of the 'world' or the 'cosmos' is to entertain a concept *within* which all intuited events occur. These events are by definition more or less orderly and differentiated, but the entire cosmos cannot be so regulated. It is Nietzsche's 'Dionysian world' with no beginning, no end, and no 'parts'. In modern (quantum theory) terminology it consists of particles whenever we observe them or of waves of energy whenever we are not looking. But in truth we have created or postulated the particles and the waves. Such process of creation is mere exercise of will to power: this is how we individually exist and how all things exist. Thus Being in its entirety (a concept in Kant, ever-living Fire in Heraclitus) consists of will to power.

III

That everything is, in its inner nature, not 'will to power' but simply 'will' was the decisive understanding that Nietzsche took over from Schopenhauer. Today people interested in Nietzsche know this perfectly well, but it seems likely that only a proportion read the highly-readable Schopenhauer himself (though this situation is probably changing). However, certain qualities and ideas in Nietzsche become more accessible when one has read Schopenhauer; in particular, the 'genealogy' of will to power clarifies this world-conception and gives it greater resonance. Schopenhauer expounds what he calls the 'First Aspect' of 'The World as Will' in Volume I of *The World as Will and Representation*, along roughly the following lines.

First of all, the will of a human being is not some sort of agent apart from the body, but *is* the body known and experienced directly. When we perceive our bodies from the outside (I look at my hand or see myself in a mirror) we represent them as we do all other beings, but when we experience them from the inside – as inclinations, revulsions and so forth – we are immediately aware of ourselves as will. Hence, I suppose, the oddness of one's reflection in a shop window: this strange figure is a stranger to one's will, which is one's inner constitution. Now, says Schopenhauer, every other thing must be similarly constituted, for what else could it conceivably be? For example, there is no point in speaking of a 'force' pushing a plant up through the soil, as though the force in question were external to the plant. From our position as observers the plant just comes up, but inwardly it must struggle towards the light rather as I might force my way through some dense material, and the fact that I supposedly know what I am doing and where I am going while the plant is utterly unconscious makes no difference. For my consciousness of any destination is not the *cause* of my will but its objectification. I intend to get through the material anyway, this driving impulse being blind, but I might picture the happy outcome. On all occasions, visualising some result is a *consequence* of the striving of the will. We proceed in this way, by blind will, which invents for itself purposes and destinations. This remains true whether one intends to do something banal or to perform the most soulful and heroic of tasks: the so-called 'intention' is spontaneously devised to give colour and meaning to the will, which in itself is colourless and meaningless. Thus my highest and most complex self-determination is a *phenomenon* or outward manifestation of the will. The will is the true reality.

The will in all beings is groundless. When the will, which is the reality of a being, urges that being in a certain direction, it does so pointlessly – just as mass-energy hurtles pointlessly through space.

So the will is primary and also free, since it is not produced, impelled or coerced by any other force. Insofar as the will is not grounded, it must evidently be free. On the other hand, the will, like the Being of Aristotle, has any characteristic or none; in other words, it takes on whatever characteristic might at any moment suit its purpose. While we know the will directly and immediately in ourselves, we know it in other beings only through its effects. Such effects are phenomena and *all* phenomena are effects of will. These naturally belong in the world of sense and are therefore not free. In this way, the will is free although its effects are not. The distinction is most important, since it puts paid to the seemingly endless debate about free and unfree will.

Being groundless, the will does not depend upon knowledge, although in the human race it uses and presumably devises knowledge as its servant. In lower animals it operates continually without knowledge, as it does for that matter through the autonomic processes of human beings. For this reason, when a person imagines he is willing something or other, he has merely (at best) raised a somatic impulse to partial consciousness and given it a goal.

The essential point in the above is, of course, that the will functions throughout nature, taking specifically human forms in people, as it takes other forms in other beings. To Schopenhauer the will somewhat resembles the mover of substances in Aristotle, though Schopenhauer does not mention Aristotle and this is my comparison. On the other hand, 'will' forges that connection between human beings and other beings which science, no less than Christianity, has tended to break. Wherever there is energy (which is to say everywhere) we can readily say there is 'will' in this inclusive sense: 'For this word indicates that which is the being-in-itself of everything in the world, and is the sole kernel of every phenomenon.'[23]

Someone might justifiably complain that from what I have mentioned so far it is still not easy, or even possible, to work out what one is to say of the will of inanimate things. Schopenhauer's answer, in brief, is this: our understanding of how things behave, and indeed of how they are, consists of characteristics, visible signs and so-called 'laws', all of which are qualities *assigned by us*. Such qualities are inextricably connected with one another but they leave the essence of each thing untouched and unknown. To use an example which will immediately be linked to an example in Schopenhauer, a stone appears to be a chemical compound and a physical object, but is it nothing more? The features ascribed by science and common perception leave the stone itself out of account. These are humanly-devised characteristics, rather as if one were to be described by another person solely in terms of his perceptions, omitting the essential component which one knows from within as one's will.

Schopenhauer notes Spinoza's remark (Letter 67) that, 'if a stone projected through the air had consciousness, it would imagine it was flying of its own will'. Schopenhauer continues, 'I add merely that the stone would be right.'[24] No doubt this must still seem a remarkable and exceedingly questionable assertion, for Spinoza's point is that the stone would be wrong, as we are wrong when we postulate free will, since we, like the stone, are in reality doing whatever universal forces decree. Nevertheless, Schopenhauer's reasoning holds up. We are in error to suppose we know something when we have merely ascribed certain qualities to it. We do not know the stone (or Aristotle's piece of wood), for we can only form a view of it – as it can only 'form a view of itself'.

But there is another dimension of Schopenhauer's reasoning which I have not so far emphasised. This is that he finds the will indivisible as well as universal. It functions through bodies, it phenomenalises itself, but remains independent of the varying and often conflicting phenomena it employs. Schopenhauer writes:

> Indeed, since all things in the world are the objectivity of one and the same will, and consequently identical according to their inner nature, there must be between them that unmistakable analogy, and in everything less perfect there must be seen the trace, outline and plan of the next more perfect thing.[25]

On this utterly vital point the mature Nietzsche differs, since, while he speaks generally of the will to power, he has in mind a universal quality which exists and manifests itself *only* in particulars. The 'will' in Schopenhauer is completely generalised, while in Nietzsche the 'will to power' is completely particularised. Nietzsche does not contemplate the will to power as something behind or apart from phenomena. At first, in *The Birth of Tragedy*, Nietzsche is probably confused about this point and makes Schopenhauerian use of Schopenhauer's expression, *principium individuationis*, but he fairly soon abandons the notion of an all-pervasive, free-floating force called 'will'. By now the *principium individuationis* is clearly to be contrasted, not with the will but with the Dionysian world, which, like the god Dionysus himself, exists in appearances. However, there is nothing else behind appearances; these alone are real.

Even now I have not shown how Schopenhauer discovers will in inanimate objects. Matter, he says, either attracts or repels (other forms of matter). This is the lowest and most elementary exercise of will. Presumably when rain falls on stone, the will objectified in the rainwater, which is matter, is repelled by the will objectified in the stone. Notice: the will *always* objectifies itself. When we proceed up the scale to the sphere of vegetation, we find the will-as-plant responding to stimuli, to the mere warmth of the sun, for instance. When we finally reach the animal kingdom, stimuli lead to the creation and use of knowledge. For human beings pre-eminently, the world becomes representation; that is, the entire cosmic and local environment becomes as we represent it to ourselves – but this representation is the superior (more subtle and comprehensive) exercise of that self-same will already objectifying itself in the simplest and most static objects.

In modern times physics comes to our aid, though it also entails a danger. In the 1880s Nietzsche thought in terms of a balance of atoms making for inertness, an imbalance producing restlessness (or 'life') – a reasonable inference at that time. But modern physics chiefly thinks of energy; everything is energy, so that a stone is energy, albeit in frozen form. And certainly the more we contemplate the Einsteinian and post-Einsteinian universe, the more we are impelled to see all beings as energy. Up to a point, this energy of physics is reasonably akin both to what Schopenhauer designated 'will' and to what Nietzsche later called 'will to power'. But leaving aside the difference mentioned above between will and will to power, the concept 'energy' depersonalises even persons (or else, oddly, leaves them aside as observers), while, conversely, the concepts of the two nineteenth-century philosophers personalise every universal thing. Either way, we extract the human species from its exclusive sphere – the sphere, namely, of special beings made in God's image, or, alternatively, of sole and potentially accurate interpreters of the cosmos – and place them firmly back in nature. As between Schopenhauer and Nietzsche, the argument involves, on the side of Schopenhauer the need for persons to remove themselves from the world so far as possible by suspending their wills, while on the side of Nietzsche, the will to power stands supreme as the very soul of the universe. The way towards the soul is called 'wisdom', and it employs knowledge as its means.

The will to power, 'working from within, incorporates and subdues more and more of that which is "outside"'.²⁶ This assertion, in
The Will to Power, refers to 'Life' which is thus identified with 'will to
power', but by now we have surely come to see that what we, along
with Nietzsche, call 'Life' is purely a mode of will to power, so the
business of incorporating and subduing occurs universally: it is the
universal process.

Notice first, then, that this will to power works from within;
it is the self and core of every being. Secondly, this core-being
incorporates and subdues that which is outside, *cumulatively*. The
being, by its nature takes over more and more of what is at first felt
to be other than itself. This procedure of taking over others may wear
any mask whatsoever, including, for example, such masks as love
and submission. In every case the accomplishment is that a being
brings others into its design. I am sure it cannot be necessary to
state that there is nothing cynical about these observations (no touch
of La Rochefoucauld: love 'in the soul . . . is a passion to dominate
another'), because cynicism is obviously founded upon disbelief or
despair. On the other hand, Nietzsche positively believes in will
to power as a world-affirmation; it includes and *ennobles* whatever
is contemplated. For example, the lover who wishes to bring the
beloved into his design, *and knows he does*, will strive above all to
cultivate what he already recognises as a seed in the beloved. The
procedure will be creative, and if it is ever cynical it will be so only
as a means of blocking false directions.

In addition, whereas the cynical assumption is always to the effect
that whatever one does is in one's own interest – 'interest' being
interpreted as self-regard and self-preservation – Nietzsche's idea
is almost the complete contrary. He sees the basic creative instinct as
a kind of eager and adventurous drive that overreaches itself, ending
in destruction. Even the protoplasm 'takes into itself absurdly more
than would be required to preserve it; and, above all, it does
not thereby "preserve itself," it falls apart . . .'.²⁷ Nietzsche does
not say so but this protoplasmic procedure is reflected in human
society when someone 'overreaches' himself. This is what happens
essentially in the great tragedies and is the source of the spectators'
awe, for the spectators obscurely realise that they are witnessing a
creative act worthy of nature, as opposed to the usual expediencies
of social beings. Prometheus, Oedipus, Antigone (and, yes, even
Clytemnestra) take into themselves more than would be required
to preserve them: the principle is not preservation but enlargement,

this constituting, so far as Nietzsche is concerned, the very principle of life.

It will be seen that we are now certainly giving to Aristotle's 'Being' definite character, content and value. The word 'Being' is no longer empty, ready to be filled by anything whatever that merely 'is'. It can be filled only by will to power. So far we have noted Nietzsche's view that will to power takes into itself more than is needed for self-preservation, and indeed tends towards its own destruction. Plainly 'power' means dominion in some sense, but in what sense? The being, say the protoplasm, extends its very own domain. The 'world', in this case the sphere available to the protoplasm, is progressively brought into the being of the protoplasm, and becomes, therefore, no longer 'outside'. It seems there is no fixed entity called 'the protoplasm' which, so to speak, 'reaches out its tentacles'; rather the protoplasm is a continually growing being which enhances itself by infusing elements from without. It does not first exist then grow, for being *is* growth. So we may assume that power in the everyday sense is at best a crude misrepresentation of real power, as Nietzsche understands it. Real power can proceed only from within a being and may not take a *purely* social form; thus it manifests itself in creative rather than political people. And, as we have suggested, Nietzsche has in mind a subtle and completely effective process of assimilation.

Certainly one must assimilate what is actually present (within one's range), which means that the will remains unsatisfied, or hungry, when it misreads the signs. Rough-and-ready bullying, for example, takes no account of the nature of the victim, other than to observe that he can be bullied. But this failure to take account is a misinterpretation, for the victim-nature of the other is not what the signs proclaim; they proclaim something else, something subtler and entirely personal. In this way the being of the bully is not remotely enlarged – which is his actual, though misconceived objective. Alternatively, when one being properly interprets another, he thereby enlarges himself. 'Properly' means in accordance with the signs that present themselves, but such will be 'misread' by weakness and need. There is no question of an infallible interpretation, and moreover, it is not necessarily a good thing that the interpreted one agrees with the interpretation. Evidently the best exerciser of will to power is the one most able to expand himself in accordance with the signs presented. For example, Plato was able to do this strikingly well in regard to the signs presented by

Socrates, but it does not follow that Plato was somehow 'right' about Socrates. In all probability he was 'wrong' from the point of view of Socrates himself. In this way, when the manifest quality of the other is incorporated, the will to power is properly exercised. This is not a culpable thing to do, though certain moral prejudices speak against it. Indeed, alternative forms of behaviour are inferior, *ontologically* inferior; the behaviour just analysed precisely *is* behaviour, whenever a being is doing what it (or he or she) is cut out to do.

Actually if we wanted at this stage to raise up an ethical standard, it would be easy enough to do so simply by saying that the best interpretation (thus the best exercise of will to power) entails spotting a potential in the other being. Zarathustra repeatedly does this in his numerous encounters, but it is clear that his own shortcomings (or hungers, or needs) do not enter into these particular proceedings. Perhaps we should also note in passing that any such potential is likely to cut across conventional moral categories and in that sense to be 'immoral'.

Nietzsche remarks as follows:

> The will to power *interprets* (– it is a question of interpretation when an organ is constructed): it defines limits, determines degrees, variations of power. Mere variations of power could not feel themselves to be such: there must be present something that wants to grow and interprets the value of whatever else wants to grow. Equal *in that* – In fact, interpretation is itself a means of becoming master of something. (The organic process constantly presupposes interpretations.)[28]

I have chosen this comment on will to power rather than other, possibly better-known ones, because the above seems to me the most promising. Let us consider the various associated items. First of all, while everything is will to power, it is clear that in this context Nietzsche is concerned with the nature of will to power at the organic level. The inorganic is here thought of as the pre-organic, that out of which organisms may be or will be sooner or later constructed. When this process of constructing an organism takes place, somehow or other the not-yet-organic works towards the organic *by means of interpretation*. The energy frozen in the lump of matter starts, as it were, to 'unfreeze'. Something very roughly of this sort must indeed occur, and Nietzsche is not being fanciful here but just naively unscientific. But the point is that this unfreezing of the hitherto inert matter is defined as interpretation. Nietzsche has in mind an elementary form of what we do in our advanced and complex fashion. The matter moves towards the condition of an organism by defining limits, determining degrees and thus positing variations of power. Note: power is not discerned but *posited*. From its own position of power the incipient organism confers power upon neighbouring beings. For an organism to form it must, in the process of self-formation, check the advance of neighbouring forces. This is how it defines limits or determines degrees and variations of power. By this same means, however, it continually defines, which is to say, *shapes* itself. We think first of elementary organisms which indeed form themselves into shapes. On the other hand, complex animals, human beings, cannot be confined to physical shapes but organise themselves by all manner of cultural and intellectual means as well. The self-shaping (which entails giving limits to other beings) must at this level of development reach out from the core of the being to what we designate 'spiritual' designs.

Nietzsche further suggests that it is the way of all organisms, from the most elementary to the most elaborate, not just to reach a safe and satisfactory limit, but to exceed the present limit, whatever it is. This means that a limit is posited to be reached, then exceeded. The process is one of first setting then surpassing limits, so that fresh limits come into being continually. An over-ready acceptance of present limits is just what produces stasis and thence decline to the inorganic level once again. Conversely, going beyond limits is always violent and destructive, but also fruitful. (Once more we can possibly discern here the 'biological' basis of pre-Euripidean tragedy.) The chief point is that there is a fundamental procedure in all nature of setting and reaching boundaries, then a self-surpassing on the part of the stronger (consequently more self-destructive) energies as they proceed towards ever-fresh boundaries. The universe thus grows, in terms not of mass-energy but of range.

This business of positing limits is what Nietzsche calls 'interpretation', meaning that human modes of interpretation (say, atomic physics) are of the same fundamental kind as the interpretations practised by the protoplasm. Interpretation is not exclusively a human or even an animal activity but a universal one: it is the universal activity of will to power. In this way, 'interpretation' means not finding out what something indicates, but rather giving the thing a significance of such a kind that one *commands* it.

We are left with a problem which cannot be solved but only specified. Nietzsche maintains that 'mere variations of power could not feel themselves to be such'. This sort of argument goes back to Aristotle. Over and above the mere distinction between one power and another there must be (Nietzsche logically insists) 'something that wants to grow'. If this were not so, then material energies interact with one another *ad infinitum*, and our own interpretations must be utterly inconsequential and misleading. This in turn would mean that our human role in the universe must be futile. On the other hand, if we accept Schopenhauer's demonstration of will as the universal agency, we have also to appreciate that will 'interprets' in some fashion, and proceed to ask: *Who* interprets?

Nietzsche puzzles out this question for himself (that is, not for publication) and, in a manner that echoes Aristotle, believes there needs to be something beyond physical energy – *as we normally understand such energy*. In other words, energy itself is possessed of a dimension or aspect that can only be called 'will to power'. *Physis* cannot be enough, if this word is taken to include only matter that may (in principle) be discerned and quantified – the material of the old physics. Will to power is the 'soul' of beings, so to speak, meaning the self-interpretation of energy.

The relation between will to power and energy might helpfully be compared to that between the Prometheus of Aeschylus and Zeus. The god can enchain but cannot destroy the Titan and the day will come when this most powerful god will require assistance from Prometheus. That is the argument of Aeschylus' play. Zeus is supreme yet he cannot calculate or imagine, while Prometheus is the one who can foretell events. In truth this prophetic capacity of Prometheus is nothing other than a mode of creation. What Prometheus specifically foretells is that the raw energy of the universe needs the human race in order to become meaningful and fruitful. Clearly this is but nominally a prediction, for in fact it is a recognition. And Prometheus is not a Titan so much as a figure of human knowledge under the tutelage of human wisdom. And who is Zeus but raw energy, the brute waste of the universe without its human interpreter? Zeus and Prometheus are both immortal but the first is energy and the second the recognition of energy. Likewise in the new physics energy only is because we recognise and name it. Energy must be named, which is as much as to say *spiritualised*, to make it as we know it, or as it essentially is. There needs to be will to power as the pioneering quality of energy that enables it to recognise and create itself. The agents of this self-creation are human beings, the ones who first call up the name 'energy' and then redefine it more explicitly as 'will to power'. In this way we have moved from 'Being' in Aristotle to 'will to power' in Nietzsche, though we might remember that the outline of this very movement was prefigured in ancient drama.

6

Ariadne and the Labyrinth

Ariadne's origins are undiscoverable and her story acquired so many variations in ancient times that we cannot guess what she once meant, but it is certain that she should be seen in a religious light and not confined to her role as abandoned lover. What we might be tempted to think of as her 'romantic' life emerges from a profoundly religious world. Even Plutarch, writing his life of Theseus in a comparatively late phase of polytheism, and believing in the reality of both Theseus and Ariadne (though not that of the Minotaur or the Labyrinth), treats her as little more than a vulnerable princess. But this part of Ariadne's career has to be completed by reference to her later alliance with Dionysus, or, in brief, her elevation. Plutarch mentions this but thinks of it as just another fable. However, if we view Ariadne appreciatively, we are impressed by her rising above the sphere of mortality, while Theseus himself, the unifier of Attica, is never raised to godhood.

How is all this to be rescued from its mere charm or perhaps absurdity for a modern philosopher? Nietzsche alone restores Ariadne to something approaching her original status. In a special sense he 'sanctifies' her. He treats her as occupying a midway point between the realm of everyday life and the realm of divinity. Thus he lifts her clear of Plutarch's conception and also snatches her from the hands of scholars. She remains human in the obvious sense of belonging to humanity but ceases to be mortal. Nietzsche regards her as somehow more than an individual; yet she is the purest distillation of every individual.

Of course Nietzsche did this knowingly and inventively, not in a credulous fashion, and, I fancy, this was more or less the case even when he identified Cosima Wagner with Ariadne. He, the mad Nietzsche, or Nietzsche in the process of going mad, conferred Ariadne-status upon Frau Wagner, in a spirit of love and reverence. Nietzsche came to focus all that he personally meant by 'Ariadne' through Cosima. In a letter of 3 January 1889 he addressed her as the

131

'Princess Ariadne, my Beloved'.[1] Just as the actual Cosima is thus idealised as Ariadne, the latter is no longer an episode in a hero's life but has entered the rapturous place of her own destiny. Now, like Dionysus himself, she slips the bonds of finitude. Cosima as Ariadne has been magnified in Nietzsche's untethered judgement to include all essential womanhood, or preferably, in the words of Nietzsche's sister, the human soul. Walter Kaufman, commenting upon Elisabeth Förster-Nietzsche's idea, says that she is not 'entirely wrong', though Jung's conception of the 'anima' would be nearer the mark.[2] However, the Jungian anima is a male image of femininity while Nietzsche's Ariadne encompasses all spiritual needs. I believe Frau Förster-Nietzsche's interpretation is actually better: Ariadne, though *immediately* associated with Cosima Wagner, means the human soul to Nietzsche. To say this is nevertheless only one step towards clarification, for we still need to discover what Nietzsche meant by 'the soul'. In *Ecce Homo* he asks, as an exclamation rather than a proper question, 'Who besides me knows what Ariadne is!'[3] So far we can merely suggest that the soul in Nietzsche is somehow 'feminine', although its meaning is as comprehensive as it is in Plato.

Most of the poem, 'Ariadne's Complaint', one of Nietzsche's *Dithyrambs of Dionysus*, first appears in the form of words spoken – or 'wailed' – by the Sorcerer in Part IV of *Thus Spoke Zarathustra*. In Zarathustra it is not dithyrambic but histrionic and has nothing to do with either Ariadne or Dionysus. When it later appears (with some alterations) it is supposed to consist of words spoken by Ariadne, to which 'complaint' Dionysus himself gives an oracular reply. The translator of *Dionysos-Dithyramben*, R. J. Hollingdale, states several things: that the two contexts in which the poem appears are 'artistically irreconcilable with one another'; that the poem is 'irresolvably ambiguous'; that when the words are imagined as being uttered by Cosima Wagner (in the *Dithyrambs*) they have a kind of truthfulness but when they are supposed to be delivered by Wagner (in the guise of the Sorcerer or, conceivably, a sort of Theseus-figure) they have less truth, or perhaps none.[4] These observations cannot be discussed thoroughly at this stage, but we can make one or two preliminary remarks.

First of all, the poem as it occurs in *Zarathustra* is perfectly 'truthful' in the special sense that it accurately represents what Nietzsche, in 1884–5, though about Wagner as one of the 'higher men'. It is *dramatically* truthful. Despite his shortcomings, nicely sketched in the figure of the Sorcerer, Wagner was a higher man because he aimed to outsoar the crowd. If we understand the Sorcerer to be a portrait of Wagner in the first instance, and secondly an exemplification of a type, then the words the Sorcerer delivers are appropriate. They are so when understood, correctly, as the pose of a 'penitent of the spirit', a category strikingly represented by Wagner. A penitent of the spirit elaborately bewails his badness. He moans, as does the Sorcerer, that he is afflicted by God. He wants to be punished for his pride.[5] In late twentieth-century terms, I take such a person to be the one who makes frequent reference to his (and our) guilt, the much-concerned moralist. He is thoroughly theatrical and his sense of guilt is a means of filling his emptiness. Zarathustra has earlier stated that he sees penitents of the spirit coming along, having grown out of the poets of former ages.[6] Nietzsche believes that poets have always required audiences; they are peacocks who spread their tales before buffaloes (stolid people, though *ein Büffel* is also, appropriately, a laborious student). Nietzsche means that poets do not much care how imperceptively they are heard, provided they are heard. Our contemporary penitents are of the same self-advertising sort.

Let us now turn our attention to the second form of the poem as it appears in the *Dithyrambs of Dionysus*. It has become the complaint of Ariadne, or the human soul, which is no longer loved and so resembles Ariadne abandoned on Naxos. Thus the whining of the Sorcerer has died away, since Nietzsche has found a better use for his poem. Once it was the expression of a mere psychological type, now it is an image of the soul. But this is the soul in modern times, forsaken by the hero and mockingly importuned by a god. The soul is no longer consummated by heroism but is prodded and disturbed by a 'cruel huntsman', an *unknown* god.

Why should Ariadne feel so desolate or half-dead? The first verse expounds this cold, unloved condition: Ariadne is unutterably cold, trembling, pierced by arrows of frost, and yet her feet are warmed. Unseen, behind the clouds, is a huntsman for whom she is the prey. But why?

Nietzsche is not referring, in what has since become a familiar fashion, to the 'vegetative' modern soul, for such a soul cannot, by definition, experience such torment as Ariadne's. And why, furthermore, is *our* soul abandoned specifically by 'Theseus', in other words, the spirit of heroism? Is it not the Platonic-Christian code, as opposed to the code of honour, from which we are thought to be increasingly estranged? Moral criticism in our day takes the form of saying that we have become something between the vacuously agreeable and the casually (or mechanically) atrocious. Evil is banal and therefore rather meaningless. So we would expect Ariadne to be simply unaware of a cruel huntsman god. Nietzsche himself speaks quite often and prophetically of such a morally comatose condition, for example in Part Three of *Zarathustra*, in the section entitled 'Of the Virtue that Makes Small'.

The answer to this question has to do with Nietzsche's undemocratic attitude. So far as he is concerned, the majority are never in question, for they scarcely change from age to age. In the section of *The Will to Power* entitled 'Discipline and Breeding' are included many private observations of an emphatically undemocratic nature. To summarise such subtle remarks is difficult, but, roughly speaking, Nietzsche time and again considers how the majority might be caused unwittingly to produce a necessarily limited number of people who justify the earth. This supreme activity of justification cannot take the form of a grim, teeth-gritting task but must be at once joyful and painful.

Nietzsche's theme is that the notion of equality is a 'superstition',[7] meaning precisely a belief founded on fear and ignorance. We believe in equality because inequality is dangerous, producing all manner of resentments and evils. Indeed, inequality is widely supposed to be the root of all evil.

Now, what happens to those who feel themselves to be, not equal to others but exceptional? Geniuses, says Nietzsche, flatter the non-geniuses by providing works which extol crowd-virtues.[8] Meanwhile, the truly exceptional cannot easily be separated from the rest, or recognised, because 'real value' – as opposed to spurious social value – is not manifest. On the contrary, real value consists not of recognised talents (e.g. for sport or learning) but of multifariousness, a combination of contrary impulses. 'Renaissance man' is an image of such value, but a being of this kind cannot now be prominent or influential in society, for his quality is deep-rooted, spiritual and not a matter of varied technical accomplishments. He must disguise himself as mediocre, giving both his good and his evil qualities the semblance of socially acceptable traits. In any case the value of a person whose nature is 'higher' is intrinsic and incomparable, having nothing to do with effects on society. Nietzsche stresses this in *The Will to Power*, 'But the "higher nature" of the great man lies in being different, in incommunicability, in distance of rank, not in an effect of any kind – even if he made the whole globe tremble.'[9] Such great men are usually other than the great ones of history. They do not engineer historical movements, except perhaps incidentally, but constitute a *'higher, brighter humanity'*, being 'colder, brighter, more far-seeing, more solitary' than the general run. Notably they do not aspire, are not ambitious, for they already possess the powers they require.[10]

The words I have just quoted give an accurate impression of their context, a passage in *The Will to Power* where Nietzsche expresses his idea of a vital distinction in society. This distinction is the only one that matters now, excluding, as it does, such admired types as 'heroes, martyrs, geniuses and enthusiasts' on the grounds that these are not subtle or patient enough. Nietzsche sees no further use for the visible hierarchies of hereditary nobility, wealth, political power, education, or even talent. Nevertheless, some people, here and there, wait and work patiently for what Nietzsche famously calls a new 'order of rank'. Patience is a prerequisite, since the future these people want is not guaranteed. A vast homogeneity is undoubtedly coming; we ourselves are near enough to see that quite clearly, and the farsighted Nietzsche could see it a hundred years ago. Before long there will be a worldwide similarity of culture and of certain amiable, cooperative values. In such a biologically fertile and perhaps extremely durable society no order of rank appears to be possible, for, inevitably, the society must be set against all but the most superficial distinctions. Nietzsche realised that, in regard to the durability of the human species, this kind of society might well be the best. Certainly it is what most people want. This is something approaching the 'millennium' and perhaps it can come to pass.

On the other hand, if our species perpetuates itself by these means, we shall lose all or most of our value. To avoid facing up to this fact there are two ruses we can try. We might say, first of all, that our value lies precisely where it has always lain: in helping one another, in neighbourly cooperation. Secondly, we could contrive to suppose that whatever our value, the universe as a whole must possess incalculable worth. Such manoeuvres will not work for everyone, since a few will realise immediately that worthwhile human cooperation must have a goal beyond itself – and beyond mere survival. Self-perpetuation or race-perpetuation is useless without a purpose. But 'purpose' is exactly what we have to sacrifice in order to place the highest value upon mere cooperation. The latter must be self-sufficient and, the moment a further purpose is proposed, human cooperation becomes subordinate – not the highest value but the means to the highest value.

The second point is no doubt more problematic. All depends upon whether we can now readily perceive that universal value, whatever it is, is determined by us and either follows or coincides with our own. If we have none, then the universe has none. The contrary belief is still a belief in God. Even if it is more a suspicion than a belief, it involves the numerous freethinkers in a dilemma.

Whatever value we will for the universe we must also will for ourselves: to believe that we mean one thing and the world means another is the theological stratagem that no longer works. Nietzsche does not bluntly explain the following desideratum (or prophecy) but we can assume from the range of his writings that a higher humanity would envision and *thus create* the richest, ripest and most multiform universe. He regularly implies that the universe is *our* creation because we alone can envision it as a whole. I mean that we are humanly obliged to form concepts and images of it. 'Totality' is a Kantian category, a 'pure conception of the understanding', as Kant calls it, which means, in effect, that whenever we contemplate a number of items as assembled we detect a totality. Thus totality is a mental construct and is obviously so when it comprises the cosmos or the 'All'. But the 'All' is our created notion. Other beings than human beings form their own expedient, self-preserving and self-enhancing means of grasping their neighbourhoods. In other words, 'the whole' is our corresponding frame of reference.

Nietzsche assumes that the idea of the universe as a vastness of which we are a part, but from which we somehow stand aside for purposes of discovery, is not even worth mentioning, except as a *device*. For him this is liable to be the modern variant of the age-old modesty (or fear) which disowns awesome human creations. An argument for Nietzsche's attitude might take the form of declaring that the quantitative and qualitative excess of the universe over what we can apprehend of it is non-existent. To talk of 'unknown beings' is to make a portentous noise: the being of unknowns being is either an emotional impression or else nonsense. The words of Parmenides may not be contradicted:

> For never shall this be forcibly maintained, that things that are not are, but you must hold back your thought from this way of enquiry, nor let habit, born of much experience, force you down this way, by making you use an aimless eye or an ear

and a tongue full of meaningless sound: judge by reason the strife-encompassed refutation spoken by me.[11]

Whatever we do not know about the universe *is* not – has no existence – and to maintain through force of habit that something we do not know might nevertheless be is to use a tongue full of meaningless sound. Conversely, whatever we know, *is*. It *is* because we know it, and requires no proof. We have to rid ourselves of the habitual notion of hypothetical being, except for its function as hypothesis. It is difficult to hypothesise something without instantly giving credit to the something. Parmenides rightly contends that a hypothesised being exists nowhere outside the hypothesis. Therefore the universe is what we know of the universe and nothing else.

Our next step is to point out that the All consists of interactive modes and forces of creation. The human mode demands a conception of the totality, but this conception varies from age to age and no variety can be independently assessed. Neither can one totality be nearer the truth than the others, for each is self-validating and is not 'on the way' to some final truth. Totalities are relatively shortlived contrivances of human beings who have chosen in the course of recent centuries to check their impulses and storytelling capacities by means of observations and measurements. We now demand to *see* monsters; we require evidence for the authenticity of relics; the incidence of disease must be measured. Such procedures are not in some unqualified way better than pre-empiric practices but they may be classed as cleverer. However, the cleverness is purely inventive. They enable us to maintain an 'overview' of the universe, of which we are peculiarly capable. Now, although this capability is 'grand' in relation to the lesser perspectives of other beings, it is not yet grand enough, since it fails to accommodate, in equal measure, our cosmic observations and our most thoughtful judgements on those observations. We shall return to this point in due course, but in order to do so we first need to strike out in another direction, namely to work a little way towards an understanding of continuous creation. This means continuous radical *re*-creation.

Continuous radical re-creation necessitates two beliefs, the first of which was probably held by Heraclitus and the second of which is a modern overturning of Plato – though Plato's own arguments have to be accepted up to a point. The first belief is that both 'beginning' and 'end' are human arbitrations which we can never fail to employ although they have outgrown their usefulness as 'facts'. This applies to all beginnings and ends, from the most trivial and localised to the universal. Yet scientists still talk about the beginning and end of the universe. This is valid if the universe is not held to be the entirety of being. There is a hiatus here between what we can – or must – logically infer and what we observe. We observe and make deductions (or guesses) about the universe, but we also make an inference about the 'All', which cannot have begun and cannot end. Alternatively, the universe, according to our observations, appears to have begun, and according to our reasonable assumptions may very well end. However, the sort of thing that goes on cannot logically be supposed to have begun to go on in empty space – in a something called a 'nothing'. Complete emptiness is conceivable only within boundaries beyond which must lie 'non-emptiness'. Accordingly, we have to maintain with Parmenides that whatever is, always is, in some form or other.

This, then, is the first, or Heraclitean belief to the effect that limits are creatively set. The second and modern belief involves a reference back to Plato on whom it rests, though it is anti-Platonic in the end. We have earlier argued (in Chapter 3) that we still cannot do without the concept 'soul', and presumably will never be able to do without it. In our consideration of a strand in certain dialogues of Plato (the *Philebus*, the *Phaedo*, the *Republic*, the *Symposium* and the *Phaedrus*) we recognised that the soul cannot be regarded as mortal – that is to say, it does not exist and therefore cannot die – but we did not satisfactorily deal with the soul's supposed immortality. At this stage let us mention once again that while we, as opposed to Plato, are apt to attach souls rather firmly to bodies (each person has his or her own soul), we still do not understand how the soul can utterly depart. The notion here is that what one peculiarly experiences (a pattern, a complex, not a mere aggregation of distinct 'experiences') constitutes one's soul and may not be said to pass away into nothingness.

Contrariwise, this soul does not *in any recognised sense* endure. Even if one is an artist and represents one's soul-pattern, the representation, which may endure for long enough, cannot be identified with the soul itself. The essential objection of the Platonic Socrates (in the *Phaedo*) can be rephrased in modern style to mean that the soul cannot be identified with any operation of the mind or body. Neither can it be taken to refer to any complex of operations, but must stand above and apart from these. This point – that the *pure* soul is not tainted by either physical or mental activities – must be taken to mean that the soul neither comes nor goes, for it is the strangest of all beings, namely a being that does not belong to the sphere of existence. Unlike everything else, it cannot be destroyed by its own corruption. In this special sense the soul does not even 'endure', since endurance occurs through time, a dimension with which the soul has an uncanny relationship.

Up to now we have been following Plato, as we said we would. Here comes the point of departure. We, unlike Plato, are convinced that time does not stretch out to eternity but rather 'fits into' eternity. That is to say, we think of time as measurable (it corresponds to the range of the expanding universe), while eternity stretches out before and after the universal expansion. Time, however, is what the soul detects and measures. The soul somehow comes together with time and cannot be said to have been 'before time'. The soul can indeed contemplate eternity but purely as a word and a concept that limits and 'places' time. Eternity has contents of course, but it is inconceivably more than its contents. Once again, I do not think this assertion is anti-Parmenidean, for we are not ascribing any qualities to eternity. It *is*, but is without qualities other than its 'isness'. Eternity is the one and only quality-less being, which is why dictionary definitions of it are more or less ridiculous – 'endless time' and the like, but time itself must be timed and cannot be unlimited.

Thus the soul is neither mortal as other beings are mortal (since it survives as long as the human species) nor eternal, since it grasps eternity as either a deduction or a mystical experience. When the soul experiences eternity, is it not permissible to argue (from the standpoint of one denied such an experience) that the experience could not have occurred before a certain stage in the evolution of our race? In brief, the experience of eternity proves nothing and only appears to transcend proof.

However, where we (following the Nietzsche of 'Ariadne's Complaint') most interestingly depart from Plato is that we take the soul to be subject to transformations over long periods of time. The soul in Plato is necessarily unchanging, while the soul in Nietzsche (named 'Ariadne') passes through phases, which are the great phases of human culture. (By a 'great phase' I mean, for example, the heroic or the Christian.) On the other hand, someone might wish to maintain, or at least to suggest, that while the soul changes its form, the pure reality behind the form is constant. But to Nietzsche there is no reality of the soul apart from its form – in any epoch.

At this point we can resume our attempt to qualify Ariadne. She is the soul in our epoch, or at the commencement of an epoch characterised precisely by the loss of faith and value. Let us be quite clear: faith and value have not been temporarily lost but only seem to be so to the typically diminished soul in modern times. Ariadne is the full potential of the modern soul, which feels forsaken by all comforting, 'warming' beliefs, especially the belief that faith and value, *as absolutes*, will return. This soul is pursued by a *thought* which is also the 'Unutterable, veiled, terrible one!/Huntsman behind the clouds!'

The soul is hunted by its own thought, yet finds this thought undecipherable. How can one have a 'veiled' thought? The word is *Gedanke*, 'thought' or 'idea', not 'feeling' (*Gefühl*) or 'awareness' (*Bewusstsein*), so Nietzsche appears to mean that one obscurely thinks something or other that cannot be brought into focus and formulated in words. Nevertheless, this is a thought as opposed to a feeling or even a cognition. Plainly, Ariadne feels her terrors and bewilderment, but the thought itself is not to be identified with these. She is afflicted by fear but is somewhat in the position of one suffering from phobic anxiety; that is to say, behind the fear as its stimulus, is a thought which will no longer produce fear once it is clearly apprehended.

We would be in error to think of Ariadne, or the soul, as first subsisting and then, as it happens, hunted by a thought, for in such a case the thought would not have made its presence known. On the contrary, the (modern) soul is precisely the prey of *this* thought and would be only in a miserably reduced condition if it were not prey. We should not regard the soul as possessing an aspect which makes it prey for the thought but rather as nothing but prey. It now exists as a being hunted by a god-thought. But the god-thought is Ariadne's own thought, or it would be if she acknowledged and formulated it.

And yet Ariadne fails to seize hold of this necessity, this fate. Nietzsche's poem, after all, is her complaint. So Ariadne complains about the condition as if she were more or other than the condition. Again, like someone who experiences an anxiety-state, she cannot but think of the state as an accidental visitor: she would remain, and indeed be restored to health and wholeness, if the state went away. 'Why – torment *me*?/ you malicious, unknown god?' she asks, as though another being might satisfy this god. We are drawn into the supposition that the god depends upon Ariadne and has not just selected her from the multitude of beings. He cannot be whatever he must be without her; perhaps (though this seems incredible at first) he cannot exist at all without her. Does a god's existence depend upon the human soul? Plainly Nietzsche contends that it does. Our error is to assume that we can get rid of gods then live happily ever after, but Nietzsche believes that this particular god *informs* us, as we inform him. He is our belongingness in nature. However, Ariadne suffers from a delusion of independence. The modern soul imagines itself to be independent of gods and this is really Ariadne's problem: she thinks the god, whatever he is, is external to her.

At times Ariadne wishes the god would kill her, but this is just a comforting fantasy of extinction which will never be fulfilled. The soul is kept alive, so it seems, precisely by the cruel god whose hidden presence makes it want to die. In fact the god is the dynamic of the soul and if he departed, the soul would sink into torpor. Conversely, so long as the soul flourishes the god lives – and proceeds with his malicious oppression.

Here we can see why the Ariadne of the legend is a perfect image of the latter-day soul. She is vitally the one abandoned by her heroic lover. Theseus gave meaning to the life of this princess but she gave her life to him, thus deserting her father, the priest-king Minos, and the island of Crete. When Theseus left her, for whatever reason, she became simply the abandoned one. She had been 'brought to life' by Theseus, in the sense that this young hero, raised at Troezen, destined for Athens, provided her with meaning. Theseus was the meaning of Ariadne; now, alone on Naxos, she requires a new meaning. Are we to assume, therefore that the human soul, having given up the code of heroism, has been torpid throughout the centuries of Christian faith? My guess is that Nietzsche would have replied as follows to such a question: 'No, the soul has not been torpid; on the contrary, it has acquired subtlety and depth, but the current of the last twenty centuries has been towards nihilism – this is a more fundamental movement than Christianity and indeed the thrust of Christianity itself.'

Now in Nietzsche's poem Ariadne cannot appreciate that the huntsman-god, the hangman-god, is her meaning-to-be, not, I repeat, an interloper who might just as well (and preferably) be absent from the scene. The god is the next act in Ariadne's tragedy and comes as a thought within her.

The god is oppressive and jealous 'yet', as Ariadne cries, 'jealous of what?' She cannot understand her worth to this god which is as much as to say she cannot understand her worth as such. Ariadne does not recognise her exalted fate, since she regards herself as belonging to the sphere of mortality. She has yet to appreciate her immortality, the immortality of the soul which, having cut loose from Christianity (and indeed from Plato's 'true world'), has not thereby become mortal. To suppose that it has is another instance of human diffidence. Ariadne knows the hateful importuner to be a god and cannot work out what a divine being might want with her. Moreover, he does not simply want her, as one might want one of a number of playthings. For some terrible reason he wants to climb into her very heart, to learn her 'most secret thoughts' and to steal her innermost being. Until he achieves his end he will continue to torture her (and will he stop even then?). But she is worthless, 'no more' than human. What Ariadne cannot comprehend, will not summon up the courage to comprehend, is that she, the human soul, is *supremely* valuable. Now, since what I have just said probably sounds commonplace, it is necessary to stress that this is the reverse of the traditional Christian assumption. In Christianity the soul is valuable because it is loved by God. God's perfect love has no needs but among mortals love always implies need. Here, however, in Nietzsche's poem, the soul is sought, or indeed demanded by a god *because he needs it.* His very godhood is a correlative of the soul.

It should be noted that the contemporary humanistic attitude, which attributes a soul equally to everyone, is not in question here. For such soul-attribution is just a socio-political stance and has nothing to do with divinity; that is to say, to the extent that one thinks of the hidden god one ceases to think in terms of society and equality.

It will be noted that Ariadne's concealed god calls for an appreciative response that she will not and cannot give (as yet). To be precise, she does not understand *what* response he calls for. One thing is certain, however: this called-for response may not take either a purely reactive or a passive form; Ariadne is not to be moulded by the god into whatever he desires. In Nietzsche reactiveness is misguided, both as a description of what happens in nature and as a principle of human conduct. But reactivity informs all human culture or certainly the bulk of it. In this extraordinary sense, therefore, human culture is relatively inadequate even at its best, although here and there (in the plays of Sophocles, for instance, or in the Old Testament) culture has at least approached a healthy condition.

The most detailed study of this aspect of Nietzsche is made by Gilles Deleuze, in his *Nietzsche and Philosophy*, especially chapter 5, Section 8, entitled 'Is Man Essentially "Reactive"?' Deleuze's theme is as follows: human beings, alone of all beings, have turned natural forces into reactive forces, so that every universal action is interpreted as something caused, something brought about in consequence of something else. Deleuze himself does not speak in quite this way, so that I am rather freely interpreting him, but this seems to be an immediately useful account of what he means. The point to bear in mind is that the basis of our thinking is reactive, with the result that we find it difficult and almost absurd to imagine purely active force. But it is we and we alone who transform the action of active force into reaction. We contemplate universal forces themselves in this very way: the Big Bang produced universal expansion, from which everything else follows. But this supposition *as it stands*, is merely evidence of reactive human nature; we cannot, without difficulty, see originary, originative force, in and for itself.

Here it seems reasonable to suspect some Leibnizian influence upon Deleuze, in respect of ideas of substance. Leibniz expresses his seminal understanding of this question especially but not solely in the *Monadology* and the essay, 'On the Reform of Metaphysics and of the Notion of Substance'. For example, in the latter he asserts:

> For active force [meaning 'force' as such] differs from the bare power familiar to the schools, in that the active power or faculty, of the scholastics is nothing else than the possibility ready to act, which has nevertheless need, in order to pass into action, of an external excitation, and as it were of a stimulus. But active force includes a sort of act or entelecheia, which is midway between the faculty of acting and the action itself, and involves an effort, and thus of itself passes into operation; nor does it need aid other than the removal of impediments.[12]

Liebniz gives the illustration of a heavy body hanging on a rope and straining the rope. To explain what is probably obvious: this means, according to Leibniz (and I do not see how one could fault him), that such a hanging body, dead or alive, *actively* pulls on the rope. As a body in its present situation it is partly or wholly composed of this force of pulling. In brief, weight is an activity rather than an inactive state. We need simply to comprehend that movements of all kinds are held by Leibniz to be fundamentally non-mechanical. They are, rather, processes of bodies themselves, stimulated to be sure, but impossible to explain adequately unless one attributes to each body entelechies or monads, each of which is self-acting (and indeed acts continually).

Plainly this topic deserves and comes near to demanding much more space than we can find here, but I wish to make just the point that Deleuze sees nature as 'alive' in this way (which has nothing to do with animism) and attributes a similar vision to Nietzsche. Almost certainly the monadology lies behind Deleuze and he is correct in interpreting Nietzsche according to his own somewhat Leibnizian understanding. In the same view, the seeds of Nietzsche's 'will to power' can possibly be detected, not (embryonically) in Schopenhauer alone but also in the utterance of Leibniz that every present state of a simple substance (a monad) 'is big with its future' – for this is the neatest possible way of summarising what Nietzsche intends by 'will to power'.[13]

We are concerned with Nietzsche's belief that human thought has been predominantly reactive and has thus distanced itself from other processes of nature, which are exclusively active. In this way, thought is a *perverted* natural process. Reactiveness, as Nietzsche analyses it, finds its most subtle expression in ascetic ideals, especially as those ideals are set forth (in all innocence) by philosophers. Philosophers want to 'float above life', as Nietzsche puts it, regarding compulsion, daily tasks, noise, disturbance of all kinds (not to mention the exasperations of politics) as beneath them, for they wish to think their crystal-clear thoughts.[14] In our century logical positivists have gone so far as to fashion a way of doing philosophy that is largely self-reflexive. All the rest of philosophy is seen by them as disguised egoism – as indeed it is, but why must we imagine that egoism can be conquered or that logical philosophy is a technique of doing so? The more basic explanation for ascetic ideals is that they are artifices for the preservation of human life. This is how human beings combat the sickness of their species. The secret design is to soothe pain (by means of emotions, including 'painful' emotions, by suitable and suitably complex thoughts; by faith in 'facts'; by inventing 'causes') and thus to sustain the species – but for what purpose? Clearly the goal is the supremacy of our race, or the replacement of fated existence by our own will. But what does our will require? We presumably wish to 'deaden the nerve-ends' or at least to keep our responses at the pitch of little, controllable jolts of excitement.

This, then, is the contemporary aspiration. Ariadne-as-soul rises above the aspiration but not yet far enough to recognise her own genius. Perhaps – so she imagines in her desperation – the hangman-god requires a ransom from her. This means he wants her to surrender some minimal possession. He will go away if she gives him something she scarcely desires, but this conjecture is known to be nonsense as soon as it enters Ariadne's head. In any case, what can she be said to 'possess'? She has not reached the stage of conferring a sort of seriousness, or even sacredness, upon things and qualities purely by enfolding them within her arbitrament. Such a stage must, of course, be the future version of Ariadne's ancient confidence – the confidence she possessed when Minoan culture rendered the world sacred. But at present Ariadne's pride can only 'instruct' the god to demand a high price, since she is worth much. Her 'other pride' tells the god to be brief; he must not detain her with long-winded speeches. Then suddenly she faces up to the fact that he requires, not a ransom at all, not a possession to be plucked from her and handed to him, but her entire being: '*Me* – you want me'? / me – all of me? . . .' The first, italicised 'me' stresses her amazement and diffidence. This really expresses Nietzsche's prediction that if and when the soul flourishes again, it will acquire colossal self-esteem and colossal responsibility also. For this reawakened soul must acknowledge its own responsibility as creator – the creator not of matter but of meaning (all the meaning formally ascribed to gods, heroes, the moral law and empirical discovery).

In return, this mocking god (so different from God) offers Ariadne love. She is contemptuous, partly on account of her current low self-esteem and partly because her years of isolation have taught her to prefer enmity. To be exact, she wants not so much enemies in general, but this very god as her supreme, 'cruellest enemy'. Naturally, therefore, he should yield to her, not the other way round. It is scarcely surprising that Ariadne cannot understand how she might yield. Either the god is her master or she is his, and if the latter, how can he be a god?

Presumably the conception is that the modern soul (Nietzsche's own soul, for example, feminised and 'generalised' as Ariadne) toys for long enough with the possibility of making specific contributions to an utterly amorphous being called 'life'. This is the ransom Ariadne speaks of. We think of contributing by means of our professional work, perhaps, or through assistance to a scarcely less amorphous being called 'society'. One might aid specific others, but this too (as a sort of ransom) is nowhere near enough. It is reasonable to compare such latter-day stipulations and reservations with those of some in the early years of Christianity who did not grasp that Christ wanted *everything* – not petty sacrifices and offerings, not money or corn or formalised little duties. Admittedly Ariadne's holding back is connected with her modesty and puzzlement, but these are not virtues so much as delaying-tactics. So Nietzsche is declaring that the soul of today, no less than the soul of two thousand years ago, is required to surrender itself, but not, this time, to Christ.

In return the soul will be loved and warmed. Here we approach the final realisation. The theory of this is no great matter, since nothing matters much at the theoretical level. Briefly, the soul, in venerating itself, venerates the god. For the soul is the god. If we wish to maintain that the soul merely partakes of the god (which is a perfectly acceptable view) we must imply that all the beings we apprehend as external truly *are* external just as we apprehend them. That is to say, Kant is wrong and our intuitions are windows on to the world. If, on the other hand, we accept Kant's Copernican Revolution, we are obliged to identify the soul with some sort of incessant creative procedures. Thus the modern soul is no longer (as it is in Plato) a pure being beyond all substances and excitations.

But if the soul and the god are two ways of looking at the same being, who is this being? At the end he reveals himself to Ariadne as Dionysus, saying,

'Be wise, Ariadne! . . .
You have little ears, you have ears like mine:
let some wisdom into them! –
Must we not first hate ourself if we are to love ourself? . . .

I am thy labyrinth' [15]

The little ears of Ariadne mean simply that she, like Dionysus himself, is fashioned by nature to be intelligent, receptive, the reverse of an ass.[16] The point is that Ariadne should hear the wise suggestion that to reach the goal of proper self-regard it is psychologically necessary to start out from self-distaste. That is a verbose way of putting what Nietzsche puts so simply. The soul wants to love itself and at present hates itself. Very well, the soul is in the right condition from which to proceed towards its goal. I take Nietzsche to mean that no one ends up accepting himself unless he finds himself wanting at the start. Is this not true? Apparent self-acceptance at the start is mere ignorance and social adaptation; only the one who doubts and finds fault with himself fashions a self he positively likes. But the fashioned self is not a model or a pose taken from outside, for it must be a strengthened and sharpened development of one's original self. By this route alone is someone forced to come round to a proper appreciation of his or her singularity, for by this route alone does the singularity reveal itself.

That is the first point. Next, what is far more important is that Dionysus declares himself to be Ariadne's labyrinth. Ariadne has a labyrinth, not as a possession but virtually as a predicate: Ariadne = labyrinth. And this Ariadne-labyrinth is not remotely an underground maze for amusement or to trap people. Ariadne must proceed through the world as if by way of a winding, endlessly deceiving set of passages. This is the way of the modern soul. There is no end (for which read 'belief') because the soul must always revert to the beginning. If there were a belief, as in the ages of faith, the maze would not be a true one but rather a bewildering, perhaps terrible journey – the sort of journey, for example, undertaken by Bunyan's Christian. As it is, there can be no end, since endlessness is the insight our metaphysical progress has attained. This is Nietzsche's world, a 'monster of energy, without beginning, without end . . .'. It is also 'without goal, unless the joy of the circle is itself a goal; without will, unless a ring feels good will towards itself . . .'.[17]

In the poem Nietzsche is apparently telling us that such an understanding is more or less buried in modern people so that the soul will reawaken and grow wise when it decides *conclusively* to explore, purely for the sake of exploration. No thread could lead us out of the labyrinth, for nothing is outside it, or, rather, the 'All' is labyrinthine and purposeless.

A question still poses itself, surely. While Dionysus is Ariadne's labyrinth, is he not more than that? Elsewhere, as we well know, Nietzsche thinks of Dionysus as 'the religious affirmation of life, life whole and not denied or in part . . .'.[18] Dionysus was to the Greeks, so Nietzsche declares, the 'mysterious symbol of the highest world-affirmation and transfiguration of existence that has yet been attained on earth'.[19] More famously, Nietzsche states that,

'The word *"Dionysian"* means: an urge to unity, a reaching out beyond personality, the everyday, society, reality, across the abyss of transitoriness . . . an ecstatic affirmation of the total character of life . . . the feeling of the necessary unity of creation and destruction.'[20] So, if Dionysus is the affirmation of the totality, he must (one might think) be more, vastly more, than the human soul, or Ariadne, or her Labyrinth.

But in fact this question resolves itself into ways of looking. If we try to deify the whole of life (every cosmological activity) by naming this whole 'Dionysus', we naturally imagine we subordinate the human soul. For the soul is, from this point of view, no more than a part. Otherwise it could not have a specific name or certain functions. On the other hand – and this is what the words of Dionysus mean in the poem – the totality is grasped by the soul alone and so the pair, soul and totality come together, although under normal circumstances when the present enquiry is not under way, each is differently conceived.

So far, however, we have not put forward a necessary reason why either or both should be a labyrinth. The idea is resoundingly anti-Platonic, for it means that far from there being a final Form of the Good (towards which some labyrinthine dialectical journey might lead) there is nothing but a maze, an endless creative movement of energies, one leading into another. For Ariadne to recognise this would be for the soul no longer to distinguish itself from the world. To be sure, it must continue to distinguish itself formally and procedurally, but not as regards its composition.

This is a difficult idea to grasp *as an idea*, since the root of the matter does not seem to be ideational. It means that affirmation of a scene or event has to coexist with philosophic enquiry. One no longer enquires in order to amend the scene. Socrates has to affirm tragedy, say a specific tragedy of Sophocles, and then conduct an enquiry into what Sophocles has demonstrated. He has no object other than the one he avows, namely to follow the trail wherever it leads. He does not set out to vanquish tragedy and if he wishes to vanquish Sophocles (with whom we would not readily think of comparing him) it is only by way of competition.

Socrates was right: one knows nothing, or to be exact, one takes things as 'known' for the sake of managing in life, but for no other reason. Here we return to the question we posed in the last sentence of Chapter 2. What Socrates did may now be regarded as a sort of brilliant travesty of what Nietzsche has in mind. Socrates enquired endlessly, but as Hippias points out in the *Hippias Major* (see above page 149), he always failed to recognise the 'magnitude and continuity of the substances of which reality is composed'. Now, to accept the Sophoclean tragedy and, in addition, to conduct an enquiry on that basis, are alike ways of saying 'Yes' to life as a whole. Here are two seemingly different routes – the one of tragedy, the other of dialectic – both of which are movements in the universal labyrinth. Tragedy has this advantage over dialectic: it denies the possibility of a radical change in the human condition. Contrariwise, dialectic gives a certain spiritedness and play to the human intelligence. But both tragedy and dialectic remain ways of formalising what has to be recognised *in advance* as formless. We have, then, two strategies instead of one, but neither can lead us out of the labyrinth, which is the soul's apprehension of the world. Dionysus tells Ariadne, 'I am thy labyrinth', meaning, 'I am the one who comprises the whole' – the 'All' of the human soul, which 'All' must now be seen in the terms of a neverending and painful adventure.

Thus the god Dionysus is the way of the soul. However, the way and the soul come together, so that they are only theoretically distinguishable. This is why Ariadne's attempts to evade the god have been futile. Similarly, her definition of the god as a cruel huntsman, a torturer and a hangman must be traced not precisely to the pain he causes but to her assumption that the pain is gratuitous. In other words, the human soul has sought to avoid the pain which is the root of its own being.

The soul has sought to do this, namely to smother the Dionysian awareness, by means of a belief in Plato's Good or the redemptive God. Nietzsche is, of course, saying that the soul must now accept itself as the creator of all it has hitherto deemed unapproachably divine, or otherwise unapproachable (for example, a distant galaxy or the distant past). This may sound easy enough to some modern thinkers but Nietzsche does not mean that we can arrange the world to please ourselves. After all, even Nietzsche's all-powerful Dionysus cannot (as yet) gain access to Ariadne; it is not a matter of willing or wishing. If every meaning we light upon is imposed by us, as is the case, the meaning must be other than us in some sense. That is to say, it must be other than our desires. In order to give ourselves a meaning we need to judge ourselves 'from the outside'. On the other hand, there is no outside. Therefore, when one judges oneself from this crucial vantage-point, one takes hold of whatever is *crucially* present and elevates that as a criterion. In the past we supposedly stood outside ourselves by means of belief or faith; now this situation has to be reached by an elevation of what is within. But it must be within the *singular* individual and it must be an elevation. This enhanced spirit is the god and he has nothing essentially to do with our desires. One might go further and say that he will always trivialise our desires and override them.

7

Overcoming the Greeks

I

Nietzsche concludes a passage in *The Gay Science* by exclaiming, 'Alas, my friends, we must overcome even the Greeks!'[1] It is a matter for regret that we have to overcome the most philosophically gifted people hitherto. But why must we do this? Why may we not just continue to build on the Greeks' achievements?

The question is not one of how to compete with the Greeks; nor is it, in the usual sense, a question of 'progress'. The aim is not to surpass individuals or a body of work, as a pioneer scientist surpasses his predecessors. To the contrary, as we noted earlier, Nietzsche sees every important philosopher more or less in isolation, each having his own, strictly unsurpassable theme. By what means, therefore, and why are we to overcome the Greeks as a whole?

One way is repeatedly demonstrated by Heidegger who examines the meanings of certain formative terms: *Logos, Moira, Aletheia* and, above all, the etymology of 'Being' and 'beings'.[2] To do this, to return to the beginning of philosophy, and indeed to the cultural situation before the beginning of philosophy (for example, to Homer's grasp of 'beings') is certainly a promising method of 'putting the Greek influence to one side', as it were. The influence must naturally remain, but would come to be seen, distinctly and constantly, as nothing more essential and inescapable than an influence.

For a different purpose (a purpose connected with the psychology of Western values) Nietsche too wants us to return to the Greeks *as a first step*, no longer in a spirit of scholarship but in order to contemplate the procedure they bequeathed to us as merely one possibility, a choice made by an individual, namely Socrates. Now, it would be easy enough to speak of this subject in exclusively modern terms (that is, to fix a knowing, modern eye upon the Greeks) but then we would be indulging in a familiar sort of academic exercise. And this would be to contemplate the Socratic influence from *within*

151

that influence. Plainly there was nothing comfortable about Socrates' original exchanges, but now we interrogate things as a matter of course. Thus our interrogations are roughly 'Socratic' from the start. Conversely, what Nietzsche puts forward as a necessity is a struggle with a *governing* belief by first exposing its psychological origins.

Let us consider further why Socrates is thus singled out; why does overcoming him alone amount to overcoming the Greeks in general? So far as Nietzsche is concerned, Socrates diverted the Presocratics or cast them into shadow. To this day earlier thinkers, including such formidable figures as Heraclitus and Parmenides, have to be reckoned as 'Presocratics'. To us they remain oddly impressive individuals whose remarks tend to be regarded through a Socratic lens. Parmenides, say, is someone about whom we might argue, or, in more recent years, we might signally fail to argue, because (despite our scholarship) we no longer really care. Whatever he meant, we desire only to discuss it. This reluctance to take a view is seen as a virtue, or at least as the absence of a vice. But Nietzsche's opinion (surely correct) is that Socrates has led us to the notion that careful exposition and honest argument constitute the sole valid procedure; everything else is unenlightened or at worst barbaric. Thus 'overcoming the Greeks' means regarding Socrates' methods as merely methods, useful and fruitful at times but far from the entire basis of philosophy.

However, that is only a subordinate point. It is more important to realise that Socrates, wisely but exclusively, made a splendid strength out of what must *finally* be seen as a weakness. I say 'finally' because the fearless vigour of Socrates countered the disarray of his own instincts; it was the bringing-to-order of an urge to dissolution. Such an urge was a weakness, biologically speaking, though the spiritual strength of Socrates was correspondingly immense. Some commentators on Nietzsche, judged with reference to Nietzsche's own remarks, are apt to misrepresent this point. Kaufman will not acknowledge the biological weakness of Socrates, while Gilles Deleuze will not admire the vigour.[3] In the relevant section of *The Gay Science* (Book Four, Section 341) Nietzsche implies that Socrates was the crucial figure in Greek cultural history, who made a world-historical judgement. Socrates was the *nonpareil* of cultural endeavour, the one who knowingly but surreptitiously taught us to survive by means of an illusion. Nietzsche tacitly suggests that Socrates himself lacked the illusion he passed on to us – to subsequent humanity. Presumably that is what Nietzsche means but he does not quite say as much because such an achievement would have been daemonic. The notion is that Socrates' own wisdom consisted in his meeting human needs by cunning manipulation of human possibilities. Could he have done this? Whether he did or not, Nietzsche recalls that at the end Socrates said, 'O Crito, I owe Asclepius a rooster.' This was a proverbial expression which meant that one was recovering from a disease and therefore ought to give the god of medicine a token of one's gratitude. Nietzsche concludes that Socrates, 'who had lived cheerfully and like a soldier in the sight of everyone' was glad to be on the verge of death because, after all, his life had been a burden. This, once again, is what I mean by Socrates' 'weakness' out of which he fashioned his prodigious strength. (The word 'prodigious' is not meant as a hyperbole).

It is important, also, to remember that this power of Socrates, a transformation of biological weakness, was what enabled him to displace his philosophic forerunners. Thus, when we now examine Parmenides, we do so not merely in a scholarly spirit or with dialectical presuppositions, but with certain beliefs – beliefs in 'goodness' and 'justice' – at the back of our minds. This distorts our reading of Parmenides or puts him in a certain light as essentially one who came before what may as well be called 'the revelation of virtue'. So overcoming the Greeks means overcoming one of the noblest Greeks who was also the one who despatched us on a specific route.

Remember, too, that Aristotle in 'Problems' ask himself why 'those who have become eminent in philosophy or poetry or the arts are clearly of an atrabilious temperament?' and he gives, as recent examples, Empedocles, Plato and Socrates.[4]

The matter under discussion is an attitude of both mind and body, which Nietzsche interprets as 'pessimism' and Aristotle as 'restlessness' or 'agitation'. In Aristotle it is clear that those of such a disposition cannot shake it off: it *is* them; they are made of it. On the other hand, in Aristotelian metaphysics, we, as moving beings, as beings constantly in motion, are also formed of God – formed not *by* God but *of* him. It is God who causes us to do whatever we do, down to the tiniest and most 'earthy' activities. This is Aristotle's distinction: the substance of a being is what that being is composed of, while God is the mover of the being. But God, the mover, and the non-divine substances he moves, are coexistent and coeternal. Not one of them, not God himself, can be apprehended as existing without, or before, the others.

Nietzsche's view, as we have appreciated in Chapter 5, is not so much a contradiction as a development of Aristotle's. He believes that one's make-up is channelled by will to power. The make-up is primary, but so, indispensably, is will to power. To consider one's chemical composition as though it were distinct from will to power is just a trick of thought; really there is no such distinction. From the beginning, therefore, an atrabilious physical constitution (manifesting itself psychologically and behaviourally as dissatisfaction) is shaped by will to power. The shaping and the material shaped are in truth one and the same.

In Nietzsche's eyes, then, Socrates was *fundamentally* dissatisfied, as a matter of both physique and will to power, indissolubly linked. All his soldierly cheerfulness merely camouflaged his temperament. For this reason he experienced life as burdensome. Socrates 'carried his life around with him', so to speak, strenuously and painfully, as one might carry a heavy burden, and when the time came, he was relieved to let it go. Nietzsche is not suggesting that life is ever 'weightless' for anyone, but there are people who carry their weight, *light or heavy*, in an equable or assenting way, and sometimes with an undercurrent of joy. The mere feeling of weight, even excessive weight, does not produce sorrow. Pessimists, nevertheless, experience their weight as positively unpleasant. This was true of Socrates and of course he was representative of others. Pessimists have naturally affected, or even conditioned culture, so that many people of another temperament have managed to share the same rueful belief. You do not have to be one of nature's pessimists to think pessimistically.

Socrates felt that it was best for him to leave life behind. Many Greeks had what superficially sounds like a similar attitude; hence, according to Nietzsche, the Greek folk story of how Silenus, the companion of Dionysus, told King Midas that human beings ought never to be born. Silenus continued: 'But the second best for you is – to die soon.'[5] This was folk wisdom as well as tragic wisdom. The tale suggests that the Dionysian dithyramb and, subsequently, tragic drama itself, did not impose a sorrowful pathos upon an otherwise sanguine people but rather expressed a deep-rooted assumption. Just the same, the pessimism of Socrates took a new form, or else gave fresh value to an old and vulgar form. His alternative was to the effect that life should be not simply lived but most energetically *thought*. The sheer intensity of Socrates' thinking is what, more often than not, still escapes us. We feebly imitate such thinking, but for it to have any chance of success – not as politics or rhetoric but as root-and-branch therapy – it needs to be abnormally intense, free from repetition, wishful argument, habits, self-indulgence, indifference, faith in one's own stylistic manoeuvres, all the usual vices of disputation. It has to be at once serious and unserious, as was the practice of Socrates himself. Everything must be broken down, again and again; no structure of history or tradition must, as a prerequisite, be left standing. This alone is dialectical thought as the way of virtue, yet even Socrates left virtue itself intact. A specific virtue might be more or less satisfactorily examined, though the mere idea of virtue as the supreme human way of life may not be questioned. At the very end, however, the procedure is possibly revealed by Socrates himself to have been, not a failure but little more than a stratagem. I believe the point is already implied by Aristotle in his diagnosis of Socrates as 'atrabilious'. In our terminology, when Aristotle develops his point, he ascribes to Socrates an overriding urge to interfere, to meddle, to mould things – this, of course, on a heightened scale of genius. Thus the disease of life of which Socrates was 'cured' by the hemlock produced in him the very practices which led to the hemlock. From one point of view this is a perfectly 'tragic' outcome. Perhaps we might see Socrates as somewhat 'Promethean', but even then, it is necessary to remember that Prometheus in Aeschylus' drama, discerns, though cannot remotely influence the operations of Necessity. We seem close to establishing that interrogation, however thorough, cannot be fundamental; something always lies beyond it. This something seems to be specific but it is really the sheer tangle of forces and events.

But did Socrates expect people ever to reach an end by means of dialectic? Plainly he did not, and we have already demonstrated that for him dialectic was the neverending way of virtue. Nevertheless, there is another point to be made here: if questioning never reaches the end – since there is no 'end', and, for that matter, only an arbitrary beginning – this confirms tragedy, Socrates' enemy, as the victor.

The thought of Socrates always aims to lead us 'out of nature'. As we have remarked, it does so, according to Hippias in the *Hippias Major*, by breaking the naturally unified into unnatural fragments.[6] But what other kind of thought is there? What kind leaves us 'within nature', and how does it do this? It happens that in 1875 Nietzsche confided the following observations to his notebook:

With Empedocles and Democritus the Greeks were well on the way toward *assessing correctly* the irrationality and suffering of human existence; but, thanks to Socrates, *they never reached the goal.* An unbiased view of man is something which eludes all Socratics, who have those horrible abstractions, 'the good' and 'the just,' on their minds.[7]

Nietzsche goes on to maintain that Greek myth and tragedy are wiser than Plato and Aristotle, at least in the field of ethics. Homer and Aeschylus each exhibits a naive ethical viewpoint wiser than the ethics of the philosophers, just because the poets do not think about such matters. The clever thought of Socrates, Plato and Aristotle actually spoils their considerations of right and wrong. Such considerations are best left unthought.

We are rushing ahead and there are several questions to be pondered here. First – to return to Nietzsche's view quoted above – the task, it seems, is to assess correctly the irrationality and suffering of human existence. Socrates himself (never mind the Socratics with 'those horrible abstractions, "the good" and "the just," on their minds') already led us astray by his mere practice and his belief that one's 'higher nature', specifically one's dialectical gifts, must be marshalled and intensified until the disease of life is at least modified and held at bay. That attitude of Socrates was enough; that was *the* anti-tragic assumption.

Thus while Socrates acknowledged the irrationality and suffering of our existence, he nevertheless urged us to fight against these qualities. Consider what is being asked here: that we should proceed against unreason and pain, even though these are inescapable. For all that, in the second half of the twentieth century a certain perverse attitude, a hopeless vulgarisation of Socrates, reigns supreme. The good person, who may even be something of a hero, is the one who rebels against all suffering; this indeed is his imperative. So what is the alternative attitude to life of Empedocles and Democritus that the young Nietzsche regarded as superior? Here it is necessary to proceed in a different way from the contemporary fashion, for it is the thrust of the two thinkers that needs to be characterised rather than the detail of their ideas.

Nietzsche maintains that these two were 'well on the way towards *assessing correctly* the irrationality and suffering of human existence'. He presumably does not mean that the Presocratics (in contrast to Empedocles and Democritus) were not already on *their* way towards assessing human existence correctly. Our understanding must be that the most remarkable Presocratic thinkers (Heraclitus and Parmenides) each postulated a way of being of all nature which, though true and undeniable, seemed to cast aside as useless even the highest human capacities. In this peculiar sense the two older thinkers did not assess *human* existence correctly; they left us to our own meagre devices.

We cannot actually live as Heracliteans, unless the rare madman can do so for periods of his life, since no civilisation could be built, for example, on the insight that 'all things are one', or, perhaps more strikingly, that 'You could not step twice into the same rivers . . .' Heraclitus himself survived by courtesy of a social ethos, a masquerade, which he despised. This indicates that one may accept Heraclitus as an unparalled truth-teller, but then, in order to endure, one has to adopt or create some necessary fictions. In other words, one must pretend that all things are as they distinctively appear to be, namely *not* one, and that this river into which I now step is indeed the river I stepped into yesterday. It follows that Heraclitus must be borne in mind and cannot be refuted, while the thought-devices by which we live should ideally be recognised as devices.

As for Parmenides, he straightforwardly declared the way of Truth to be unliveable, so that we must get by with 'mortal opinions'. We have to think of Parmenides as compromising to a degree with his town of Elea, knowing full well – to put the matter figuratively – what the goddess had told him about Truth (for instance, that there is strictly no such thing as 'the past').

So now to the burden, first of Empedocles which may well be viewed as taking its rise from Parmenides. Guthrie, for instance, has a section in his chapter on Empedocles entitled 'Escape from Parmenides: The Four Roots', or, as an alternative title, 'Echoes of Parmenides'. Somewhat similarly, in a chapter called 'The Atomists of the Fifth Century' Guthrie regards Democritus as attempting to reconcile the 'audacious' thought of Parmenides with the demands of what we might pardonably call 'empiricism'.[8]

Empedocles, it should be noted at the outset, completely integrates what we have long regarded as two separate spheres: the sphere of matter on the one hand, and the spiritual-moral sphere on the other. In this respect he follows his predecessors, but in him the integration is more striking because the Empedoclean cosmos is governed by the two great forces, Love and Strife. That is to say, his scheme gives overwhelming prominence to what we see as either wholly or partly spiritual qualities. When Love dominates the world, all things are fused into a perfect sphere; when Strife is dominant (as it has been, in our observations, since the universe began), the whole is apparently divisible into countless masses.

Here it is scarcely necessary to consider this alternation of Love and Strife in doxographical fashion, beyond the point at which we seem to have lighted upon the Empedoclean thought that Nietzsche would have judged to be *psychologically* valuable. Thus the first comment to be made is that Empedocles regards Love as a strictly physical (natural) agency making for union. Love joins substances together. This notion is admirable, because it unifies what may be unified – or what may be allocated to a single unifying principle. Love, we now say (in defiance of the Platonic centuries), is physically grounded even in its highest reaches; it is an activity of matter. Well, Empedocles already said as much. Similarly, we can readily see Strife as both psychical and physical. We quite regularly think of forces as engaged in some sort of 'strife', while at the same time we properly give that label to purely human and animal antagonisms.

Before we proceed it is advisable to mention that Nietzsche would probably have regarded Empedocles' ideas as pointing to a radical, undeniable truth. Really they point in the direction of Heraclitus' 'War is the father of all and the king of all'[9] or his 'We must know that war is common to all and that strife is justice, and that everything comes into being by strife . . .',[10] at least in the sense that Empedocles, like Heraclitus, places us in the midst of a universe of competing forces (and not, of course, as mere observers). Empedocles' non-Heraclitean addition of Love as the opposite pole of cosmic activity is perhaps his way of accounting for what we perceive as harmony. Heraclitus says there is no harmony, except the harmony of a game enjoyed by the gods. However, since we perceive harmony, the condition exists in some fashion. To this extent at least, Empedocles is an advance on Heraclitus; he accounts for a condition which we cannot but perceive; without which Heraclitus himself could not fashion his gnomic utterances. Harmony, like Strife, appears to occur, to be a 'fact of life'. Therefore it *is*. To Nietzsche, moreover, Empedocles is so far working on the right lines, attempting to explain what we observe, without recourse to non-observable or purely spiritual principles.

Next, Empedocles does not see the universe as an integrated system. There is no hint of a teleological explanation. The cosmos of

Empedocles has neither design nor goal. This extremely old vision of the world as, if you will, a 'monster of energy' is, of course, consistent with Nietzsche's post-Kantian belief that the mind itself provides design. Here again, however, we should stress that at or near the beginning of philosophy it was perfectly possible for a thinker to conceive of a 'pointless' world; a world, admittedly, organised on the basis of a large general principle (the alteration of Love and Strife) but not organised *for* an ultimate purpose – say, that of universal Love – or by a divine organiser. It is worth adding that this Empedoclean notion of all things as essentially bits and pieces which collide and sometimes form bodies, but commonly fly apart, and in any event behave randomly, is at least vaguely similar to the modern world of quantum mechanics.

Perhaps we can venture another comparison between the Empedoclean and the modern understanding, or certainly between the Empedoclean and the Nietzschean, to the effect that non-living things are in a manner animated. The hylozoistic belief is nevertheless not animism, not the familiar, early assumption that matter houses spirits, but is more akin to our understanding that the organic (even in its highest forms) is not essentially different from the inorganic. Once again, Nietzsche would have seen this as a promising line of thought blocked for over two thousand years by Platonism. Related to this viewpoint of Empedocles is the further notion that everything has some sort and degree of awareness. A stone, for example, is, in its stony way, 'aware' of the soil in which is it embedded. As we have noted, the selfsame opinion is adopted by Nietzsche.

It is also to the point that Empedocles sees change in the world – every form of motion, in other words – as at once necessary and uncaused. Nothing causes fragments of matter to move, to collide with one another, and sometimes to form compounds; it is merely in their nature to do so. Rather, it is, or should be, unthinkable that they might remain motionless. For what external cause of motion could there be? On the other hand, the specific movements are, so it seems, utterly necessary. Since something has occurred, it had to occur. The leaf had to fall from the tree – in precisely the way it fell. But if this is true of everyday physical occurrences, why does it not also apply to events in human history? A great war, a revolution, a birth, the death of an individual comes about precisely when and how it comes about, accidentally or predictably: such occurrences are both necessary and causeless. This is a view of events which Plato scorns as though it were intrinsically senseless. It is certainly 'senseless' so far as Socratic–Platonic reasoning can determine, but to Nietzsche, as to Empedocles of old, it is by far the most 'reasonable' explanation of events, specifically that they unfold by chance *and* by necessity. (Actually 'unfold' is the wrong word, for it implies a flowing *sequence* as opposed to a Parmenidean entirety of presentness.)

Finally an important element of Empedocles' thought which might – or 'must' as it seems to me – have impressed itself upon the young Nietzsche is more problematic, more 'a matter of opinion'. Empedocles regarded life, his own life in particular, as deeply guilt-ridden. Notice how inexorably he fastens guilt upon himself, for it consists in neither criminal acts nor impious thoughts but in the mere business of eating flesh. One eats flesh in order to live and this is sinful, because animal meat is, or might be, the present form of a dead person. The dead person could well have been noble, which is to say destined ultimately for godhood.

Nietzsche does not acknowledge 'guilt' in any sense, ancient or modern; at the same time he proclaims that it is impossible to remove suffering from life. To Nietzsche, I suspect, Empedocles' guilt is readily translatable into the terms of suffering, or, more likely, it is regarded as a fifth-century attempt to account for a crucial discrepancy, namely the discrepancy between how a few people experience life and the heights to which they aspire (Empedocles being such a one and Nietzsche another). Empedocles regarded himself as a *daimon* or divine being condemned for a period to mortal existence: this he clearly states in his poem 'Purifications'. As for Nietzsche, he apprehended himself as a 'destiny', meaning one who alters, not so much the course but the *value* of all events. It is not fanciful to compare Empedocles' self-estimate with that of Nietzsche. The latter resolved to make a radiant meaning out of his suffering. Thus the blamelessness of Nietzsche's pain, as perceived by him, is allied to his lifelong, formative need to elevate himself 'beyond man and time', towards a prefiguration of the *Übermensch*. To strive towards this condition was Nietzsche's endeavour, as it had been that of Empedocles. This was not an absurd imperative, for it expressed Nietzsche's rather persuasive idea of how nature works. In a certain sense there was no self-glorification but, on the contrary, a recognition of the self as inescapably 'natural', as behaving naturally and thus openly exercising will to power. It was the others, all the others, the rest of the human race, who sought to evade their fates and so crept about the earth as purely social creatures. In this way both Empedocles and Nietzsche are, very consciously, *sufferers* and each sees this fact as a means and motive of his progressive elevation. Such a fundamental correspondence is more important by far than the difference between the 'guilt' of Empedocles and the 'innocence' of Nietzsche.

II

Why Nietzsche added the name of Democritus to that of Empedocles is marginally less transparent, but perhaps clear enough. In *Philosophy and Truth* Nietzsche is quoted as saying that to Democritus, 'the world is totally lacking in reason and instinctive drive; it has all been shaken together. All gods and myths are superfluous.'[11] At the outset we should emphasise that Nietzsche correctly sees Democritus as denying the world 'instinctive drive' as well as reason. This means that animals are not motivated by instinct and nothing is driven by some such force as 'will to power'. Nietzsche comes to disagree with this belief, yet at this early stage in his own thinking (1875, the period of *Untimely Meditations*) he is probably not much dissatisfied with Democritus' exclusion of spiritual or mental forces. If anything, Nietzsche is invigorated, so one would think, by the elementary removal of obviously doubtful notions – notions such as 'instinct' and 'spirit'. Even so, Nietzsche, throughout his career, attributes a non-physical dynamic to the physical universe.

Unlike Empedocles, Democritus says nothing about guilt or self-enhancement, and our knowledge of his ethical writings (which were, in any case, only a small proportion of his life's work) takes us no further than a banal doctrine of prudence, of maintaining one's good spirits by not attempting too much. However, it would certainly be wrong to think of Democritus as little more than an early physicist, and this for a reason which is doubtless well understood but seldom expounded. His thought is *inclusive*; he simply does not contemplate nature as a mechanistic sphere distinct from the mind or spirit. Whatever nature is, it comprehends gods and myths, but does so superfluously. If the human race could eliminate gods and myths, what would be left over would not be a vast machine. On the contrary, the very idea of a machine, or nature-as-mechanism is itself a myth.

The essence of the world is its atomic structure. Just the same,

Democritus goes further than other atomists contemporary with him (and further than modern physicists) in trying not merely to describe atomic structure but also to give intellectually coherent, all-embracing explanations. He seems to balk at nothing. But the vital difference that defines or characterises Democritus as a philosopher rather than a physicist is that he knows his explanations for what they are, specifically *attempts*. Nothing is certain. Knowledge is not progressive. But this does not rule out the possibility that some of the things we claim to know might in some way be 'valid'; it merely rules out the *question* of validity. It is no longer a pertinent question.

For instance, Democritus notes that our senses commonly deceive us, or at least give us varying and thus 'senseless' reports. A modern scientist merely answers, 'Of course', and either thinks no more about the matter or else classifies the kinds of deception, describing how they came about. But Democritus instantly asks: since the senses are unreliable, what, in contrast, may be said to be reliable or truthful? Plato's supposition that intellection or reasoning takes place independently of the senses and is the soul's highest activity has apparently not occurred to him, or if it has, has been dismissed as the kind of belief some people need to hold. The twentieth-century derivative of this, to the effect that propositions may be verifiable, we diagnose as having the supreme motive of plucking certainty (however trivial) from the phantasmagoria. On the other hand, Democritus remarks that 'either nothing is true or it is unclear to *us*'.[12] One cannot proceed beyond this statement. Thus our assertions are normally conventions. We call something 'sweet' says Democritus, while in reality only atoms and void 'exist'.[13] The quality of sweetness does not 'exist', by which Democritus means that sweetness is merely a judgement, an opinion, and has no *further* existence. Atoms and void, however, are at the furthest reaches of (non-dialectical) thinking and therefore lie beyond the scope of opinion. Sooner or later, possibly, atoms and void might join the ranks of mere opinions, but at present we arrive at their being – for, of course, a void must also be said 'to be' – by a process which transcends opinion. For what is an opinion but a belief which is either true or untrue? But atoms and void cannot, at present, be held to be untrue. Already, of course, we think of atoms, not as the smallest units but as composed of yet smaller units, but, philosophically speaking, that is beside the point, for sooner or later one comes down to a particle of some sort. However much we divide units up, something else – another 'thing' – remains. This is not because there actually is a further, smaller thing but because we are obliged to assume there is.

At all events, Democritus joins Parmenides in relegating almost all our thought to convention. Even the 'true' (that is, the undisputable) thought of the atom has been more or less a convention since the atomists first lighted upon it. Nevertheless, 'For each of us,' Democritus declares [despite our conventionality], 'there is a reshaping – belief!'[14] That is to say, to the limited extent that we escape from convention, we shape (or create) and believe; we do not truthfully discern. The moment I stop calling this thing in my hand 'a pen' and begin to contemplate it thoroughly, what actually happens? I shape the thing afresh and believe it to be something no one else believes it to be. In other words, I now create it. On the one hand is the convention 'pen'; on the other hand is my creation.

This means, of course, that my impression of the so-called pen should not and strictly cannot be subordinated to a true idea, since the latter is nonexistent. In practice, we (at best) lurch from convention to impression, but the impression is an utterly personal and private creation. In fact it should not be called an 'impression', if by that term we mean to confer priority upon an original entity of which an impression is formed. There is no such entity outside the merely serviceable sphere of convention.

My impression is also, as Democritus originally said, a 'belief'. I honestly and inwardly believe the pen to be as I see it. In what other mode can it exist? Nearly all the time, however, I falsify my perceptions and beliefs in order to survive. I do not wish to be a bedlam creature, forever seeing what I alone see (or hear, etc.). By this means, however, I say, for example, 'This is sweet', and so amount to nothing, playing no part in the universal scheme. The choice is between playing a part, which is fatal (tragic), and not playing a part, which is nugatory.

Democritus already implies all this, so it is no wonder that Nietzsche saw him, along with Empedocles, as being on the right track. But Democritus does not make a tragic 'fuss' about our immense dilemma; he simply goes on thinking. He thinks not dialectically, and perhaps not even scientifically, but in a purely adventurous way. To him thinking is the royal road, not of virtue (as it is for Socrates) but of human creation.

I would argue, for example, that the main feature of the atomism of Democritus (to us, though not necessarily to Nietzsche, 120 years ago) is that by this route he pursues a question which we still cannot confidently answer. Yet this question concerns the basis of our sensory perceptions, in other words, the raw material (even to Kant)[15] of our knowledge. Democritus (along with others, it should be said) teases out the problem of how objects can exist and can relate to other objects, even though, as distinct objects, they are evidently separated by nothingness. In brief, how can anything *be* unless it is separated, from other things by intervals of non-being? Modern answers are to the effect that, except for whatever lies beyond the bounds of the universe (and perhaps not even there), there is no nonbeing. Between my eyes and yonder tree is not void space but an interval randomly occupied by imperceptible particles. The tree itself is a comparatively dense aggregation of particles which, because of its density, emits rays of light to me. The rays are focused in the form of an image in my perceptual apparatus. So I have knowledge of the tree when I recognise it, calling its optical image 'tree'. But in thus naming the image I am incidentally seeing it as composed of parts. A seemingly indivisible element – such as a particle – is not in itself knowable but must remain at the level of a supposition, a postulate which exists unknowably, because we nevertheless cannot proceed without it.

Now, if we are willing to think of the process of seeing as a sort of 'touching', since the light-wave emitted by the tree reaches my retina, we arrive at the position of Democritus. He worked out that all perception (including taste and hearing) is a form of touching. How indeed could it be anything else? Thus there is no actual void but only a comparatively empty space, in many cases so empty (so infrequently and irregularly occupied) that for all practical purposes we might well regard the seeming void as merely the 'opposite' of a substantial body. This is indeed how we tend to regard it (for all our modern science) but we are simply being expedient when we do so.

So far, then, Nietzsche would see Democritus as one thinking matters out without recourse to non-physical postulates. That makes him, in our terms, a 'scientist', if not a materialist. But there is a further dimension to Democritus as follows: he believed that bodies in space collide with one another and rebound for absolutely no reason. This is the entire basis of universal activity, up to and including the mental processes of human beings. As for the movement of a body before it 'bounces off' some other body, that is simply what occurs and always has occurred. Nothing gave rise to movement as such. Thus there was no first cause of movement, but to us today, in the great period of physics and belief in the Big Bang, this remains a riddle. Logically it cannot ever be solved, since our thinking functions by means of limits and is unable to reckon with the illimitable. Eternal Return is Nietzsche's response – not his 'solution' – to this riddle.

To Nietzsche the thinking of Democritus is admirably devoid of what most people would like to think, and so precisely the right foundation for subsequent philosophic endeavours. It should be stressed that in Nietzsche's eyes Democritus is *not* somehow definitively correct; his work does not constitute a scientific base for us to build on. Nevertheless the procedure is exemplary because it excludes hopes and fears, or rides roughshod over them. To this extent at least, it is superior philosophy.

Democritus proceeded for the most part in logical–deductive fashion, and reached 'halting-points' rather than conclusions. Thus one attains a position beyond which thought cannot advance. That is what we still do at our best (least conformable, least politi-cal, least lazy). In this way the thought of Democritus, being philosophical, is better or healthier than the *typical* thought of a modern physicist – by which I mean a physicist who (unlike Werner Heisenberg, for example)[16] refuses to notice philosophy. The point is that Democritus recognises all genuine thought as a species of creation, albeit creation on the part of one whose own development is unashamedly included – or even emphasised. Scientists who exclude their singular evolution (and of course philosophers who do the same) merely stunt themselves.

At this point we can begin to appreciate fully why Nietzsche sees the thrusting-aside of Empedocles and Democritus by the 'Socratics' as regrettable. Neither of these two contemporaries of Plato required an abstraction such as 'the good' or 'the just'. But this means that such abstractions were always strictly unnecessary. They were indeed fruitful; to call them 'useless' would be absurd. The invention of 'the good' and 'the just' by Socrates constituted a great increase in our armoury of thought. From what Aristotle says, that is what Socrates meant it to be: an augmentation of thinking (thence, I suppose, of virtue, in Socrates' sense of the word).[17] But those whom Aristotle calls 'the others', meaning followers of Plato and possibly Plato himself, took such a term as 'the good'; to refer to a universal, independent of the mind, having what Aristotle describes as an 'independent existence'. Likewise 'the just' became an ascription for an action or a thought determined by 'justice', so that the latter indeed became the independent origination and cause of the just occurrence.

Platonism in this sense clearly persists, for we have not found another way to structure our existence. We might, in our sophistication, regard 'the good' as purely a concept, but it remains such a masterful concept, the 'sovereign' one, in Iris Murdoch's phrase,[18] that for many it is hard to circumscribe. In other words, the sovereign concept, 'good' is always ranging outside its conceptual territory. 'The good' still appears to have a quasi-independent existence, and so, perhaps just as obviously, does 'the bad'.

At present, then, these terms remain ontological as much as ethical requirements. It is not simply that without 'the good' there would be no particular good, but that in its absence there would be – so it seems – no meaning whatsoever. But once it was absent and yet there was meaning – Empedoclean meaning, for example, and behind that a number of Heraclitean and Parmenidean pointers to what is probably the undesigned and shapeless reality of the universe.

So let us proceed to an attempt to describe what, in Nietzsche's judgement, knowledge and wisdom should be taken to be. Although Nietzsche's understanding of the matter (or of these intertwined matters) has been suggested quite regularly in this book, the point still needs to be made, and the making of it will require, not a summing-up, not a restatement, but an exploration.

Our consideration should certainly begin with the simplest notions which we have hitherto more or less taken for granted. We have not thought even to interpret the Socrates of the *Theaetetus* when he declares that knowledge must be of compounds, since there can be no knowledge of unanalysable beings. This is admittedly evident, for we can have no knowledge of subatomic particles, whose existence we merely postulate. Everything we know is divisible into either parts or aspects. It may be equally important and it is certainly rewarding to think of knowledge as the apprehension of relations. One knows something by perceiving and defining it in space and/or time. These are well-worn observations but it is necessary to recall them here. Thus we understand the procedures of knowledge to be either synthetic or analytic.

Socrates sets Western philosophy on its course of assuming that knowledge is virtually of a piece with language, more generally with representation and symbolisation. A wordless infant cannot be said to 'know' the garden in which he finds himself today for the tenth consecutive day of warm weather. No doubt the infant recognises features of the garden but recognition is not enough. Socrates himself does not deal with a child's lack of knowledge; rather he uses examples of animals: a pig or a baboon does not know what it nevertheless recognises. At this point in the discussion, Socrates is dealing primarily with Protagoras. He interprets 'Man is the measure of all things, of those that are that they are, and of those that are not that they are not' to mean that each individual perceives (therefore 'measures') individually. Socrates disagrees with this subjectivist or 'perspectivist' view, but not in the least with the alignment of knowledge with representation. Is it not the case, however, that Socrates thus initiates an arbitrary definition of knowledge? I do not mean a wrong definition, simply one that should be questioned in a dialogue dealing precisely with the *question* of knowledge.

In a consideration of Nietzsche we have to set this Socratic (and normative) notion of knowledge against whatever we can infer about the notions of Heraclitus. Heraclitus is the one who draws a contrast between the Word (the *Logos*) and language in general. The Word which (whatever else it is) is that to which one 'listens' if one is wise, stands apart from what we ordinarily take to be knowledge. It seems that a person is wise to the extent that he or she pays attention to the Word. Therefore the Word should either be designated 'true knowledge' or else take precedence over 'knowledge'. Heraclitus explicitly asks his readers to listen not to him (that is, to his words) but to the *Logos* instead. By this means they will grow wiser. Mainly, however, as a result of listening to the Word they will gain 'knowledge' of some sort, though not of the customary sort.

None of the synonyms for *Logos* seems to apply to what Heraclitus is talking about. The Word is not simply language or speech, still less is it thought or reason. The Word, as distinct from the sayings of Heraclitus, for example, is that to which one should pay heed. Insofar as Heraclitus or anyone else expresses his thoughts in words, one is not to take much notice of such misleading utterances. On the other hand, Heraclitus is not laying stress upon reason; the way he recommends has nothing to do with 'reasoning things out'. He states that 'Eyes are more accurate witnesses than ears',[19] which suggests that reasoning is, if anything, a deviation from the path of wisdom. In what immediately follows I am discussing *Logos* in Heraclitus, *not elsewhere*, for this common-enough expression is used quite differently in Heraclitus than it is, for example, in

Aristotle. It would be reasonable to question why Heraclitus, for all his proud peculiarity, should be distinguished in just this way: why should his use of a familiar word be set apart from the general use? The answer is that Heraclitus gives *Logos* such pre-eminence that he cannot be following the normal practice; at the very least he is emphasising a significance which others, in their chatter about gods and customs and cosmological origins, all too easily forget. To understand what Heraclitus means by *Logos* we should not artlessly refer to other authors. He alone goes to the root of the matter. By this I mean the psychological root insofar as this can be detected in, or behind, the etymology of the term. The uniqueness of Heraclitus' use of *Logos* has led to an immense amount of confusion, not to mention a path of thought against which he (disdainfully) warned his contemporaries. It is best to take *Logos* in Heraclitus to signify 'meaning': 'Listen, not to me but to the meaning.' Thus the Heraclitean meaning of something stands apart from what anyone says about it, and when we appreciate that fact, the intention of Heraclitus becomes clearer. He emphasises that all our talk about percepts distracts us from their essential import. The latter can be grasped quite readily, not by means analogous to an Husserlian *epoché* but by paying close attention to them, or 'listening' to them. The Word consists of spontaneous, culture-free perception, or to be precise, that is the form it initially takes. Some sort of culture will normally be associated with the perception, for example a name, but one should remain clear about the distinction between the name and the perception. The Word is clearly not a social interpretation of a percept or 'field' of percepts, for if it were, it would be formalised and therefore distanced from whatever it purported to explain. Such perception need not be difficult to attain, and in fact it must not be. In this way the Word which is neither uttered nor even considered in a predominantly verbal mode, can only be an untrammelled but *conscious* recognition that the scene is as it evidently is. How, then, is such a recognition 'conscious'? It is so because one forms a strong image of it and remembers it. That is to say, the image recurs. Note: 'strong' does not necessarily imply 'distinct'; the image might be confused but it must stand out and emphatically 'be'. One apprehends such a scene, or rather the image of the scene, as the sole and primary 'truth'.

In addition, this scene tells one about all things everywhere, at all times; nothing is concealed and there is nothing to puzzle out. Further, since the Word tells the hearer that 'all things are one', it acknowledges 'all things' as belonging inextricably together, as being unified in apperceptions.

Heraclitus should be taken to imply that if one extracts a supposed 'entity' from one's field of perception and tries to say something about it (if, in other words, one proceeds to analysis and knowledge), one joins the ranks of fools ('wont to be in a flutter at every word'), losing sight of the obvious oneness of reality. It is 'in reality' – as opposed to the realm of words – that 'Good and bad are the same',[20] that 'Couples are wholes and not wholes';[21] or that 'The beginning and end are common.'[22]

It is striking, however, that the Word, which according to the above remarks we would assume to be tied to individual observations, is somehow common to all who hear it. Everyone who hears the Word grasps the same (wise) meaning. Since our perceptions cannot but vary, the meaning must transcend them but not in anything resembling the sense introduced by Plato and not as the accepted definition of a word may be said to 'transcend' an individual perception. We must deduce that while everyday language *falsely* defines our observations, they were originally unified anyway – in the unity of the Word. The Word, as opposed to diction and utterance, constitutes our awareness of the world as movement: we apprehend in a way that countermands the rigidities of knowledge, recognising the world as essentially movement and contra-diction. For instance, we can see perfectly well (though we cannot in the ordinary sense 'know') that 'Couples are wholes and not wholes'.

This is the 'one divine law' which, contrary to what we suppose, nourishes all human laws. A human law is not necessarily a law in the technical sense but rather any socially-accepted belief. Therefore a human 'law', or formulated belief, lives insofar as it is nourished by the divine law, which it nevertheless attempts to contravene.

At this stage I wish to make the following point: the pig, the baboon and the wordless infant all perceive what is before them, without falsifications, but cannot hear the Word which 'names' the scene. This simply means they are unconscious of their perceptions. It is convenient now and again to speak of 'naming', but this should not be taken literally, for what is meant is the formation of an image which corresponds to the scene and does not impose a meaning upon it (as an ordinary use of words must). Of course, the image itself is laden with meaning but such meaning is irreducible to words and is for that very reason – in the terminology of Heraclitus – 'ever true'.

At this stage we need to consider how people (as opposed to animals) can be conscious of experiences which absolutely may not be verbalised. It is not simply that 'words are inadequate' but that they have absolutely nothing to do with the experiences. If the essence of consciousness is verbalisation, how does this exceedingly familiar sort of experience occur? There must be another sort of specifically human consciousness which is neither pre-verbal nor in any sense remotely verbal and yet is vitally different from animal consciousness.

In fact this is our confused fundamental consciousness, the consciousness we falsify as a matter of course for the mere purpose of living, so that for many people (some the least primitive) it scarcely exists. Insofar as it exists, it does so to be worded and thus refined or purified. We more or less happily acknowledge that language distorts the *pathos* of an experience and we necessarily (so it seems) philosophise in this distorting medium. Nevertheless, words are held to be the province of truth. Is it not this absolutely normal, indeed inescapable distortion to which Heraclitus, more than any other philosopher (more even than Parmenides), points?

Up to now in this discussion of *Logos* I have begged the most elementary question: how can a meaning exist unless it is expressed? Philosophy has, of course, followed just the route indicated by this question. It is true also that in psychology and in everyday usage a person is fully conscious of something only when the thing is, or may be, rendered in words. The Freudian unconscious is precisely the wordless. I believe that Heraclitus was already aware of this crux, while Socrates, despite his formidable wisdom, was not.

To Heraclitus an experience is 'true' precisely to the extent and in the manner that it stands clear of attempts to define it. *That an experience cannot be formulated is what guarantees its 'truth'.* However, such a 'true' reality is not intrinsic, not a property of things perceived, but is entirely bound up with one's experience. For all that, an experience is quite different from what an animal could undergo. This difference, if we could indicate it, would take us closer to what Heraclitus meant by the 'Word'. Now the answer grows clearer: the baboon cannot 'know' anything, not just because lower animals are unable to put their perceptions into words, but primarily because they do not fashion images. It is image-formation rather than word-formation that Heraclitus takes to be the basis of wisdom. The image stands apart from the percept and so gives meaning to the percept. The latter on its own would be meaningless, although of course no human being, as opposed to an animal, ever experiences an image-free perception. But the image which, for us, must always accompany a perception, is the meaning. And the meaning is always something added. It must be added. However, this addition, when it is the Word and not the usual clutter of interpretations and opinions, coincides with the percept. The remarkable, or indeed 'magical' fact about the Word is that it coincides with the percept and yet does not forfeit its distinct identity. Magically it stands apart as awareness of the percept, but also matches the percept in every particular. (Note: *the percept, not the thing-in-itself*.) So when *this* addition coincides with the percept, what we have is truth, or preferably *Aletheia*, albeit not a linguistic so-called 'truth', not a predicate. This is indeed the Word – and is 'ever true'.

III

If we left matters at this stage we would have radically departed from Western philosophy, but Nietzsche, for all *his* radicalism, does not diverge from the tradition here. He realises instead that wisdom, thus interpreted as fidelity to one's 'truthful' images, has to engage in a continuing struggle with knowledge. Knowledge is not to be despised and discarded just because it is untrue and unwise. In this way – so it seems to me – Nietzsche proceeds ahead of both Heraclitus and Socrates; he at least begins to overcome the Greeks.

Here let us recall and emphasise that Socrates claims not to know what knowledge is. Socrates is not teasing or in any way being perverse. Further, he regards his ignorance as a part – perhaps indeed the foundation – of his wisdom. When Nietzsche takes up this argument, which he does without reference to Socrates, he nevertheless assails another philosopher, Kant, from a semi-Socratic point of view. This happens in *The Will to Power* and takes the form of asserting that Kant wants 'knowledge of knowledge', which is a 'piece of naivety'.[23] But so far as I can see, Kant merely wants what anyone might want, that is, to define knowledge. He does this at the end of the *Critique of Pure Reason* by arguing that there are three degrees of conceptualisation, viz. Opinion, Belief and Knowledge. Opinion is a 'consciously insufficient judgement, subjectively as well as objectively'. Belief is 'subjectively sufficient' but 'objectively insufficient'. Knowledge, finally, 'is both subjectively and objectively sufficient'.[24] These are elementary definitions but Kant is not being naive since he has kept at the forefront of his mind that the objectivity he here refers to is not at all the objectivity of science and everyday belief. 'Objective sufficiency' is not a measure of independent reality.

Although such observations are not a product of naivety, Nietzsche certainly improves on them by 'looping back' behind Kant to Socrates and then going beyond Socrates in a fresh direction. To Nietzsche knowledge is neither more nor less than judgement. And what is judgement? It is what Kant means by opinion fortified by authority. In other words, Nietzsche ruthlessly (or cheerfully) eliminates the whole idea of objectivity while recognising that an attitude of profound respect is required towards knowledge. This is because such an attitude trains the soul; it is a sort of piety. Thus one respects the law of gravity far more than a political argument, but not on the grounds that the former is objectively true and the latter questionable. The reason is that Newton's law holds one's being in check; it is a real hurdle for scientists to jump and not just a preference.

So far we seem to be dethroning knowledge, however, and this, of course, is what modern nihilists would have us do. Everything is 'a matter of opinion'; all viewpoints are perspectives; 'nothing is true, everything is permitted'. Here I have especially in mind the frivolity, often masked as anguish, of contemporary artists, authors and moviemakers. The notion is that one can think or create whatever one wishes; there is neither a criterion of reality nor a spiritual trap into which one can tumble. However, Nietzsche himself characterised this kind of behaviour as merely 'weak nihilism'.

Nietzsche offers a solution to exactly the problem under discussion by, first of all, respecting knowledge greatly, despite its lack of firm *external* foundation. How can anyone do this? How can one subordinate wishes and fears to a field of thought – say physics – which one understands to rest upon a highly selective and therefore precarious foundation? Physics abstracts from the cosmos precisely those features which establish and fortify its own requirements. But outside the realm of knowledge (that is to say, 'in reality') such features wholly belong to waves or currents of energy (such metaphors display one's incapacity) and are indistinguishable. For that very reason we need a *metaphysical* base for physics itself, even though modern physics appears to do away with metaphysics. The building of such a base starts with the realisation that nothing, absolutely no occurrence, can be reduced to physics. This is not because everything has an externally fashioned purpose but because each thing, by which I mean each monad, proceeds from what Leibniz calls an 'internal principle'. By definition every such principle is beyond analysis and, since it is the ultimate basis of the discipline we know as 'physics', cannot itself be subjected to that discipline. Now while every such principle takes precedence over knowledge, it works by means of organising its environment, which is to say, so far as human beings are concerned, largely by means of knowledge. In this way knowledge *is* founded and is indispensable, even though it is not founded upon anything outside the principle of the monad itself. We should take it as read that the monadic principle takes precedence over wishes and fears; indeed it is the director of the entire personality.

To proceed more cautiously: there is a clear distinction between the knowledge singularly gained and employed by a monad and public knowledge. When an individual (since it is preferable to return from Leibnizian terminology to everyday language) avails himself of public knowledge, he should 'ideally' control and shape that knowledge. The individual does not, or should not, despise and discard public knowledge, even in areas where it is unnecessary for survival, but ought preferably to engage in some kind of negotiation, or indeed struggle with the knowledge in question. This is what Nietzsche means by the struggle between knowledge and wisdom. It would be an absurd struggle if one simply despised the item(s) of knowledge. The 'foe', which is the knowledge-fragment, needs to be vastly respected. One should respect the knowledge in the sense of skirmishing with it logically like a very Socrates. But always one's powers of thought must determine the outcome, whether this is decisive or aporetic.

The point about respecting knowledge has nothing to do with either courtesy or common sense but indicates that this procedure was, to Nietzsche, a strengthening of the soul. The soul does not grow more powerful as a result of despising knowledge, or readily manipulating it (the techniques of a weak nihilist) but just by engaging in such struggles as a constant exercise. The soul must always win, yet it has only the appearance of winning when it merely fails to engage itself with whatever knowledge confronts it. Even Socrates failed to engage himself with tragedy, which, in principle, he could have regarded as a mode of knowledge. In Nietzsche's view, however, Socrates regarded tragedy as blocking his own theoretical procedures. No doubt at that time, in the fifth century, Socrates had no alternative but to rule tragedy out of court, yet for us today (as a result of Socrates' revolution) we can bring tragedy into the reckoning. Now, if thought relegates knowledge, and these two take precedence over everything else, including tragedy, of course, *but also including even virtue* (neither viewing the first as antiquated nor the second as beyond consideration), then, in Nietzsche's eyes one is finally proceeding as a philosopher. This is what Heraclitus, Parmenides, Empedocles and Democritus supremely did in the ancient world.

Accordingly, when Nietzsche speaks highly of science, as he does, for example, in *The Gay Science*, he emphasises the courage and steadfastness it requires. Science demands severe and inexorable service. 'This "severity of science"', Nietzsche writes, 'has the forms and good manners of the best society: it is frightening for the uninitiated. But those who are used to it would never wish to live anywhere else than in this bright, transparent, vigorous, electrified air – in this *virile* air.'[25]

In using the word 'virile', Nietzsche is typically provocative, but he chiefly intends to specify a quality of character possessed, he believes, by every ardent scientist. From our point of view Madame Curie, for instance, was 'virile'. The supposition is that scientists (who need not be professional scientists) cast aside their desires, or believe they ought to do so, when they get down to work. Scientists are secretly ashamed of themselves if they become merely political or utilitarian; whenever their work is put to some non-scientific end, even (or especially) that of virtue.

At this point it might be said that I am following Nietzsche along the path of a transparent error, namely that of accepting certain qualities as virtues (steadfastness, civility and the rest), although these should strictly be questioned. I believe there is one answer to this charge: the sort of firmness of soul which Nietzsche has in mind is the unquestionable quality of being. It is far beyond the level of a virtue. Without this quality, the monad, the 'element' of a thing (as Leibniz calls it) cannot be. Hence the thing 'disowns itself', as it were. Such a disowning of self occurs only or at least mainly in human beings among whom it is actually the norm. The point is that the monad-being is as unanalysable philosophically as it is physically and if its mere quality is what we regard as a virtue, then such virtue is originary; it cannot be supported and requires no support. We shall say a little more about this in a moment.)

What I have outlined above remained Nietzsche's attitude towards *Wissenschaft* as a whole. It is not knowledge that counts (and certainly not the results or application of knowledge); it is the character-building discipline that searching for knowledge entails. Likewise, science is not, in itself, enough. In *Beyond Good and Evil*, published four years after *The Gay Science*, Nietzsche declares that 'Compared to a genius . . . the scholar, the scientific average man, always rather resembles an old maid: like her he is not conversant with the two most valuable functions of man.' The scientist is 'not noble, with the virtues of a type of man that is not noble, which is to say, a type that does not dominate and, is neither authoritative nor self-sufficient . . .'.[26] Such remarks apply to learning in its widest sense. Here Nietzsche emphasises the dependency, the self-subordination and lack of creativity of even a very good scientist who is not, however, audacious. The small company of truly major scientists are creative before they are conscientious. As is well-known, Einstein simply disregarded the lack of proof for his general theory; proofs of some sort would infallibly manifest themselves in due course. Such a person is a genius, a law-giver as opposed to a scientist.

It is now clear why knowledge and wisdom should be seen as fruitfully antagonistic: they are locked together, though in agonistic mode. This is why wisdom is not remotely that histrionic-hierophantic quality cultivated by elders of the tribe; still less does it consist of shrewd social manipulation. At the same time, the hoarding of impersonal knowledge is a mark of emptiness. 'A scholar can never become a philosopher,' writes Nietzsche, 'for even Kant was unable to do so but, the inborn pressure of his genius notwithstanding, remained to the end as it were in a chrysalis stage.'[27] Thus Kant remained 'a great thinker', as distinct from a philosopher. This may be unjust to Kant (who was nevertheless excessively thorough and laborious) yet if we subtract the example of Kant, we can see what Nietzsche has in mind.

It seems that the 'philosopher' in Nietzsche's sense must be wise, but what does this mean, since it means something quite distinct from dictionary definitions and popular images? The quality is personal, or preferably, *singular* and consists in the persistent exploration of one path. For example, Parmenides guides himself by a sort of negative image of the Way of Truth, an understanding that culture is by definition truthless. A modern example is that of Heidegger, who impels himself on the pursuit of 'Being'.

Here one is forced to an unnerving conclusion: such people are or become nihilists, though of the strong variety. By that I mean they are obliged to override traditional values; their knowledge, disciplined by their wisdom, takes precedence over both virtues and ideals. Virtues in the usual sense (that is to say, apart from the one virtue of 'self-propulsion') must themselves be subject to scrutiny, since virtue lacks *Grundwahrheit* or rock-bottom truth. It remains the case, nevertheless, that Socrates, the philosopher who more than any other speaks of virtue and is utterly directed by it, will not investigate virtue itself. Thus this field of thought remains, not impenetrable but unpenetrated.

Perhaps we are still not clear how knowledge should be directed. How can we exercise any control over it, since political legislation is obviously useless? The legislator of knowledge is indeed wisdom, provided we grasp that word correctly. 'Wisdom' implies that the individual 'knows' in a way that has nothing to do with knowledge. This is not meant as a paradox. He or she knows what is personally required. Such people do not need what their mere preferences suggest. Sophocles' Antigone, for instance, does not 'prefer' to be entombed, but she is 'wise' (as opposed to impetuous or stubborn) when she continues to oppose Creon. Her action is not *primarily* brave or good; it is merely wise, which is to say, propelled from within (or by an 'internal principle', as Leibniz would say).

The guiding knowledge that such people possess is prior to all other forms of knowledge. It is also prior to both prudence and philosophy – in the sense of the 'history of philosophy'. Such guiding knowledge cannot be founded upon anything, for it is already the foundation and neither seeks nor needs support. Resting upon this foundation, a philosopher in Nietzsche's understanding of the term has 'an immediate perception of things' and 'serves himself as a reflection and brief abstract of the world'.[28] One with such perception sees neither 'what is there to be seen' nor what the culture prescribes. The utterly healthy vision is always an interpretative and evaluative *force*, constrained by no other force. A person of this kind serves himself as a reflection and brief abstract of the world because that is what the individual as an individual does. Even so, such a knowledge-seeker's estimate of formalised knowledge is, we must repeat, respectful and even, in general terms, admiring. Certainly he *wants* the sort of knowledge that impels his admiration. The principle is that concepts and words themselves are to be subordinated to 'immediate perception'. They are not demeaned but respectfully weighed and valued from *above*, as an honourable legislator weighs the facts and opinions presented to him. The difference, however, is this: the legislator has an 'open mind' while the philosopher knows what he is looking for. This may be, as with Thales, a means of unifying the universe, or, as with Nietzsche, a means of willing the eternity of all things.

Notes

PREFACE

1. Nietzsche, Friedrich, *Beyond Good and Evil: Prelude to a Philosophy of the Future*, translated with commentary by Walter Kaufmann (New York: Vintage, 1966), Part One, 'On the Prejudices of Philosophers', 23, p. 32 (BGE).
2. Kant, Immanuel, *Critique of Pure Reason*, translated by J. M. D. Meiklejohn, introduced by A. D. Lindsay, (London: J. M. Dent New York: E. P. Dutton, 1934), 'Introduction', VI, 'The Universal Problem of Pure Reason', p. 36.

1 KNOWLEDGE AND WISDOM IN THE TRAGIC AGE

1. Russell, Bertand, *History of Western Philosophy*, p. 44.
2. Aristotle, *The Complete Works of Aristotle*, The Revised Oxford Translation, edited by Jonathan Barnes, Bollinger Series (Princeton, New Jersey: Princeton University Press, 1984). 'On the Heavens, 294a, 27–32, Vol. I, p. 484. 'Metaphysics', Book 1, 983, 9–10, 20, Vol. II, p. 1556.
3. Nietzsche, Friedrich, *Philosophy in the Tragic Age of the Greeks*, translated with an Introduction by Marianne Cowan (Chicago: Regnery Gateway, 1962), p. 45 (PTG).
4. Ibid., p. 44.
5. Ibid., p. 41.
6. Nietzsche, Friedrich, *Philosophy and Truth*, Selection from Nietzsche's Notebooks of the early 1870s, translated and edited with an introduction and notes by Daniel Breazeale and foreword by Walter Kaufmann (New Jersey: Humanities Press; Sussex, Harvester Press, 1979), No. 24, p. 6 (PT).
7. Guthrie, W. K. C., *A History of Greek Philosophy*, Vol. 1, *The Earlier Presocratics and the Pythagoreans* (Cambridge: Cambridge University Press, 1962), Chapter III, p. 96.
8. Ibid., p. 98.
9. Ibid., p. 85.
10. PTG, p. 48.
11. See Kirk, G. S., Raven, J. E., and Schofield, M., *The Presocratic Philosophers* (Cambridge: Cambridge University Press, 1957), p. 108.

12. PTG, p. 45.
13. Heracleitus, *On the Universe*, Fragment XX, see *Hippocrates* Vol. IV and *On the Universe*, with an English translation by W. M. S. Jones, (Cambridge, Mass.: Harvard University Press; London: Heinemann, 1979), p. 477. Note: in references to the title of this edition, but not elsewhere, 'Heracleitus' is spelt thus.
14. Ibid., Fragment XXX.
15. Guthrie, W. K. C., op. cit., pp. 469–77.
16. PTG, p. 57.
17. Heracleitus, *On the Universe*, Fragment 1, p. 471.
18. Ibid., Fragment LIX, p. 489.
19. Ibid., Fragment LXXIX, p. 495.
20. PTG, p. 62.
21. Op. cit., Fragment LVII, p. 489.
22. Ibid., Fragment XLI, p. 483.
23. Nietzsche, Friedrich, *The Will to Power*, translated by Walter Kaufmann and R. J. Hollingdale, edited, with commentary, by Walter Kaufmann (New York: Vintage, 1968) (WP), No. 617, p. 330.
24. Kirk, Raven and Schofield, *The Presocratic Philosophers*, p. 243.
25. PTG, p. 89.
26. Kirk, Raven and Schofield, p. 358 (Fragment 1).
27. Ibid.
28. Ibid., p. 363 (fragment 12).
29. Ibid.
30. Ibid., p. 366 (Fragment 11).
31. PTG, p. 50.
32. See WP, Book Four, 'Discipline and Breeding', III, 'The Eternal Recurrence:' p. 550.
33. Ibid.
34. Ibid., Book One, 'European Nihilism', p. 7.
35. Nietzsche, Friedrich, *Thus Spoke Zarathustra: A Book for Everyone and No One*, translated with an introduction by R. J. Hollingdale (Harmondsworth: Penguin, 1980), See especially 'Zarathustra's Prologue', pp. 45f.(Z).
36. Kirk, Raven and Schofield, p. 252 (Fragment 8).
37. Nietzsche, Friedrich, *On the Genealogy of Morals*, translated by Walter Kaufmann and R. J. Hollingdale, and *Ecce Homo*, translated by Walter Kaufmann (New York: Vintage, 1969) (GM and EH) EH, 'Why I am So Clever', 10, p. 258.
38. Adair, Robert K., *The Great Design: Particles, Fields, and Creation* (New York: Oxford University Press, 1987), p. 3.
39. Heidegger, Martin, *Nietzsche, Vol. I, The Will to Power as Art*, translated with notes and an analysis by David Farrell Krell (London: Routledge & Kegan Paul, 1981), p. 61. First published in this translation in New York by Harper and Row, 1979.

2 SOCRATES AND DIALECTIC

1. Nietzsche, Friedrich, *The Birth of Tragedy* and *The Case of Wagner*, translated , with commentary, by Walter Kaufmann (New York: Vintage, 1967). (BT and CW). BT, 13, p. 94.

2. Nietzsche, Friedrich, *Human, All Too Human A Book for Free Spirits*, translated by R. J. Hollingdale, introduction by Erich Heller (Cambridge: Cambridge University Press, 1986) (HAH). 'The Wanderer and His Shadow', No. 86, p. 332.

3. Nietzsche, Friedrich, *The Gay Science*, translated with commentary, by Walter Kaufmann (New York: Vintage, 1974), No. 340, p. 272 (GS).

4. BT, 'Attempt at a Self-Criticism', 1, p. 18.

5. Ibid., Section 9, pp. 67f.

6. Heracleitus, op. cit., Fragment 104, p. 503.

7. See Kirk, Raven and Schofield, p. 252 (Fragment 8), and Chapter 1, above, p. 27.

8. Nietzsche, Friedrich, *Twilight of the Idols* and *The Anti-Christ*, translated, with an introduction and commentary by R, J. Hollingdale (Harmondsworth: Penguin, 1968) (TI and AC). See TI, 'The Problem of Socrates', 12, p. 34.

9. WP, Book Three, 'Principles of a New Evaluation', No. 530, p. 286.

10. See Kant, Immanuel, *Critique of Pure Reason*, 'Transcendental Doctrine of Method', Chapter II, Section III, 'Of Opinion, Knowledge and Belief'.

11. Plato, *The Collected Dialogues*, edited by Edith Hamilton and Huntingdon Cairns, Bollingen Series LXXI (Princeton, New Jersey: Princeton University Press, 1985), *Theaetetus*, 176a (Cornford's translation).

12. BT, Section 12, p. 82.

13. TI, 'The Problem of Socrates', 9, p. 33.

14. The meaning of *aletheia* has been often enough discussed but is perhaps not very firmly grasped. What I say here is a crude but just adequate rendering of Heidegger's accounts in Section II of the Introduction to *Being and Time* and in the first and second essays of *Early Greek Thinking*.

15. See above, especially pp. 13 and 37.

16. Z, Part One. 'Zarathustra's Prologue', p. 44.

17. GS, Book Four, 'Sanctus Januarius', 324, p. 255.

18. PT, 'The Philosopher: Reflections on the Struggle Between Art and Knowledge', No. 31, p. 9.

19. WP, Book Four, 'Discipline and Breeding', No. 906, pp. 506f.

20. TI, 'The Problem of Socrates', 9, p. 33.

21. BT, Section 9, p. 68.

22. PT, 'The Philosopher: Reflections on the Struggle Between Art and Knowledge', No. 143, p. 48.
23. Aristotle, op. cit., Volume Two, 'Problems', Book XXX, 953a.
24. *Plato, The Collected Dialogues*, p. 1555. The translation is by Jowett.
25. Kaufmann, Walter, *Nietzsche: Philosopher, Psychologist, Antichrist* (Princeton, New Jersey: Princeton University Press, 1974) First published 1950. Part IV, Chapter 13, 'Nietzsche's Attitude toward Socrates'.

3 PLATO'S 'REAL WORLD'

1. TI, 'How the "Real World" at last Became a Myth', p. 40.
2. *The Complete Works of Aristotle*, Vol. II, 'Metaphysics', Book XIII, 1078b, 25, p. 1705.
3. EH, 'Why I Am So Clever', 1, p. 236.
4. PT, 'The Philosopher: Reflections on the Struggle Between Art and Knowledge', 19, p. 4.
5. Tejera, V., *Nietzsche and Greek Thought* (Dordrecht: Martinus Nijhoff, a member of the Kluwer Academic Publishers Group, 1987). See especially Chapter V.
6. AC, 15, pp. 15f.
7. GS, Book One, 54, p. 116.
8. Plato, *Philebus*, 24–7.
9. Ibid., 30b.
10. See WP, Book Four, III, 'The Eternal Recurrence', 1062, pp. 546f: 'If there were for it [the universe] some unintended final state, this must also have been reached.' Nietzsche is contending that nothing can lie beyond perfect harmony and completeness; on reaching such a condition a body must come to an end.
11. Plato, *Parmenides*, 141.
12. Ibid., 130.
13. In Gilbert Ryle's *The Concept of Mind* (Hutchinson, 1949) it is, of course, the mind rather than the soul which is denied and termed a 'category-mistake', but the soul is likewise a category-mistake, if one assumes the soul to be a sort of (abstract) entity.
14. GM, Second Essay, Section 16, p. 84.
15. See Kant. *Critique of Pure Reason*, Part First, Section II, 'Conclusions of the Transcendental Aesthetic'.
16. Plato, *Phaedo*, 80b.
17. PT, No. 86, p. 33.
18. WP, Book Four, 'Discipline and Breeding', No. 1067, p. 550.
19. Ayer, A. J., *Language, Truth and Logic* (Harmondsworth: Penguin, 1971), p. 202. First published by Gollancz in 1936.
20. Heidegger, Martin, *Nietzsche*, Vol. II, *The Eternal Recurrence of the*

Same, translated with notes and an analysis by David Farrell Krell (San Francisco: Harper & Row, 1964), p. 156.
21.   See above, pp. 39ff.

4   THE LEGACY OF EURIPIDES

1.   BT, Section 11, p. 77.
2.   Aristotle, Vol. II, 'Poetics', 13, 1453, 29–30, p. 2325.
3.   BT, Section 10, p. 73.
4.   WP, Book Four, 'Discipline and Breeding', 1050, p. 539.
5.   Quoted in H. A. Reyburn's *Nietzsche: The Story of a Human Philosopher* (London: Macmillan, 1948), p. 33.
6.   WP, Book Four, 'Discipline and Breeding', 1067, p. 550.
7.   BT, Section 10, p. 73.
8.   Op. cit., 'Introduction', I, 'Of the Difference Between Pure and Empirical Knowledge', p. 26.
9.   See BT, Sections 11 and 12.
10.   Op. cit., Fragment 1, p. 471.
11.   BT, Section 10, p. 73. See above note 7.
12.   Idem, Section 12, p. 82.
13.   Idem, p. 83.
14.   WP, Book Three, IV, 'The Will to Power as Art', 794, p. 419.
15.   Z, Part Two, 'Of Self-Overcoming', p. 138.
16.   WP, Book Three, IV, 'The Will to Power as Art', 796, p. 419.
17.   See Derrida, Jacques, *Spurs: Nietzsche's Styles*, translated by Barbara Harlow (Chicago: University of Chicago Press, 1979), especially pp. 39f. First published in Paris, 1978.
18.   *Reading Nietzsche*, ed. Robert C. Solomon and Kathleen M. Higgins (New York: Oxford University Press, 1988).
19.   Ibid.
20.   BT, 'Attempt at a Self-Criticism', 2, p. 19. Kaufmann's translation speaks of 'perspective' rather than 'optics', but Nietzsche in fact refers to 'die Optik'.
21.   WP, Book Three, 'Principles of a New Evaluation', 821, p. 435.
22.   EH, 'Why I Am So Clever', 10, p. 258.
23.   WP, 575, p. 309.
24.   I refer especially to sections 27 to 47 of *The Anti-Christ*.
25.   WP, 569, p. 307.
26.   Idem.
27.   PT, Section 1, p. 7.
28.   GS, Book Four, No. 324, p. 255.
29.   Nietzsche, F., 'Schopenhauer as educator', *Untimely Meditations*, translated by R. J. Hollingdale, with an introduction by J. P. Stern (Cambridge: Cambridge University Press, 1983), p. 143 (UM).

5 ARISTOTLE'S 'BEING' AND NIETZSCHE'S 'WILL TO POWER'

1.   Aristotle, Vol. II, 'Metaphysics', Book XI (K), 1059ᵃ, 18, p. 1673.
2.   Ibid., Book XI (K), 1060ᵇ, 31–2, p. 1676.
3.   Ibid., Book VI (E), 1025ᵇ, 16, p. 1619.
4.   Ibid., Book I (A), 981ᵇ, 27–8, p. 1553.
5.   Ibid., Book II (a), 993ᵇ, 10–11, p. 1570.
6.   Ibid., Book II (a), 994ᵃ, 1–2, p. 1570.
7.   See WP, Book Four, 'Discipline and Breeding', 1067, pp. 549f.
8.   'Metaphysics', Book IV, 1003ᵃ, 22–3, p. 1584.
9.   Ibid., Book IV, 1010ᵇ, 30–1, p. 1596.
10. Ibid., Book IV, 1010ᵇ, 35–8, p. 1596.
11. Ibid., Book XII, 1071ᵇ, 6, p. 1693.
12. See the *Critique of Pure Reason*, 'Transcendental Doctrine of Elements', Part First.
13. 'Metaphysics', Book XII, 1072ᵇ, 8–9, p. 1693.
14. Ibid., Book XII, 1072ᵃ, 9–10, p. 1694.
15. Ibid., Book XII, 1072ᵃ, 21, p. 1694.
16. Ibid., Book XII, 1072ᵃ, 24–6, p. 1694.
17. Ibid., Book XII, 1072ᵇ, 29–31, p. 1695.
18. See Spinoza, Benedict De, *The Ethics*, Part I, 'Concerning God', Propositions XIV to XXV.
19. WP, Book Three, 'Principles of A New Evaluation', 'The Mechanistic Interpretation of the World', 621, p. 333.
20. WP, Book Three, 'Principles of a New Evaluation', 642, p. 342.
21. Ibid., 569, p. 307.
22. *Critique of Pure Reason*, 'Transcendental Dialectic', Chapter II, Section IX, p. 311.
23. Schopenhauer, Arthur, *The World as Will and Representation*. Translated from the German by E. F. J. Payne (New York: Dover, 1969), Vol. I, p. 118.
24. Ibid., p. 126.
25. Ibid., p. 144.
26. WP, Book Three, 'Principles of a New Evaluation', 681, p. 361.
27. Ibid., 651, p. 345.
28. Ibid., 643, p. 342.

6 ARIADNE AND THE LABYRINTH

1.   This letter is included in *Nietzsche Briefwechsel* (Vol. III 5, Colli and Montinari edition (Berlin, New York: Walter de Gruyter, 1984), pp. 572ff.
2.   Op. cit., p. 34.
3.   EH, 'Thus Spoke Zarathustra', 9, p. 308.

4. See Nietzsche, Friedrich, *Dithyrambs of Dionysus*, Bilingual Edition, Translated and Introduced by R. J. Hollingdale (London: Anvil Press Poetry, 1984), pp. 83–5.
5. See Z, Part Four, 'The Sorcerer'.
6. Idem, Part Two, 'Of Poets'.
7. WP, Book Four, 'Discipline and Breeding', No. 864, p. 461.
8. Idem.
9. Ibid., No. 876, p. 468.
10. Ibid., No. 993, p. 517.
11. Kirk, Raven and Schofield, p. 248 (Fragment 7).
12. I haved taken this translation from an old collection of the works of Leibniz, *Leibnitz* (so spelled), *The Philosophical Works*, translated with notes by George Martin Duncan (New Haven: Tuttle, Morehouse and Taylor, 1890), pp. 69f.
13. Ibid., 'The Monadology', No. 22, p. 221.
14. GM, Third Essay, No. 8, pp. 108ff.
15. *Dithyrambs of Dionysus*, op. cit., p. 59.
16. Cf. EH, 'Why I Write Such Good Books', 2, p. 261. Here Nietzsche comments that he, unlike the animal that has long ears, has 'the smallest ears' and this 'is of no small interest to women,' for he will 'understand them better'.
17. WP, Book Four, 'Discipline and Breeding', 1067, p. 550.
18. Ibid., 1052, p. 542.
19. Ibid., 1051, p. 541.
20. Ibid., 1050, p. 539.

7 OVERCOMING THE GREEKS

1. GS, Book Four, 'Sanctus Januarius', No. 340, p. 272.
2. See especially Heidegger, Martin, *Early Greek Thinking*, Translated by David Farrel Krell and Frank A. Capuzzi (San Francisco: Harper & Row, 1984).
3. Kaufmann, Walter, *Nietzsche: Philosopher, Psychologist, Antichrist* (Princeton, New Jersey: Princeton University Press, 1974), Chapter 13, 'Nietzsche's Attitude toward Socrates', and Deleuze, Gilles, *Nietzsche and Philosophy*, translated by Hugh Tomlinson (London: The Athlone Press, 1983). See especially Chapter 1, 'The Tragic'.
4. Aristotle, *Complete Works*, Vol. II, 'Problems', Book XXX, 953a, 10 and 17, pp. 1498ff.
5. BT, Section 3, p. 42.
6. See above, Chapter 2, pp. 52ff.
7. PT, 'The Struggle Between Science and Wisdom', No. 196, p. 136.
8. Guthrie, W. K. C., *A History of Greek Philosophy*, Vol. II, *The Presocratic Tradition from Parmenides to Democritus* (Cambridge:

Cambridge University Press, 1965). See especially pp. 138–44 on Empedocles and pp. 389ff. on Democritus.

9. Op. cit., Fragment 44, p. 485.
10. Ibid., Fragment 62, p. 491.
11. PT, 'The Struggle Between Science and Wisdom', No. 195, p. 135.
12. Kirk, Raven and Schofield, p. 410.
13. Idem.
14. Idem.
15. See Kant, *Critique of Pure Reason*, Introduction, p. 25. 'But though all our knowledge begins with experience, it by no means follows that all arises out of experience.' Kant means, of course, that our empirical knowledge guided through impressions must be augmented and organised by *a priori* knowledge supplied by the workings of the mind. But without our raw knowledge obtained by the senses there could be no knowledge at all, no thought, no reason, no *mind*.
16. See Heisenberg, Werner, *Physics and Philosophy*, Introduction by Paul Davies (Harmondsworth: Penguin Books, 1989). First published in New York by Harper & Row, 1962.
17. See Aristotle, 'Metaphysics', Book XIII (M), 1078^b, 12–32, p. 1705.
18. The allusion is, of course, to Iris Murdoch's *The Sovereignty of Good* (London: Routledge & Kegan Paul, 1970). The title is completed by the phrase 'over other Concepts'.
19. Heraclitus, *On the Universe*, Fragment 15, p. 475.
20. Ibid., Fragment 57, p. 489.
21. Ibid., Fragment 59, p. 489.
22. Ibid., Fragment 70, p. 493.
23. WP, Book Three, 'Principles of a New Evaluation', 530, p. 287.
24. Kant, *Critique of Pure Reason*, 'The Canon of Pure Reason', Section Third, p. 466.
25. GS, Book Four, 293, p. 235.
26. BGE, Part Six, 'We Scholars', 206,, p. 125.
27. UM, 'Schopenhauer as Educator', 7, p. 181.
28. Idem.

Bibliography

When not specified, the place of publication is London.

Ackrill, J. L., *Aristotle the Philosopher* (Oxford: Oxford University Press, 1981).

Adair, Robert K., *The Great Design: Particles, Fields and Creation* (New York: Oxford University Press, 1987).

Aristotle, *The Complete Works of Aristotle*, The Revised Oxford Translation, edited by Jonathan Barnes, 2 vols (Princeton, New Jersey: Princeton University Press, Bollinger Series 71–2, 1984).

Barnes, Jonathan, *Early Greek Philosophy* (Harmondsworth: Penguin, 1987).

——, *The Presocratic Philosophers* Vol. I, *Thales to Zeno* (Routledge & Kegan Paul, 1979).

Blum, Alan F., *Socrates, the original and its images* (Routledge & Kegan Paul, 1978).

Calder, Nigel, *Einstein's Universe: A Guide to the Theory of Relativity.* (New York: Viking 1979: London: Penguin 1982).

Conversations with Nietzsche, edited and with an introduction by Sander L. Gilman, translated by David J. Parent (New York: Oxford University Press, 1987).

Cotterell, Arthur, *The Minoan World* (Michael Joseph, 1979).

Deleuze, Gilles, *Nietzsche and Philosophy*, translated by Hugh Tomlinson (The Athlone Press, 1983).

Derrida, Jacques, *Spurs: Nietzsche's Styles*, translated by Barbara Harlow (Chicago and London: The University of Chicago Press, 1978).

Exceedingly Nietzsche: Aspects of Contemporary Nietzsche-Interpretation, edited by Daniel Farrell Krell and David Wood (Routledge, 1988).

Gosling, J. C. B., *Plato* (Routledge, 1973).

Gulley, Norman, *The Philosophy of Socrates* (Macmillan, 1968).

Guthrie, W. K. C., *A History of Greek Philosophy*, Vol. I, *The Earlier Presocratics and the Pythagoreans* (Cambridge: Cambridge University Press, 1962).

——, *A History of Greek Philosophy*, Volume II, *The Presocratic Tradition from Parmenides to Democritus* (Cambridge: Cambridge University Press, 1965).

Hare, R. M., *Plato* (Oxford: Oxford University Press, 1982).

Hegel, G. W. F., *Phenomenology of Spirit*, translated by A. V. Miller with analysis of the text and foreword by J. N. Findlay (Oxford: Oxford University Press, 1977).

Heidegger, Martin, *Being and Time*, translated by John Macquarrie and Edward Robinson (New York: Harper & Row, 1962).

——, *Early Greek Thinking*, translated by David Farrell Krell and Frank A. Capuzzi (New York: Harper & Row, 1984).

——, *An Introduction to Metaphysics*, translated by Ralph Manheim (New Haven, Conn.: Yale University Press, 1959).

——, *The Metaphysical Foundations of Logic*, translated by Michael Heim (Bloomington: Indiana University Press, 1978).

——, *Nietzsche, Volume I, The Will to Power as Art*, translated with notes and an analysis by David Farrell Krell (Routledge & Kegan Paul, 1981).

——, *Nietzsche, Volume II, The Eternal Recurrence of the Same*, translated with notes and an analysis by David Farrell Krell (San Francisco: Harper & Row, 1984).

——, *Nietzsche, Volume III, The Will to Power as Knowledge and Metaphysics*, translated by Joan Stambaugh, David Farrell Krell and Frank A. Capuzzi, edited with notes and an analysis by David Farrell Krell (San Francisco: Harper & Row, 1987).

——, *Nietzsche, Volume IV, Nihilism*, translated by Frank A. Capuzzi, edited with notes and an analysis by David Farrell Krell (San Francisco: Harper & Row, 1982).

Heisenberg, Walter, *Physics and Philosophy: The Revolution in Modern Science*, introduction by Paul Davies (Harmondsworth: Penguin, 1989). First published by Harper & Row, New York, 1962.

Herbert, Nick, *Quantum Reality: Behind the New Physics* (Rider & Company, 1985).

Kant, Immanuel, *The Critique of Judgement*, translated with analytical indexes by James Creed Meredith (Oxford: Clarendon Press, 1989).

——, *Critique of Practical Reason*, translated with an introduction by Lewis White Beck (New York: Macmillan, London: Collier-Macmillan, 1956).

——, *Critique of Pure Reason*, translated by J. M. D. Meiklejohn, introduction by A. D. Lindsay (J. M. Dent, 1934).

——, *Prolegomena*, translated by Paul Carus (La Salle, Illinois: Open Court, 1990).

Lampert, Laurence, *Nietzsche's Teaching: An Interpretation of Thus Spoke Zarathustra* (New Haven and London: Yale University Press, 1986).

Leibniz, Gottfried Wilhelm, *Philosophical Writings*, translated by Mary Morris and G. H. R. Parkinson, edited by G. H. R. Parkinson (J. M. Dent 1973).

Magee, Brian, *The Philosophy of Schopenhauer* (Oxford: Clarendon Press, New York: Oxford University Press, 1983).

Marek, George R., *Cosima Wagner* (Julia MacRae Books, 1983). First published in New York by Harper & Row, 1981.

Mates, Benson, *The Philosophy of Leibniz: Metaphysics and Language* (New York and Oxford: Oxford University Press, 1986).

Melling, David J., *Understanding Plato* (Oxford: Oxford University Press, 1987).

Murdoch, Iris, *The Sovereignty of Good* (Routledge & Kegan Paul, 1970).

Nietzsche, Friedrich, *Beyond Good and Evil: Prelude to a Philosophy of the Future*, translated with commentary by Walter Kaufmann (New York: Vintage, 1966).

——, *The Birth of Tragedy* and *The Case of Wagner*, translated with commentary by Walter Kaufmann (New York: Vintage, 1967).

——, *Daybreak: Thoughts on the Prejudices of Morality*, translated by R. J. Hollingdale, introduced by Michael Tanner (Cambridge: Cambridge University Press, 1982).

——, *Dithyrambs of Dionysus*, Bilingual Edition, translated and introduced by R. J. Hollingdale (Anvil Press Poetry, 1984).

——, *Friedrich Nietzsche Briefe* Januar 1887–Januar 1889, edited by Giorgio Colli and Mazzino Montinari, Berlin and New York: Walter de Gruyter, 1984).

——, *On the Future of our Educational Institutions* and *Classical Philology*, translated and introduced by J. M. Kennedy (Edinburgh and London: T. N. Foulis, 1909.

——, *The Gay Science*, translated, with commentary by Walter Kaufmann (New York: Vintage, 1974).

——, *On the Genealogy of Morals*, translated by Walter Kaufmann and R. J. Hollingdale, and *Ecce Homo*, translated and edited with a commentary by Walter Kaufmann (New York: Vintage, 1967).

——, *Human, All Too Human: A Book for Free Spirits*, translated by R. J. Hollingdale, introduced by Erich Heller (Cambridge: Cambridge University Press, 1986).

——, *Philosophy and Truth: Selections from Nietzsche's Notebooks of the early 1870s*, translated and edited with an introduction by Daniel Breazeale, foreword by Walter Kaufmann (New Jersey: Humanities Press: Sussex: Harvester Press, 1970).

——, *Philosophy in the Tragic Age of the Greeks*, translated with an introduction by Marianne Cowan (Chicago: Regnery Gateway, 1962).

——, *Thus Spoke Zarathustra: A Book for Everyone and No One*, translated with an introduction by R. J. Hollingdale (Harmondsworth: Penguin, 1961).

——, *Twilight of the Idols* and *The Anti-Christ*, translated with an introduction and commentary by R. J. Hollingdale (Harmondsworth: Penguin, 1968).

——, *Unpublished Letters*, translated and edited by Karl F. Leidecker (Peter Owen, 1960).

——, *Untimely Meditations*, translated by R. J. Hollingdale with an introduction by J. P. Stern (Cambridge: Cambridge University Press, 1983).

——, *The Will to Power*, translated by Walter Kaufmann and R. J. Hollingdale, edited, with commentary by Walter Kaufmann (New York: Vintage, 1968).

Parmenides, A Text with translation, commentary and critical essays by Leonardo Tarán (Princeton, New Jersey: Princeton University Press, 1963).

The Philosophy of Socrates, A Collection of Critical Essays, edited by Gregory Vlastos (New York: Anchor Books, Doubleday, 1971).

Plato, *The Collected Dialogues of Plato including the letters*, edited by Edith Hamilton and Huntingdon Cairns, Bollinger Series LXXI (Princeton, New Jersey: Princeton University Press, 1961).

Plato, *Early Socratic Dialogues*, edited with a general introduction by Trevor J. Saunders, translations by Trevor J. Saunders, Ian Lane, Donald Watt, and Robin Waterfield (Harmondsworth: Penguin, 1987).

——, *The Trial and Execution of Socrates*, translated with an introduction by Peter George, drawings by Michael Ayrton (The Folio Society, 1972).

Plutarch, *Plutarch's Lives*, translated by Bernadette Perrin, Vol. I (London: William Heinemann, New York: Macmillan, 1914).

Popper, Karl, *The Open Society and its Enemies*, Vol. I, *The Spell of Plato* (Routledge & Kegan Paul, 1945).

Reading Nietzsche, edited by Robert C. Solomon and Kathleen M. Higgins (New York: Oxford University Press, 1988).

Rist, John M., *The Mind of Aristotle: A Study in Philosophical Growth* (Toronto: University of Toronto Press, 1989).

Russell, Bertrand, *A Critical Exposition of the Philosophy of Leibniz* (Cambridge: Cambridge University Press, 1900).

——, *History of Western Philosophy* (George Allen & Unwin, 1961).

Ryle, Gilbert, *The Concept of Mind* (Hutchinson, 1949).

——, *Plato's Progress* (Cambridge: Cambridge University Press, 1966).

Santas, Gerasimos Xenophon, *Socrates' Philosophy in Plato's Early Dialogues* (Routledge & Kegan Paul, 1979).

Sayre, Kenneth M., *Plato's Late Ontology: A Riddle Resolved* (Princeton: New Jersey: Princeton University Press, 1983).

Schacht, Richard, *Nietzsche* (Routledge & Kegan Paul, 1983).

Schopenhauer, Arthur, *On the Fourfold Root of the Principle of Sufficient Reason*, translated by G. F. J. Payne, with an introduction by Richard Taylor (La Salle, Illinois: Open Court, 1974).

——, *The World as Will and Representation*, translated by E. F. J. Payne, 2 vols (New York: Dover, 1966).

Silk M. S. and Stern, J. P., *Nietzsche on Tragedy* (Cambridge: Cambridge University Press, 1981).

Spinoza, Benedict de, *The Chief Works*, Vol. II, translated with an introduction by R. H. M. Elwes (New York: Dover, 1951).

Studies in Nietzsche and the Classical Tradition, edited by James C.

O'Flaherty, Timothy F. Sellner and Robert M. Helm (Chapel Hill, North Carolina: University of North Caroline Press, 1976).

Tejera, V., *Nietzsche and Greek Thought* (Dordrecht: Martinus Nijhoff, 1987).

Teloh, Henry, *The Development of Plato's Metaphysics* (University Park: Pennsylvania; London: Pennsylvania State University Press, 1981).

Willetts, R. F., *The Civilisation of Ancient Greece* (B. T. Batsford, 1977).

Index